FROMMER'S

COMPREHENSIVE TRAVEL GUIDE

Sydney

4th Edition

by John Godwin

MACMILLAN • USA

ABOUT THE AUTHOR

John Godwin is a former Australian journalist and foreign correspondent now living in America. His hardcover books include the bestselling *The Baffling World* and *Murder USA*. In addition to this guide, he is the author of *Frommer's Australia on $45 a Day*.

MACMILLAN TRAVEL

A Prentice Hall Macmillan Company
15 Columbus Circle
New York, NY 10023

ISBN 0-02-860060-6
ISSN 0899-2770

Design by Michele Laseau
Maps by Ortelius Design

SPECIAL SALES

Manufactured in the United States of America

Contents

SPECIAL FEATURES

- Frommer's Smart Traveler: Restaurants *88*

- Frommer's Cool for Kids: Restaurants *91*

SPECIAL FEATURES

- Suggested Itineraries *119*

- Frommer's Favorite Sydney Experiences *123*

- Did You Know . . . ? *127*

List of Maps

What the Symbols Mean

⭐ **Frommer's Favorites**   Hotels, restaurants, attractions, and entertainments you should not miss.

💲 **Super Special Values**   Really exceptional values.

Abbreviations

The following abbreviations refer to the standard amenities available in all rooms:

A/C   air conditioning
MINIBAR   refrigerator stocked with beverages and snacks
TEL   telephone
TV   television

The following abbreviations are used for credit cards:

AE   American Express
JCB   (Japan)
MC   MasterCard
V   Visa

Trip Planning with this Guide
USE THE FOLLOWING FEATURES:

What Things Cost In   To help you plan your daily budget

Calendar of Events   To plan for or avoid

What's Special About Checklist   A summary of the city's highlights

Suggested Itineraries   For seeing the city

Easy-to-Read Maps   Walking tours, city sights, hotel and restaurant locations—all referring to or keyed to the text

Fast Facts   All the essentials at a glance: climate, emergencies, information, safety, taxes, tipping, and more

Frommer's Special Traveller Tips   Hints on how to secure the best value for your money.

Invitation to the Readers

In researching this book, I have come across many wonderful establishments, the best of which I have included here. I am sure that many of you will also come across appealing hotels, inns, restaurants, guest houses, shops, and attractions. Please don't keep them to yourself. Share your experiences, especially if you want to comment on places that have been included in this edition that have changed for the worse. You can address your letters to:

John Godwin
Frommer's Sydney, 4th Edition
c/o Macmillan Travel
15 Columbus Circle
New York, NY 10023

A Disclaimer

Readers are advised that prices fluctuate in the course of time, and travel information changes under the impact of the varied and volatile factors that affect the travel industry. Neither the author nor the publisher can be held responsible for the experiences of readers while traveling. Readers are invited to write to the publisher with ideas, comments, and suggestions for future editions.

Safety Advisory

Whenever you're traveling in an unfamiliar city or country, stay alert. Be aware of your immediate surroundings. Wear a moneybelt and keep a close eye on your possessions. Be particularly careful with cameras, purses, and wallets, all favorite targets of thieves and pickpockets.

1

Introducing Sydney

Travelers have the habit of comparing each place with another place, yet nothing annoys Sydneysiders more than being told that their city resembles San Francisco. Which, superficially, it does . . . except for being five times as big, twice as hot, and half as hilly. But the locals consider San Francisco a charming provincial backwater and their own town the metropolis and queen of the Pacific region, and find the comparison very faint praise indeed.

Apart from being the largest, oldest, and liveliest city of the Australian continent, Sydney is the only Australian city boasting an internationally recognized landmark: the pearly scallop shells of the Opera House, now nearly as familiar a symbol as the Statue of Liberty, the Eiffel Tower, or the Coliseum. Today the major effort of Sydney's people is aimed at showing the world that there is considerably more here than this celebrated piece of architectural confectionary.

Sydney is astonishingly beautiful; made so by a harbor setting for which the only term is "breathtaking." The immense harbor expanse divides the city in half, creating a foreshore of 150 miles, splintering the coastline into hundreds of inlets, coves, and bays and putting a large portion of the city within sight and walking distance of the ocean. Since Sydney is hilly, the harbor gesticulates at you from the most unexpected angles, offering an endless kaleidoscope of views. With hundreds of colored sails dotting the water, green foliage marking the shoreline, ruffles of breakers fringing golden beaches, and white ocean liners docked at the very tip of the high-rise business district, the overall effect is magical.

That wondrous ocean setting has resisted all assaults on the city's beauty by greedy developers and mediocre urban planners. They linked the north and south shores with one of the ugliest bridges extant, a clumsy slab of steel and mortar nicknamed "the coathanger," turning most of the downtown area into a chaotic, log-jammed mess. They spread an endless rash of drab red-roofed suburbs inland, with patches in between that look like mass graveyards for secondhand cars. But no matter what they perpetrated, Sydney remained a gem among cities, protected against all the ravages that myopia and a fast-buck mentality could inflict.

Sydney, which celebrated its 200th birthday in 1988, is the capital of the state of New South Wales, but not of Australia (that honor belongs to Canberra). With some 3.6 million inhabitants sprawling over 670 square miles, metropolitan Sydney today is one of the largest urban areas on the globe—something you had better keep in mind when you start sightseeing.

1 History

Early Days

THE OCEAN INLET CALLED Botany Bay was explored by the great navigator Capt. James Cook in 1770. He proclaimed the land a British possession, noted

Dateline
- **1788** The First Fleet sails into ➤

What's Special About Sydney

Beaches
- 34 ocean beaches—mostly magnificent—within city limits.

Architectural Highlights
- Sydney Opera House—the city's international symbol.
- Sydney Harbour Bridge, an immense single-span "coathanger" linking the city with the North Shore.
- Sydney Tower, a slender pillar stabbing 1,000 feet into the sky with an observation deck on top.
- El Alamein Fountain, world's first fountain to use water as its sculptural material.

Museums
- Art Gallery of New South Wales. Old European masters, Australian classics, and contemporary art.
- Powerhouse Museum. Fascinating technological grab bag, steam engines to space modules.

Events/Festivals
- Festival of Sydney, a summer carnival with happenings all over town.
- Royal Easter Show, an agricultural spectacular.
- Australia Day, with history reenacted and glorified.
- Sydney-Hobart Yacht Race, the nation's premier sailing event.

For the Kids
- Taronga Zoo, aquarium, Children's Museum, Manly Beach, Pier One, Monorail—and much more.

Shopping
- Queen Victoria Building (QVB), a marvel of interior design.
- Strand Arcade, Royal Arcade, Imperial Arcade, with shopping devoted chiefly to the glamour trade, as is Cosmopolitan Centre in chic Double Bay.

Natural Spectacles
- Sydney Harbour from any angle at any hour. Barrenjoey Head on the North Shore. The dramatic panorama of The Gap—favored by honeymooners and suicides.

After Dark
- 27 live professional theaters, the opera, the giant Entertainment Centre—plus myriad discos, nightclubs, comedy cabarets, and music pubs.
- Kings Cross—wall-to-wall stripclubs, eateries, dance dens, and unabashed brothels.

Dateline

Botany Bay with 1,044 people, including 736 convicts. Three days later two French vessels, commanded by La Perousa, arrive. Colony of New South Wales (NSW) proclaimed, comprising 2,100,000 square miles—half of Australia. Capt. Arthur Phillip appointed governor.

- **1793** Governor Phillip departs. Population of Sydney now 3,120, of whom 2,465 are convicts.

- **1806** Capt. William Bligh (of the *Bounty*) becomes governor, but is overthrown in a mutiny by army officers.

- **1840** Transportation of convicts to NSW is stopped. A total of 111,500 had been exiled there.

- **1851** Gold discoveries in NSW and Victoria bring in many "diggers" from overseas.

- **1872** Sydney is now a city of 288,000 people, supporting 3,167 taverns.

- **1901** The separate colonies unite to form the self-governing Commonwealth of Australia.

- **1908** A spot named

➤

some curious animals "like deer with the heads of dogs, which hop" and then sailed on. Nothing much else might have happened for quite a while if it hadn't been for the American Revolution.

Until then, America had been used as a convenient dumping ground that kept Britain's jam-packed prisons from bursting at the seams. After the breakaway of the American colonies, King George's government considered alternatives and came up with a perfect one: the immense empty island-continent "down under," lying 14,000 miles away—outer space by 18th-century measurements.

And so on January 26, 1788, a fleet of 11 badly battered transports dropped anchor at what is now Sydney Cove. They carried a small military escort and 736 male and female minor convicts, poachers, pickpockets, prostitutes, Irish rebels, and cardsharps. They were rowed ashore and given a first task—building their own prison.

Their real prison, however, was the gigantic wilderness that surrounded them and their total ignorance about it. Nothing was known about the continent, not even its shape. Nobody was even sure the place was an island. It was a place where the seasons were turned upside down, where the seeds brought from England wouldn't grow, where animals carried their young in pouches, and where the black, unclothed natives spoke languages unrelated to any other on earth. Several convicts attempted to escape by *walking* to China which, they believed, lay over the next mountain range.

These were the first of more than 150,000 convicts transported from Britain and clustered in a series of hellholes along the Australian coast, where only the toughest survived the early years. Rum was the universal solace and for a time the only currency; flogging post and gallows, the prime labor incentives. When Captain Bligh (of *Mutiny on the Bounty* fame) became governor of New South Wales and tried to suppress the illicit rum trade, his own officers rebelled against him and igno-miniously shipped him home. The convict heritage, which today has a certain prestige, left a lasting imprint on Sydney. It contrib-uted to the fierce egalitarianism of Austra-lians, their distrust of authority, the ribald iconoclasm of their humor, and their po-litical obstreperousness.

Colonies to Commonwealth

Gradually conditions down under im-proved. Convict transportations ceased in the 1840s and the chained "Gentlemen of the Broad Arrows" were replaced by succes-sive waves of free immigrants. Most of them came in search of gold, but stayed on to prosper from other sources. Not all, by any means. One of the worst gangs of goldfield thugs, the notorious "Sydney Ducks," moved on to California to continue their trade and were duly hanged en masse by San Francisco vigilantes.

By the turn of the century the erstwhile penal settlements had become thriving colonies, growing rich on wool, wheat, meat, and coal exports—and with develop-ment, increasingly independent. The time had come for political emancipation. In 1901 the six colonies of the continent trans-formed themselves into the six states of the self-governing Commonwealth of Austra-lia. By then Sydney had grown into a large and rather rowdy city of nearly half a mil-lion. And because it was perpetually battling Melbourne for national supremacy, a brand-new capital, Canberra, was built half-way between them.

Sydney's ethnic and cultural image around 1900 was completely different from what it is today. It was untouched by even a breath of cosmopolitanism. Its population was almost solidly Anglo-Irish, except for a few thousand Chinese who had come over during the gold rushes and now ran restau-rants, market gardens, and small shops. The enormous influx of European and Asian im-migrants, which shaped the city's present face, did not begin until after World War II.

Dateline

Canberra, halfway between Sydney and Melbourne, is chosen as site for the national capital.

- **1914** Australia enters World War I on the side of Britain, and 60,000 Australians are killed in action.
- **1923** Nightly radio broadcasts begin in Sydney.
- **1932** Sydney Harbour Bridge opens—with a disturbance. The city's population reaches one million.
- **1939** Australia enters World War II.
- **1942** Three Japanese midget submarines creep into Sydney harbor and torpedo a ferry. All three subs are sunk.
- **1947** Large influx of European migrants begins.
- **1965** Australia sends troops to Vietnam. The total number later reaches 40,000.
- **1966** Australia adopts the dollar as decimal currency.
- **1973** Elizabeth II inaugurates the Sydney Opera House.
- **1988** Sydney—and Australia—celebrate their 200th anniversary.

World War & Depression

When Australia entered World War I alongside Britain in 1914, its young men joined the armed forces in frenzied enthusiasm based on total ignorance of what was in store for them. Some 417,000 men volunteered out of a population of five million (one in every 12 people) and Sydney's Circular Quay became the scene of constant mass farewells, as the packed troop ships sailed for combat zones. The Aussies were bigger, healthier, and more spirited than their English comrades in arms—"eminently suited for assault tactics." This was their role in France, in Turkey, and in Palestine, and the resultant toll was appalling: 60,000 dead, 167,000 wounded!

The 1920s, which followed the bloodletting, were simultaneously a period of expansion and regression for Sydney. The city grew mightily, reaching one million inhabitants. But the clammy hand of wowserism kept it confined to the kindergarten stage. The bluenoses, the spiritual brethren of America's Prohibitionists, had climbed into the saddle and stomped heavily on whatever smacked of excessive *joie de vivre.*

They utilized a "temporary" wartime measure to close pubs at 6pm, keep them closed on Sunday, and render civilized wining and dining (as well as outdoor cafes) well-nigh impossible. They forced ludicrously outmoded beachwear on both sexes; placed hundreds of books, films, and stage plays on the "banned" list; padlocked playgrounds on Sunday; and would have turned off the surf if that had been technically feasible.

Sydney, however, soon had other worries than blue laws. The Great Depression hit Australia hard, rendering some 20% of the work force unemployed, heating up social conflicts to the point of violence. The semi-Fascist New Guard clashed with embittered trade unionists, and some of the uproar even spilled over into Sydney's most festive occasion.

Sydney Harbour Bridge, a colossal steel structure linking the city with the North Shore, was supposed to be ceremonially opened by New South Wales's leftist Premier, J. T. Lang, in 1932. But just as Lang was about to cut the ribbon, up dashed a mounted New Guard officer named de Groot and slashed the ribbon with his sword. De Groot was unhorsed and jailed, but he had managed to ruin the grand occasion for Lang.

Worse followed. Lang, a Labor radical, tried to ease the economic crisis of his state by suspending interest payments on loans from Britain. Murmurs of "Bolshevism" were heard, the state governor dismissed Lang, and his own Labor Party expelled him. The depression, however, dragged on until the outbreak of World War II again provided full employment.

War Reaches Australia

At the outset the Second World War seemed to be a replay of the first. Again the troop ships loaded with cheering volunteers sailed from Circular Quay, prices for wool and wheat exports rose

Greater Sydney

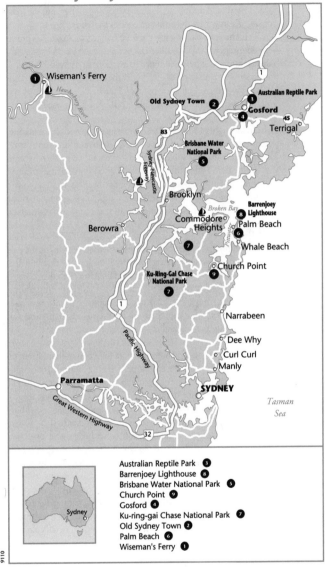

Australian Reptile Park	**3**
Barrenjoey Lighthouse	**8**
Brisbane Water National Park	**5**
Church Point	**9**
Gosford	**4**
Ku-ring-gai Chase National Park	**7**
Old Sydney Town	**2**
Palm Beach	**6**
Wiseman's Ferry	**1**

9110

IMPRESSIONS

Of all the places in the world, this is the greatest nest of rascals, male and female!
—Captain William Sturges, 1788

wondrously, and the folks at home were coining money. But the scene changed abruptly with the attack on Pearl Harbor.

With the Japanese advancing in New Guinea, on Australia's northern doorstep, with all its trained troops fighting on far-off battlefields, the Commonwealth lay wide open to invasion. Every available man—and most women—were drafted under the guideline "Don't test their eyes—count them." Japanese bombers flattened Darwin, Sydney was blacked out, the beautiful harbor foreshores crisscrossed with slit trenches.

On the night of May 31, 1942, three Japanese midget submarines crept into the harbor and torpedoed a ferryboat. Nineteen Australian sailors and all the sub crews died—the war had reached Sydney.

In the months that followed American reinforcements streamed in, and gradually the tide turned. But it had been, as Wellington said about Waterloo, "a damned close run thing." Close enough to shake Australia out of its complacent delusion that distance meant safety.

Mass Immigration

Above anything, the "empty continent" needed people. In the past Australia had severely restricted immigration for fear that non-English would drag down its standard of living. After 1945 this changed drastically. The government launched an assisted immigration scheme, paying the passage for overseas newcomers, regardless of their mother tongues. More than three million New Australians came and settled, altering the face and customs of the country almost beyond recognition.

Sydney's population zoomed to more than two million. From an Anglo-Irish stronghold the city turned into one of the most cosmopolitan on earth, with every second inhabitant either born abroad or of foreign parentage. At the same time the authorities skillfully avoided the minority enclaves. Sydney has posh and poor neighborhoods, but nothing resembling a ghetto or barrio patch.

Sydney's silhouette changed apace. It used to be that once you crossed the Harbour Bridge to the North Shore, you were in suburbia. Now the tall towers that mark downtown marched across as well, transforming both shores into skyscraperland, pushing the real suburbs out farther and farther. In the central regions, restaurants, cafes, and nightspots proliferated at a dazzling rate, generating a much-needed whiff of *dolce vita*. It was the start of the greatest upheaval Sydney had known since it ceased being a penal colony.

Conflict & Change

The winds of change that swept the world in the 1960s bowled a very mixed bag of blessings into Sydney. They spelled the end of Mother Grundy's reign, puffing away the blue laws, censorship, dress codes, and enforced Sunday observance. They brought in the so-called Permissive Society and its long-haired, beringed standard-bearers, the hippies. As author Russell Braddon commented: "Habitually stoned out of their minds, they believed themselves beautiful. They were also convinced that it was they who invented sex."

But the period also produced the most divisive conflict ever waged by Australia—Vietnam. For the first time Australia went to war without Britain, sending 40,207 men to Indochina. What created a rising tide of bitterness was the fact that nearly half of them were conscripts, drafted to fight for—nobody knew precisely what. This time Sydney's youth did not crowd the recruiting stations as they had in previous wars. Instead, they staged protest demonstrations, which grew bigger, noisier, and more violent as the war dragged on.

Others, however, lined their pockets. Sydney was the top favorite R&R haven for U.S. servicemen. Tens of thousands of them swarmed in for a spot of frantic fun before returning to Vietnam. Their demands sparked radical changes in the square mile called Kings Cross. The Cross was once a pleasantly bohemian neighborhood, sprinkled with European restaurants and low-rent studios. Now it turned into a round-the-clock red-light zone, crammed with stripjoints, bars, and brothels, thronged with hookers of every sex and price gradation.

The Vietnam tragedy left Australia an uneasy conscience and profound distrust of military adventurism. It left Sydney in particular with a very nasty drug problem that has not diminished with the years.

The positive side of the decades was expressed in an unprecedented building boom. Giant downtown complexes, such as the 50-story polygon Australia Tower and the MLC Centre, introduced an exciting mix of plazas, terraces, restaurants, outdoor cafes, theaters, showrooms, and offices, giving the effect of an Italian town square and eliminating the archaic concept of the city as strictly a place of business. The crowning moment came in 1973, when Elizabeth II inaugurated the Opera House—a group of magnificently designed structures built on the site of an old power station. This time there was no New Guard to slash the ribbon, and after the queen had flicked her golden shears Sydney had an instantly recognizable landmark.

Other advances were less spectacular but more far reaching. One of them was the quiet shelving of the so-called White Australia policy. This "policy"—never formalized but rigidly enforced—had excluded non-Caucasians from settling in Australia. Just about the only nonwhites you saw in Sydney were a handful of Aborigines and a scattering of Asian exchange students, who were obliged to depart as soon as they had completed their courses.

Now, without any official proclamation, a stream of Chinese, Malays, Vietnamese, Cambodians, Thais, and Koreans entered, adding innumerable restaurants, shops, and stalls and taking over a goodly portion of the city's transport services. The population of metropolitan Sydney shot up to 3.5 million.

IMPRESSIONS

Australia is full of surprises and adventures and incongruities and incredibilities: but they are all true, they all happened.
—Mark Twain, 1895

200th Birthday

By the 1980s, Sydney had become one of the world's great metropolitan centers, a major tourist destination, and an international financial hub. Certain penalties were attached to this new status. The urban area now sprawled over 670 square miles, commuting to and from work could be a nerve-grinding drag, and many of the outer suburbs were faceless dormitory deserts.

Yet the unmatched harbor setting, the balmy climate, superb skyline, and myriad entertainment, sporting, and cultural attractions combined to make Sydney one of the most livable large cities on earth.

In January 1988 virtually the entire population joined the festivities that celebrated the city's 200th birthday, simultaneously the bicentenary of Australia. Few places have had a less promising start than the desolate bay in which the First Fleet unloaded its chained cargo of unwilling passengers. And few places have come such a long way.

At this point in time no visitor can escape the profusion of banners, posters, and bumper stickers proclaiming *Sydney 2000*. They drive home the message that Sydney, after a hectic international tussle, beat Beijing for the honor of hosting the next summer Olympic Games. For an advance view of the preparations for the event, see the second "Organized Tours" in Chapter 6.

2   Art, Architecture & Cultural Life

Art

The advance guard of a distinctive Australian school of painting consisted of people like Sidney Nolan, William Dobell, Margaret Preston, Arthur Streeton, and to some extent, the Aboriginal artist Albert Namatjira. These and a dozen others are today considered the lodestars of Australian brushwork, and their pictures are priced accordingly. But there is a large group of young contemporaries following in their footsteps, some of them already overshadowing the pioneers. Look for the works of Brett Whiteley, Keith Looby, Ian Fairweather, and John Olsen if you want to see what moves and shakes the Australian art world today.

Versatility is the keynote of the youngest generation of Australian artists. They give you the feeling that one medium alone simply isn't enough for the torrent of creative energy that galvanizes them. This is also the chief characteristic of Sandy Bruch, who is currently carving her name on the Sydney art scene. Bruch's highly personalized creations branch into ceramics, book illustrations, and virtually every facet of graphic art. To view her work, you can call Bruch at **02/331-2262.**

Architecture

At first glance (and second and third) Sydney's architecture is a dizzying hotchpotch of styles and sizes thrown together with all the aesthetic sensibility of a bargain basement. This is because the city has no real old and new quarters; structures of every period rub shoulders and it takes time to pick out the gems from the garbage.

Most of the gems date from the early and cruellest colonial days. The wicked Georgians—whatever their failings—built beautiful houses. Their classic simplicity, clean lines, and Grecian sense of proportion are the hallmarks of convict-architect Francis Greenway, who designed the Hyde Park Barracks, St. James's Church, and the Conservatorium of Music, along with half a dozen other period prizes.

The virtuous Victorians who followed were great engineers but mediocre architects. Their concept of beauty generally was to plaster on the maximum amount of ornamentation, so that their structures frequently came out looking like a cross between a cathedral and a wedding cake. Unfortunately they reigned for a long time and had ample funding, and left Sydney awash with ornate incubi like the Town Hall, fabricated by eight different architects in what is humorously known as Victorian Baroque.

Sydney's modern architecture emerged in the 1960s and runs the gamut from execrable to stunning. Its pièce de résistance is the Opera House, actually a group of buildings designed by the Danish master Jörn Utzon. Other outstanding examples are the soaring Sydney Tower (by Donald Crone), and Australia Tower and the grandiose MLC Centre in Martin Place (both by Harry Seidler). Kings Cross boasts a unique landmark, El Alamein Fountain, the first structure ever to use water as a sculptural material. This was done by having water spout from 211 nozzles in little spheres, the whole giving the effect of a giant, shimmering thistledown, floodlit at night. The fountain, which commemorates the battle in 1942 at El Alamein in North Africa, is one of the three most photographed tourist attractions in Sydney.

The happy aspect of Sydney's architectural stew is the ingredient of surprise that makes it such a wonderful town for strolling. Suddenly and when you least expect it, you'll stumble on buildings of such grace, charm, or wild eccentricity that you'll kick yourself if you've left your camera behind.

IMPRESSIONS

In a decade the whole skyline has changed as concrete towers thrust skywards, giving the new silhouette of the city the appearance of a miniature New York. The simile is not far-fetched, because Sydney to Australia is what New York is to the United States.
—Edgar Holt, 1971

Cultural Life

Sydney suffers (or benefits) by having a curiously split personality that goes much deeper than casual visitors can see. A local journalist summed it up when he said, "We drive on the left with American road signs." On the one hand there is a certain sentimental attachment to the Crown across the sea. This is visibly symbolized by the umpteen "royal" parks, buildings, and monuments around the city, and invisibly by the tens of thousands of local sons who sailed from Circular Quay to fight and die at Britain's call in three wars.

On the other hand, Sydney has an aggressively republican, anti-establishment facet to its character. You only have to drop in on some of the "off-Broadway" stage performances to get a sulfurous whiff of these sentiments. Coupled with a lifestyle that is much closer to that of California than to any other model, these conflicting tugs on its heartstrings have made Sydney a quite contrary—and therefore very interesting—place. Where else in the world would you find families eating traditional English Christmas dinners on a beach in 90° Fahrenheit heat? And if you look at the Australian flag flying from the buildings, you will note that it still bears Britain's Union Jack in the upper-left corner above the six stars of the Southern Cross.

There is also another kind of conflict dividing the soul of Australia in general and Sydney in particular—an ongoing struggle between hedonism and wowserism. "Wowser" is Aussie for a puritan blue-nose, and has been defined as a person living in dread that someone, somewhere, might be having a good time. Wowserism has always been a strong element in Australian history, and at certain periods its disciples more or less ruled the country. From circa 1918 to about 1960 they kept the Commonwealth locked in a kind of moral and culinary kindergarten by means of legislation that made 19th-century Boston seem wildly liberal.

They saddled the nation with liquor laws that made civilized dining a near impossibility, civilized drinking a total one. They imposed a censorship that banned virtually all adult books, plays, and films, and tore gaping holes into those they allowed in. They prohibited Sunday movie and stage performances, curtailed Sunday train excursions, and in some states went so far as to lock up children's playground swings on the Sabbath. They would have locked up the beaches if that had been technically possible, but they did manage to bar bikinis long after these had become accepted swimwear everywhere else.

When the reaction to Mother Grundy's reign set in, it was understandably drastic. Today all Sydney beaches are topless, the language in vogue on local stages turns the air blue, the town boasts a nightlife district that matches that of Marseilles, and the ads appearing in periodicals would curl an American's hair. Not so long ago the word "homosexual" wasn't permitted in print. But to quote author Robert Hughes, "When urban Australia came out of the closet, as it did in the seventies, it almost ripped the doors off their hinges."

At this time wowsers are in full retreat. Only in the liquor department do you get reminders of their existence, as you'll see in the dining chapter. How long this retreat will last is anybody's guess. For puritanism is as much inherent in the Australian character as in the American—simply the reverse side of the same coin.

A Smattering of Strine

Winston Churchill once called Britain and America "two nations divided by a common language," and the same could be said about the U.S. and Australia. Volumes have been written about Down Underese, which the locals regard as the purest form of English. Leader in the field is undoubtedly Afferbeck Lauder's *Let Stalk Strine,* the title being the phonetic translation of how a native would enunciate "Let Us Talk Australian." (The author's nom de plume is Strine for "in alphabetical order.")

Australians deliver words in a flat, nasal drawl, moving their lips as little as possible in the process. Thus Sydney becomes "Sinny" and the capital of Victoria "Melbrn." They shorten words of more than two syllables, then stick a vowel at the end of it. In this manner "compensation" turns into "compo" and a garbage collector is a "garbo." They also employ diminutives whenever possible, making surfers "surfies," mosquitoes "mozzies," and vegetables "veggies."

They call their country Oz (as in *The Wizard of. . .*), but nobody these days calls anyone "cobber" anymore. Even "fair dinkum Aussie" has a distinctly sarcastic flavor. The most commonly used term in this vein is "ocker"—and it's not meant as a compliment. An ocker denotes a rural or urban redneck.

Whether or not you understand this terminology doesn't matter much. What matters are those statements you *think* you understand, but actually don't. Australian phraseology can differ quite drastically from American. If, for instance, a waitress or shop assistant inquires "Are you all right?" and you respond with "Yes, I'm fine," it means you won't get served. The question doesn't concern the state of your health but whether you need attention.

The effect can be just as unfortunate vice versa. I once watched a young Sydneysider conduct a very promising flirtation with a lass from Los Angeles. He got so far as to make a date with her for the following day. "Righto," he said, "so I'll knock you up tomorrow morning." "You will *not*," she snapped, turned on her heel, and strode off, leaving behind a sorely bewildered Aussie. She didn't know that in Strine "knock up" means to call on.

All this, however, is still not actual Australian slang, which has a vocabulary all its own. It would require the rest of this book to enlighten you on the mysteries of such expressions as "come the raw prawn" or "flat out like a lizard drinking." They're not likely to be used on you, but you will hear and wonder over expressions such as *back o'Bourke* for the bush or outback, *sheila* for girl, *chook* for chicken, *poofter* for homosexual, *daks* for pants, *pom* for an English person, *tucker* for food, *dinkum* for honest or real, and the ubiquitous adjective *crook,* which means bad for anything from the state of the economy to the quality of a sandwich.

The following is a short list of Australian terms you'll probably encounter. The translation is into American English.

arvo afternoon
bloke guy
bludger loafer
bonnet (car) hood
boot (car) trunk
brolly umbrella
bullet, getting the being fired
bumpers (car) fenders
cockies farmers
duco car paint
earbashing talking too much
entree appetizer (*not* main course)
fireplug hydrant
flake (on a menu) shark
flog sell
footpath sidewalk
full as a boot drunk
gee-gees horses
good oil the truth
good on yer term of approval (sometimes ironic)
grog liquor
lay-by buying on deposit
lollies candy
mate buddy

mean stingy
middy small glass of beer
plonk cheap wine
power point electric socket
push gang
queue to line up—for anything
ratbag any kind of villain
schooner large glass of beer
serviette napkin
shout to treat (buy for) someone
skiting boasting
smoke-o coffee or tea break
sport man, as in "Listen, man"
squatter ranch owner
station large ranch
stubby small beer bottle
sweets dessert
ta thanks
ta-ta good-bye
taxi rank cabstand
tea dinner
wogs bugs, flies

A few more points. Strine has a curious predilection for the feminine gender—nearly everything is a *she,* including the weather, the city, one's job, or the fare on the cab meter. Australians also consistently pronounce "a" as "i," turning "paper" into "piper," and "late" into "lite." The standard greeting formula "Good day, mate," comes out "G'di, mite." They will use the term *bastard* without any human connotation whatever, referring, for instance, to a stretch of road as "She's a bastard," to mean lousy.

Finally, a difference in spelling and counting that has wreaked havoc with addresses and telephone numbers. Australians say "double" whenever a letter or number occurs twice in succession. They will spell out Paddington "p-a-double-dee-," etc., and 4,466 as "double-four double-six." If they hear you repeat letters they'll quietly assume that you stutter.

3 Famous Sydneysiders

Sir Edmund Barton   (1849–1920), Australia's first prime minister. An erstwhile lawyer, Barton became the leader of the Australasian Federation League, dedicated to uniting the six colonies into one Commonwealth. When this was accomplished, on New Year's Day 1901, Barton was elected as first head of the newly united government.

Sir John Brabham   (b. 1926), world-famous racing car designer and driver. Won the world car-racing championship twice, and was named "Driver of the Year" in 1960. Knighted in 1979.

Sir William Dobell   (1899–1970), outstanding portrait painter and major contributor to Australia's modern art movement.

Herbert Vere Evatt   (1894–1965), flamboyant and controversial foreign minister after World War II. He was elected president of the UN General Assembly in 1948, and later became head of the Australian Labor Party.

Dawn Fraser   (b. 1937), only swimmer to win a gold medal in three successive Olympic Games (1956, 1960, 1964). She was named Australian of the Year after swimming the 100 meters in 58.9 seconds at the 1964 Tokyo Games.

Francis Greenway   (1777–1837), architect who became an involuntary Sydneysider after being deported from England as a convicted forger in 1814. Directed by Governor Macquarie, who eventually pardoned him, Greenway designed the colony's finest buildings, all historical landmarks today.

Thomas Keneally   (b. 1935), trained for priesthood but became one of Australia's top novelists. In 1982 his *Schindler's Ark* (*Schindler's List* in the United States) made him the first Australian to win the coveted English Booker Prize.

John Thomas Lang   (1876–1975), most turbulent premier of New South Wales. Rising from newspaper boy to head of the state Labour Party, he pushed through major social reforms, but ran into trouble in the 1930s during the Great Depression. Nicknamed "Big Fella," Lang attempted to alleviate the financial crisis by refusing to pay the interest on loans from Great Britain. In consequence, the governor of New South Wales dismissed him from office—a hitherto unheard of action—and his own party expelled him.

William McBride   (b. 1927), gynecologist at Women's Hospital who first alerted the world to the terrible danger of giving the drug thalidomide to expectant mothers. The echoes of his warning reverberated around the globe and resulted in the banning of the drug. Later he invented the first serial type of oral contraceptive.

Ken Rosewall   (b. 1934), tennis great who won the international professional single's title in 1973. Entering the Davis Cup team at age 19, Rosewall had a Davis Cup career stretching over 21 years.

Dame Joan Sutherland   (b. 1926), possibly the greatest opera singer born in the southern hemisphere. Sutherland began her working life as a typist but after winning two singing contests in Australia, she became a soprano sensation at London's Royal Opera House in 1952. She never looked back, earning her greatest acclaim in *Lucia di Lammermoor* at La Scala, Milan.

Sir Gordon Taylor   (1896–1966), pioneer of long-distance aviation. Gordon flew with Kingsford Smith on a nightmarish flight to New Zealand during which he climbed out on a wing and nursed a faltering starboard motor long enough for the aircraft to make an emergency landing.

4   Food & Drink

Sydney today is one of the world's great centers of gastronomy, but its eating facilities were created in a unique and rather tragic fashion. Every war and political upheaval around the globe generated a flood of refugees into Australia. They brought their culinary skills with them, and frequently that was all they brought. Thus immediately after World War II there was a mushrooming of Polish, Czech, Yugoslavian, German, and Romanian establishments. A little later came the Hungarians. Then the Vietnamese, Cambodians, and Koreans. At present Sydney is awash with Thai eateries. A sprinkling of Italian, Greek, and Chinese restaurants had always existed. Taken together they add up to a culinary spectrum that ranges from Argentinian to Yemenite, covering every international nuance in between.

Some 40 or so years ago the gastronomic scene was frankly dismal. Australia's national diet was standard Anglo-Irish, only slightly alleviated by the high quality of the meat and vegetables. Australians rarely drank either wine or coffee, but habitually drank tea *with* their meals. Cheese resembled flexible soap and bread was a crustless white square with the flavor of blotting paper.

Regulations enforced by the reigning wowser faction were partly to blame. They made al fresco dining almost impossible and the harmonizing of edibles and potables as difficult as humanly practicable. On one historic occasion the minions of the law actually arrested the proprietor of a top-ranking restaurant for serving genuine sherry trifle dessert (he had no liquor license).

It was in the realm of alcohol legislation that the bluenose brigade outdid itself. They used a wartime emergency act, dating back to the *First* World War, to close hotel bars at 6pm and keep them shut all day on Sunday. Since most workers got off at 5pm, the last legal drinking hour became a lunatic stampede in which you needed a shoehorn and a hand grenade to get near the bar. Restaurant drinking was restricted by constantly reducing the number of liquor licenses available for the purpose. These laws were kept in force by a strange alliance between the wowser lobby and the liquor barons. Publicans were keenly aware of the delightful advantages of the "five o'clock swill." They could sell as much grog during one frenzied hour as they would in an entire evening of leisurely sipping. The fact that they did so in conditions resembling a cattleyard didn't concern them in the slightest. So what if their bars looked like green-tiled toilets? They were saving fortunes on staff wages, light bills, furniture, and everything else they would have had to spend in order to make their establishments attractive. The fact that the blue laws virtually eliminated any meaningful competition between them suited the publicans dandy.

Only during the 1950s, after several state referendums, the influx of Europeans, and an enormous amount of media pressure, were the laws gradually relaxed. Among the wonderful by-products of this process was the flowering of Sydney's beer and wine gardens, sidewalk cafes, and outdoor restaurants that blend perfectly with the climate.

One hangover from the wowser epoch, oddly enough, works out in favor of the dining public. This is the institution called BYO, which stands for "Bring Your Own" (bottle, that is). Since liquor licenses are still expensive, many of the less pricey establishments operate without them. You buy your own potations (there is always a bottle shop in the vicinity) and the restaurant supplies the glasses. The advantage? Well, a passable bottle of Riesling costs around $A7 over the counter. Served by a waiter it would be $A10 or more.

The Cuisine

Actually there is no such thing as an Australian cuisine, but there are a number of outstanding national dishes. They don't include kangaroo-tail soup, which is difficult to obtain and mostly canned for export to the Far East. There is, however, roast spring lamb in mint sauce and carpetbagger steak (beef tenderloin stuffed with oysters). And that earthy but wonderful local combination, steak and eggs: a plate-size steak with two fried eggs on top, which some rural families still eat for breakfast. Also a selection of seafood that ranks among the world's finest: the small sweet Sydney rock oysters prepared Kilpatrick, with a slice of fried bacon; Queensland snapper, coral trout, and the tender and subtle-tasting barramundi (not obtainable anywhere outside Australia); Moreton Bay bugs, an outrageously misnamed species of miniature crustacean; Tasmanian scallops and lightly grilled John Dory, another fish found only in Australian waters; and Victorian yabbies (a small type of lobster) and their larger relative, the crayfish. (Crayfish, by the way, is the usual Australian term for lobster.) Here I must mention two Oz specialties that might be mercifully forgotten, but loom so large that they can't be ignored. One is the meat pie. This down under equivalent of the hot dog and hamburger consists of an outer crust of soggy pastry filled with anonymous meat, the whole concoction drenched in tomato sauce before consumption. It tastes nearly as gruesome as it sounds, and the inhabitants of Oz put away astronomic quantities of it.

Everybody eats them, from members of Parliament to construction workers, often two or three at one sitting or standing. A Melbourne football crowd gobbled up 40,000 of them on a single memorable Saturday afternoon. Together with chips (french fries) these pies could be said to form the basic diet of a large segment of the population. Since no one has ever quite fathomed the mystery of their meat contents, I would advise visitors to treat them with caution.

The other great Aussie addiction is to a dark and odorous yeast spread called Vegemite. "Addiction" is the right term, because many Australians seem unable to survive when deprived of it. They drag jars of the stuff along with them wherever they go, including Antarctic surveys. When residing in foreign parts they spend vast amounts of time scouring the shops for it, loudly bemoaning that none of the substitutes they find tastes like the real thing. Vegemite is not an acquired taste—you have to be reared on it from childhood. Spread *thinly* on toast, the flavor is pleasant in a salty way. But you'll never become a real aficionado unless you've had it for breakfast since you were six.

A handful of specialties aside, Sydney's gastronomic excellence is based on foreign cooking—though not necessarily cooked by foreigners. Imported—that is non-Anglo-Irish—establishments outnumber the native variety by at least five to one. The restaurant scene is dominated by hundreds of small, family-run, and modestly priced eateries dishing up Greek moussaka, Indian curries, Hungarian goulash, Yugoslav raznici, Chinese dim sum, Austrian schnitzel, Italian lasagne, Mideastern felafel, Polish dumplings, German sauerbraten, and so on—usually cooked by mom and served by pop and daughter.

The same variegated influence pervades delicatessens, which are among the best, cheapest, and most cosmopolitan found anywhere. Not even the famed New York delis can match the quality of the rollmops, salami, mortadella, Camembert, Brie, liptauer, pickled cucumbers, potato salad, and ham sold here—and generally at far lower prices. One reason for this is that a Sydney sandwich is just that, not a triple-layer vegetable pile as in America.

BUSH TUCKER

Ironically, the latest Oz food fashion is actually the oldest. These are the delicacies of the original Australians, the Aborigines, hitherto ignored or despised by the white usurpers of the continent. But a television series on bush tucker, aired for the 1988 bicentennial, evoked a tremendous public response and produced a wave of recipe books and at least one commercial enterprise that grows and packages this line of edibles, which is traditionally gathered only by nomads.

Now you can actually get a taste of such culinary curiosities as roasted witchety grubs (the flavor resembles shrimp), hairy litchi, wild ginger, burrawang nuts, green ants, and sautéed mangrove worms, alongside a portion of grilled python or crocodile steak, or goanna tail (which tastes like chicken) preceded by bunya nut soup and concluded with a sorbet made from wattle seeds.

19

Food & Drink   Introducing Sydney

A few of these items appear on the menus of some deluxe Sydney restaurants—at prices that would make an Aboriginal hunter's head spin. You can also order them by mail from **Bush Tucker Supply Company,** P.O. Box B103, Boronia Park, NSW 2111, Australia.

Drinks

Although in recent decades Australians have learned to appreciate wine, beer remains the national drink, the native nectar. Statistically, Aussies down 30 gallons of beer per throat annually, a figure that becomes even more impressive when you remember that this national consumption total counts children and teetotalers. This puts them slightly below the Belgians and Bavarians—but only slightly. On the other hand, Oz beer is so much stronger than either the continental or American brews that their intake should count about 20 points more. This seems an opportune place to warn you that you can get loaded on Australian beer very quickly, unless you ask for "light" varieties.

Every Australian state has its own brands of beer, and the quality is universally high, though New South Wales doesn't quite come up to the standard of the Tasmanian, Victorian, and Western Australian products. Beer sells in small "middies" or large "schooners," with a middy costing from $A1.40 to $A1.80, depending on where and in what manner of pub you order it. If you're drinking in a group, custom demands that you "shout" in turn, meaning that every member of the group pays for a round in sequence. But *never* out of sequence—Australians take a dim view of anyone ramming largesse down their throats, unless that person has just backed a winner at the races.

The Australian wine industry is almost exactly as old (or young) as the Californian, and in some respects strikingly similar. After generations of indifference, Australians have finally taken to their grape products with such enthusiasm that the growers can't keep pace with the demand. The most illustrious wine region in the country is South Australia's Barossa Valley, but New South Wales has its own wine country, the Hunter Region. As a whole, Australia is great for light table wines, not so good in heavy varieties, fair in the champagne range. Dry or sweet vermouth is outstanding, as are Riesling and chardonnay. Claret, Moselle, Chablis, and sauterne are a joy to drink—and cheap to boot, as long as you buy them over the counter. Once a restaurant markup goes on top, it's a different story. If you wish to delve deeper into this fascinating study, you can get highly knowledgeable and erudite brochures by writing to the **Australian Wine Export Council,** Box 622, Marden, SA 5072 (☎ **08/364-1388**).

Another drink, coffee, enjoyed an even more remarkable rise in popular favor. Just 20 years ago Australians were as devoted to tea as the English, but the present generation has switched to coffee. The chief reason for this was the introduction of the espresso machine, which changed the process of coffee making. Today these miracle contraptions have proliferated, and when you order coffee you almost automatically get cappuccino. If you don't like the froth or the chocolate shavings, order a "flat white" (unless you want it black). In Sydney the product is generally excellent, but in the smaller towns it's still safer to stick to tea. Coffee, again depending on location, ranges from $A1 to $A2.20 per cup.

5 Recommended Books & Films

Books

Australian literati gained international renown when Patrick White won the Nobel Prize for literature and thus focused attention on his writing compatriots. Today the works of Australia's leading authors— people like Thomas Keneally, Christina Stead, Judith Wright, and Olga Masters—occupy what you might call global bookshelves. Robert Hughes's historical flashback, *The Fatal Shore,* topped U.S. and British best-seller lists for months. *Schindler's Ark* (*Schindler's List* in the United States), Thomas Keneally's soul-searing account of one German's fight to stem the Holocaust, won the coveted Booker Prize in England. The variety and sheer volume of Australia's literary output make it difficult to compile a brief list of "recommended" works. Those given below were chosen mainly because *I* happen to like them and because they cover the widest possible range of subjects, periods and styles. I humbly apologize for the many, many omissions that will undoubtedly enrage Australian book lovers.

GENERAL

The Unspeakable Adams and *The Inflammable Adams* (Nelson, 1983). Collections of highly unorthodox essays by Australia's wittiest and most controversial columnist, Phillip Adams.

I, the Aboriginal by Douglas Lockwood (Rigby, 1962). A prize-winning author's searching study of Aboriginal living, thinking, and attitudes.

The Fatal Shore by Robert Hughes (Collins, 1985). The most gripping and erudite account of the grim old penal-colony period.

The New Australian Cinema, edited by Scott Murray (Nelson, 1980). Excellent survey of the down under film industry.

Australian Style by Betsy Walter (Waldon, 1991) and *Leaves of Iron* by Philip Drew (Angus & Robertson, 1985). Two vastly different aspects of the Australian art and architectural scene.

Sydney by Jan Morris (Viking, 1992). Portrait and background of a city drawn with critical astuteness and affection.

LITERATURE

Riders in the Chariot and *The Tree of Man* by Patrick White (Penguin, 1962, 1964). Two of the Nobel Prize winner's most mordant and captivating novels.

Clancy of the Overflow by A. B. "Banjo" Paterson (Angus & Robertson, 1989). Australia's most beloved bush ballad; this edition superbly illustrated by Evert Ploeg.

Careful, He Might Hear You by Sumner Locke Elliott (Pan, 1963). Novel that was the basis for an outstanding movie.

The Glugs of Gosh by C. J. Dennis (Angus & Robertson, 1980). Poetic satire on national smugness, penned in 1917.

Hunting the Wild Pineapple by Thea Astley (Putnam, 1991). Collection of highly original short stories told with a dead-on ear for contemporary dialogue.

Lillian's Story by Kate Granville (Allan & Unwin, 1982). Female view of social mores down under and elsewhere.

They're A Weird Mob by Nino Culotta (Angus & Robertson, 1955). Hilarious and astutely observed saga of an Italian Immigrant in Sydney.

Films

Australia's moviemaking has garnered world acclaim, but in the 1950s and 1960s the country produced films for which the term "turkey" would have been complimentary. They were false and faded carbon copies of American and British formulas. In order to come alive, Australian films had to find the courage to portray *themselves*—warts and all—instead of aping overseas formulas in speech and plot, performing what is known in Oz as the "cultural cringe."

Significantly, all the early Australian successes were attempts to come to terms with the country's past, especially the shadowy sides. Thus *The Chant of Jimmie Blacksmith* was a searing indictment of racism, *Breaker Morant* dealt with an Australian war crime, *Gallipoli* with an appalling military debacle, and *The Getting of Wisdom* with the tawdry snobbery of Victorian school education. Even a lighthearted story like *My Brilliant Career* had a strongly critical social undercurrent.

It was with contemporary themes that Australian filmmakers sprung their biggest surprises. For this supposedly ultra-macho society produced movies that were not only sensitively poetic, but feminist, insofar as females activated the plot instead of being merely acted upon. If you've seen *High Tide, Careful, He Might Hear You, Winter of Our Dreams,* or *Travelling North,* you will know what I mean. And having once established their identity, filmmakers could spoof it, as they did in *Crocodile Dundee,* which no Aussie regards as anything but a good-natured and pleasantly profitable joke.

But success usually carries a penalty. In this case it was the drain of the finest directors toward the fleshpots of Hollywood. Within a few years Australia lost creators like Peter Weir, Bruce Beresford, and Fred Schepisi to the American motion picture industry. And while they still made outstanding films (Weir scooped an Oscar for his *Dead Poets' Society*), they no longer made them in Australia.

In 1989 Schepisi returned home to produce the haunting *Cry in the Dark,* for which Meryl Streep acquired an astonishingly authentic Oz accent. The film, originally titled *The Evil Angels,* dealt with one of Australia's most controversial murder cases, in which an innocent woman was charged with killing her child.

2

Planning a Trip to Sydney

THIS CHAPTER IS DEVOTED TO THE WHERE, WHEN, AND HOW OF YOUR TRIP—the advance-planning issues required to get it together and take it on the road.

After people decide where to go, most have two fundamental questions: What will it cost? and How do I get there? This chapter will resolve those issues and answer other important questions, such as where to obtain more information about the destination and when to go.

---

1 Information, Entry Requirements & Money

Sources of Information

The **Australian Tourist Commission** is extremely helpful, and maintains the following offices in the United States, England, and New Zealand: **Los Angeles:** 2121 Ave. of the Stars, Suite 1200, Los Angeles, CA 90067 (☎ **310/552-1988**); **New York:** 489 Fifth Ave., 31st Floor, New York, NY 10017 (☎ **212/687-3000**); **London:** Gemini House, 10-18 Putney Hill, Putney, London SW15 (☎ **081/780-2227**); **Auckland, New Zealand:** Level 13, 44-48 Emily Place, Auckland 1 (☎ **09/379-9594**).

ENTRY REQUIREMENTS

Every visitor to Australia needs a valid passport and—unless you happen to be a New Zealander—an Australian visa, which can be obtained at an Australian consulate-general and at some Qantas ticket offices. If you apply in person at a consulate, you will generally get your visa while you wait. If you apply by mail, you should allow at least 21 working days. Visas for up to three months are free. Visas for up to six months require a U.S. $25 processing fee. An application to extend your stay after arrival in Australia costs $A200. Further information can be obtained from the following Australian government offices in the United States, Canada, England, and New Zealand.

IN THE UNITED STATES   Contact the Australian Embassy, 1601 Massachusetts Ave. NW, **Washington, DC** 20036 (☎ **202/797-3000**). There are five offices of the Australian Consulate-General: 1000 Bishop St., Penthouse Suite, **Honolulu,** HI 96813 (☎ **808/524-5050**); 1990 Post Oak Blvd., Suite 800, **Houston,** TX 77056 (☎ **713/629-9131**); 611 N. Larchmont Blvd., **Los Angeles,** CA, 90004 (☎ **213/469-4300**); 636 Fifth Ave., 4th Floor, **New York,** NY 10111 (☎ **212/245-4000**); One Bush St., **San Francisco,** CA 94104 (☎ **415/362-6160**).

IN CANADA   Contact the Australian High Commission at 50 O'Connor St., Suite 710, **Ottawa,** ON K1P 6L2 (☎ **613/236-0841**). Additionally, there are two offices of the Australian Consulate-General: 175 Bloor St. East, **Toronto,** ON

M4W 3R8 (☎ 416/323-1155); and World Trade Centre, 999 Canada Place, Suite 602, **Vancouver,** BC V6C 3E1 (☎ 604/684-1177).

IN GREAT BRITAIN AND IRELAND Contact the Australian High Commission, Australia House, The Strand, **London** WC28 4LA (☎ 071/379-4334); the Australian Consulate-General, Hobart House, 80 Hanover St., **Edinburgh** EH2 2DL (☎ 031/226-6271); the Australian Consulate-General, Chatsworth House, Lever Street, **Manchester** M1 (☎ 061/228-1344); or the Australian Embassy, Fitzwilliam House, Wilton Terrace, **Dublin** 2 (☎ 01/76-1517).

IN NEW ZEALAND Contact the Australian High Commission, 72 Hobson St., Thorndon, Wellington, **Auckland** (☎ 04/473-6411).

CUSTOMS

There is no limit on the personal funds you may bring into or take out of Australia. Visitors may bring personal effects into Australia

---

The Australian Dollar, the U.S. Dollar & the British Pound

At this writing, U.S. $1 = about $A1.40 and U.K. £1 = about $A2.10. These rates fluctuate and may not be the same when you travel in Australia. Therefore, the accompanying table should be used only as a guide. Also remember that you usually receive a less-favorable exchange rate when you buy Aussie bucks in America or Great Britain or cash traveler's checks at Australian airports or currency exchanges or hotels. The best rates are usually those offered by banks.

$A	U.S.$	U.K.£	$A	U.S.$	U.K.£
0.25	0.18	0.12	6.00	4.29	2.86
0.50	0.36	0.24	7.00	5.00	3.33
0.75	0.54	0.36	8.00	5.71	3.81
1.00	0.71	0.48	9.00	6.43	4.29
1.50	1.07	0.71	10.00	7.14	4.76
2.00	1.43	0.95	12.00	8.57	5.71
2.50	1.79	1.19	14.00	10.00	6.67
3.00	2.14	1.43	16.00	11.43	7.62
3.50	2.50	1.67	18.00	12.86	8.57
4.00	2.86	1.90	20.00	14.29	9.52
4.50	3.21	2.14	30.00	21.43	14.29
5.00	3.57	2.38	50.00	35.71	23.81

without paying duty. For those over 18 these include 200 cigarettes or 250 grams of cigars or tobacco and one liter of alcoholic liquor. Other goods to the value of $A400 for adults and $A200 for children under 18 may be included in personal luggage duty-free.

There are very strict laws prohibiting the entry of drugs, firearms, and certain quarantinable goods into Australia. These laws are enforced and penalties are severe.

Money

Australia, you'll be glad to hear, deals in dollars and cents. Paper money, however, is called "notes," not "bills." Coins come in (rarely seen) 1¢ and 2¢ copper pieces; 5¢, 10¢, 20¢, and 50¢ in silver; and $1 and $2 in brass. Notes are $5, $10, $20, $50, and $100.

TRAVELER'S CHECKS & CREDIT CARDS

Traveler's checks in U.S. dollars are accepted virtually everywhere in Australia, though most banks ask to see a passport. Australian states impose a stamp duty of around A10¢ per check, so it's cheaper to

What Things Cost in Sydney	$A
Taxi from airport to city	18.00
Bus from airport to city	6.00
Local telephone call	0.30
Double room at Inter-Continental Sydney (very expensive)	285.00
Double room at Hotel Capital (moderate)	95.00
Double room at Kirketon Hotel (budget)	68.00
One 3-course dinner, without wine, at Bennelong (expensive)	39.00
One 3-course dinner, without wine, at Balkan (moderate)	25.00
One 3-course dinner, without wine, at Kim (budget)	18.00
Can of local beer	1.60
Cup of coffee	1.00–2.20
Haircut (either sex)	16.00–18.00
Coca-Cola	1.20
Roll of ASA 100 Kodacolor film, 36 exposures	6.00
Admission to Museum of Contemporary Art	6.00
Movie ticket	11.50
Theater ticket	12.00–39.00
Pack of cigarettes (20)	4.25

stick to higher denominations. Most banks also charge a fee for the transaction. It's generally better to cash checks at a bank rather than a hotel, because the hotel exchange rate is nearly always less favorable than the bank rate. Major credit cards, especially Visa and MasterCard, are accepted throughout Australia.

2 When to Go—Climate, Holidays & Events

The Climate

Sydney's seasons are the reverse of those in North America and Europe, though not as contrasting. September to November is spring, December to February is summer, March to May is fall, and June to August is winter. The variations involved resemble southern California. While winter can get fairly frosty, it doesn't entail snow. Summer is hot, humid, and subtropical, alleviated by cooling squalls of wind known as "southerly busters." During spring and fall you are liable to get a mixture of the above, plus heavy rain. In general it's an outdoor climate, and the locals make full use of it.

Monthly Temperature & Rainfall in Sydney

	Jan	Feb	Mar	Apr	May	June	July	Aug	Sept	Oct	Nov	Dec
Max Temp (°F)	78	78	76	71	66	61	60	63	67	71	74	77
Min Temp (°F)	65	65	63	58	52	48	46	48	51	56	60	63
Rainfall (in.)	3.5	4.0	5.0	5.3	5.0	4.6	4.6	3.0	2.9	2.8	2.9	2.9
Rainy Days	8	9	12	13	12	11	11	8	8	8	8	7

Holidays

Australian public holidays batten down Sydney's hatches fairly tightly, except for Kings Cross, which generally ignores them. Holidays are New Year's Day (January 1), Australia Day (last Monday in January), Good Friday, Easter Monday, Anzac Day (April 25), Queen's Birthday (second Monday in June), Labour Day (first Monday in October), and Christmas Day and Boxing Day (December 25 and 26).

Sydney Calendar of Events

January

★ **Festival of Sydney**

This joyous hodgepodge of popular entertainments, cultural events, and ethnic presentations, with outdoor markets, crafts fairs, and sporting competitions thrown in, incorporates Australia Day (Jan 26) with its grand military tattoo and reenactment of the landing of the First Fleet.

Where: All over town. **When:** Most of January. **How:** Contact NSW Travel Centre. 19 Castlereagh Street, Sydney NSW 2000 (☎ **02/231-4444**).

• **Opera in the Park,** Hyde or Centennial Park. The famous Sydney Opera Company stages free, outdoor performances in January.

February

• **Gay and Lesbian Mardi Gras Parade** Out of the closet and rolling down the main city streets come some of the most fantastic floats and costumed paraders you're likely to see. Date varies.
• **Chinese New Year.** Celebrated throughout Australia, but especially in Sydney's large Chinatown (Haymarket) featuring impressive dragons and myriads of firecrackers. Dates vary.

March

★ **Royal Easter Agricultural Show**

Australia's top agricultural showcase offers the country's best—from livestock to wine, farm machinery to household gadgets—plus a fun park and carnival, art exhibits, fashion and flower shows, and events as varied as sheepdog trials, whipcracking contests, and polo matches.
Where: Moore Park Showground. **When:** Twelve days before Easter. **How:** Contact the Royal Agricultural Society of NSW, Box 4317, GPO Sydney, NSW 2001 (☎ **02/331-9111**).

June

• **Sydney Film Festival** Held in various theaters (check the newspapers) and in hot competition with the parallel Melbourne event, this festival brings out the latest and most innovative Australian cinematic productions. The festival generally lasts for two weeks. Quality varies, as do the dates.

August

• **Around Australia Yacht Race.** The second-biggest windjammer event in the country. Watch the start in Sydney Harbour. Late August.
• **City-to-Surf Fun Run.** A nine-mile mini-marathon that has thousands of amateur joggers and some professional runners pounding from downtown to the beach. See the papers for the exact route and date.

September

• **Rugby League Grand Final,** Moore Park Football Stadium. Aussie equivalent of the Super Bowl. Some 40,000 fans crowd in, fiercely partisan and known as "barrackers." Date varies.

December

- **Sydney–Hobert Yacht Race.** *The* canvas classic down
  under. The competing yachts look magnificent as they start
  on the race over the rough Bass Strait to Tasmania. If you
  can't get into one of the scores of spectator craft, the best
  vantage point is Lady Macquarie's Chair in the Botanic
  Gardens. December 26.

3   Health & Insurance

HEALTH PREPARATIONS   No special health preparation is
necessary unless you've recently visited regions affected by yellow
fever, smallpox, or cholera, in which case you need a certificate of
vaccination. Visitors are permitted to bring reasonable quantities of
prescribed nonnarcotic medications.

INSURANCE   Only visitors from Great Britain and New Zealand
are covered by the Australian Medicare system. All others should take
out private medical insurance. Make sure that your personal and
family policy covers overseas medical care in case of illness or acci-
dent. When renting a car, third-party insurance is compulsory, and
more comprehensive coverage is optional but advisable.

4   What to Pack

What to take depends largely on when you come, but in any case
include at least one warm sweater or jacket. Generally Sydneysiders
dress informally, but on certain occasions a bit of polish is considered de rigueur. Some of the posher restaurants won't allow male
customers in without a tie, and a few even insist on coats. Women
tend to wear more skirts and fewer pants than their American sisters, but that's entirely optional. The most widespread summer wear
for men consists of walking shorts, knee-high socks, and short-sleeved
shirt with or without tie. It looks rather smart, faintly military, and
is acceptable office garb. Women frequently wear tropical whites,
men *never*.

Women needn't bother to stock up on pantyhose. They're
sold everywhere—and cheaply—in Australia. The same goes for
cosmetics.

If you come in the Australian winter, the handiest item either sex
can bring is an all-weather coat with a detachable lining. That, combined with a scarf and a small travel umbrella, should see you through
whatever Sydney's weather has in store.

There are a few items you should bring, regardless of season. One
is a washcloth in a plastic case—very few Aussie hotels supply them.
A travel alarm clock makes you independent of hotel wakeup calls,
which are notoriously unreliable. Sunglasses. A small flashlight. A pair
of light plastic shoe trees. A magnifying glass to read the tiny print
on maps. Stationery and envelopes, since these are much more
expensive in Australia than in the U.S. The same goes for film.

And—if you smoke—a cigarette lighter. The standard Australian wood matches cost A20¢ a box.

Leave at home any kind of electrical gadgetry unless it runs on batteries or you bring along a 220–240V, flat three-pin plug converter/adapter. You should also beware of taking any cosmetic liquid in glass bottles; stick to unbreakable plastic.

5 Tips for the Disabled, Seniors, Singles, Families & Students

FOR THE DISABLED   Disabled persons can get advice on facilities and other aid from **Technical Aid for the Disabled** (☎ 808-2022) and **Consumer Information for the Disabled,** 58 Oxford St., Darlinghurst (☎ 331-2606).

FOR SENIORS   Few of the discounts available to Australian seniors apply to tourists, since you have to show an Australian Pensioner's Card to get them. For seniors' activities, contact the **Senior Citizens Clubs Information,** 34 Argyle Place (☎ 247-3388).

Several U.S. groups have programs for independent senior travelers down under. These programs include motor travel, hotel, rail, and bus discounts, and apartment bookings. The largest such organization is the **American Association of Retired Persons,** 601 E St. NW, Washington, DC 20049 (☎ 202/434-2277).

FOR SINGLES   Advice for single tourists inevitably means single women. Men are supposed to get along without—which a great many patently cannot.

Solo ladies are rarely hassled in Sydney, except in Kings Cross, which is a recognized red-light district. Even there it's safety in numbers—the streets are so thronged at all hours that a hassle seldom goes beyond a proposition. The pub scene, however, is still pretty much a male stamping ground. Women should expect some heavily inquisitive stares if they enter on their own. In pairs or groups they are readily accepted.

This does not apply to taverns featuring band entertainment. Since pubs form the major venues for rock, jazz, western, and folk combos, there is absolutely no gender discrimination among their audiences. The same goes for discos, dance clubs, or other night spots, where the scene is usually so chaotic that nobody knows who came in with whom. Or who leaves with whom, for that matter.

There are a large number of women's aid and support organizations in Sydney, including the **Women's Emergency Centre,** (☎ 516-5588), **Womens' Health Advisory Service,** (☎ 046/53-1445), and **Womens' Action Group** (☎ 428-3317).

FOR FAMILIES   Sydney offers an immense array of family facilities and entertainment. For particulars see "Cool for Kids" in Chapters 4, 5, and 6. You'll find a mass of additional activities listed in the free monthly publication *Sydney's Child,* P.O. Box 171, Beecroft, NSW 2119 (☎ 484-5334).

Family rates in Sydney hotels vary considerably. Some establishments provide free rollaway beds, others charge for them. Some allow children up to certain ages to share a room with their parents free, others charge heavily discounted rates. A few of the larger hotels provide playrooms and day-care centers, but these are mostly in the deluxe bracket. Family rates depend chiefly on the season, that is, they go up during school holidays and down during the slack winter months. Virtually all museums, exhibits, and outdoor entertainments have special children's rates or discounts for family groups. The same applies to organized tours and excursions.

Don't forget that you need a valid passport for *everyone* in your family. Children up to 18 years may either be included on a parent's passport or have one of their own.

FOR STUDENTS   You should obtain an International Student Identity Card, one of the handiest documents extant. It entitles you to special transport rates as well as discount tickets to sporting events, museums, exhibitions, and (some) theaters. Apply to the **Council on International Educational Exchange,** 205 E. 42nd St., New York, NY 10017 (☎ **212/661-1414**).

In Sydney the following outfits can offer advice and help: **Student Exchange,** 33 Ryde Rd., Pymble (☎ **418-1211**), and **Student Travel** (☎ **519-9866**).

Campus accommodation is available on the two city campuses during university vacations: mid-January to mid-February and June and July. The first is at the International House of the University of Sydney campus at 96 City Rd., Chippendale, NSW 2008 (☎ **02/692-2040**). Full board costs $A40 per day. The International House of the University of New South Wales (☎ **02/663-0418**) charges $A35 per day, full board, for students, $A45 for nonstudents. In both cases facilities are campus casual. And in both cases it's best to book ahead. Neither accepts credit cards.

6   Getting There

By Plane

Although you can also get to Sydney by cruise ship, the vast majority of visitors prefer air travel. The deciding factor is time: You can now fly from Los Angeles or San Francisco in just 14 hours and 40 minutes.

FROM NORTH AMERICA   The international carriers flying to Sydney from North America include **Qantas** (☎ toll free **800/227-4500**); **Canadian Airlines** (☎ toll free **800/367-5320**); **United Airlines** (☎ toll free **800/631-1500**); and **Air New Zealand** (☎ toll free **800/262-1234**).

The early 1990s fare war among these companies has made ticket prices as erratic as stock market charts . . . fares change from month to month, sometimes from week to week. The only way to keep up with these wild fluctuations is to query every carrier before deciding which one to take. Treat the prices I quote as guidelines rather than fixtures. They're liable to change several times over before you get to read them.

Qantas has the most flights—47 per week—from the United States and Canada, 12 of them nonstop (2 of them recently added, direct nonstops from Los Angeles to Sydney). It is also the only carrier that gives you a choice of afternoon or late-evening departures. The afternoon departure is a blessing for folks who suffer from jetlag. The flight arrives in Sydney just at bedtime, so you can catch a good night's sleep and wake up bright-eyed next morning.

The Qantas ticket offices in Los Angeles and San Francisco can also issue Australian visas to travelers. This means that Qantas ticket holders can complete their travel formalities at the same time they make their airline bookings. All flights from North America leave from San Francisco, Los Angeles, or Vancouver. To reach your point of departure, you can utilize the special add-on fares. These are very low fares from U.S. cities to the departure points. As their name suggests, add-on fares are added to your international ticket when you purchase it and cannot be bought separately.

Qantas operates a partnership service with American Airlines from New York, Chicago, Boston, and Washington, D.C. In addition, Qantas is a partner in several frequent-flyer programs. Thus, members of Alaska Airlines, Canadian Airlines, and American Airlines frequent-flyer programs can earn miles by flying Qantas between U.S. cities and destinations in Australia, New Zealand, and the Pacific. Award levels in these programs vary and frequently change, so it's best to check with each carrier for current information.

FROM THE UNITED KINGDOM British Airways (☎ **081-897-4000**) and Qantas (☎ **081-846-0466**) have the most frequent service from the United Kingdom to Australia. Air New Zealand (☎ **071-930-3434**) also flies to Australia, as do several other airlines. Qantas services seven Australian cities regularly, including daily flights from London to Sydney and Melbourne. British Airways serves Sydney, Melbourne, Adelaide, and Perth, with daily flights to Sydney from London. Stopovers may be in such places as Bangkok or Singapore.

At the time of this writing, the price of a regular economy-class fare from London to Sydney was £1245 to £1445, with a minimum stay of 14 days. The flying time to Sydney from London is approximately 21 hours, including one stopover.

AIRFARES

The key factor in determining airfares is *when* you want to travel. All airlines have different price ranges for low season, shoulder season, and high season. These seasons correspond roughly to winter, spring, and summer down under. Remember that Australian seasons are the reverse of ours—that is, our winter is summer down under, so that the highest rates apply when it's coldest here and hottest there. If you choose to travel in high season you are liable to depart from, say, a subzero New York and land in Sydney sweltering in 95°F heat.

Qantas has three seasons: basic (April to August); shoulder (March and September to November); peak (December to February). The normal price of an economy-class round-trip ticket from Los Angeles or San Francisco to Sydney, Melbourne, Brisbane, or Cairns is $2,008 basic, $2,108 shoulder, $2,308 peak. There are variations in these rates depending on whether you fly midweek (Sunday to Wednesday) or weekend (Thursday to Saturday), with midweek rates costing $50 to $100 less.

However, under the current free-for-all conditions "normal" prices come close to being exceptional—a paradox produced by the global airfare war. Every airline features limited duration discounts, some of them offering savings up to 50%. The trouble is that these cut-rate offers change so fast that they can't be contained in a book. The only way to keep abreast of them is to start inquiring a couple of months before your projected departure date.

Other bargains are of a more permanent nature (see below), but even these undergo changes in the course of a season.

SUPER-APEX   This is one of the best bargains Qantas offers. You can fly economy from San Francisco or Los Angeles during midweek in basic season for U.S. $948 round-trip, shoulder season U.S. $1,048, peak U.S. $1,248. These are point-to-point fares; no stopovers permitted. You must purchase your ticket at least 21 days before departure and stay in Australia at least seven days, but not longer than one month.

CUSTOM-APEX   This allows you one free stopover in addition to your point of turnaround. The ticket to Sydney, Melbourne, Brisbane, or Cairns costs U.S. $1,098 for midweek departure in basic season, U.S. $1,198 shoulder, U.S. $1,398 in peak season. For

---

Frommer's Smart Traveler: Airfares

1. Shop *all* airlines flying to Sydney. New, competitive carriers may have entered the field.

2. Start inquiring several months before your projected departure.

3. Try to fly on a weekday. Weekend airfares are frequently higher.

4. Currently there are no standby fares being offered to Sydney. This may change tomorrow.

5. Make use of the special discount fares offered to overseas visitors flying *inside* Australia.

6. Ask about frequent-flyer programs that will give you bonus points.

7. Ask about special discounts being offered for the flight from your hometown to your departure city.

8. If told that there are no cheap seats available, call again—and again. Low-cost seats often materialize at the last moment.

an additional U.S. $150 you can buy unlimited stopovers in Australia, New Zealand, Tahiti, and Fiji.

EXCURSION   South Pacific Excursion fares have no advance purchase requirements, but stipulate a minimum seven-day, maximum six months stay. You get a maximum of six stops plus point of turnaround on your journey, letting you visit Australia, New Zealand, Fiji, and Tahiti. Round-trip fare in basic season is U.S. $2,008, shoulder U.S. $2,108, peak U.S. $2,308.

DOMESTIC FLIGHTS   In 1993 Qantas merged with Australian Airlines, one of the two major carriers within the country. This means that you can now get to as well as all around Australia on the same airline. It also means that you can get domestic flights at reduced rates. Call Qantas for information about domestic discounts as soon as you have decided on your itinerary.

GROUP FARES   These can mean substantial savings for any club, association, or impromptu group traveling together for any purpose. However, every airline seems to have a different policy regarding group bookings, and these policies change according to season and demand. Your best bet is to contact several airline sales offices and hear what kind of deal they're offering. It will depend not only on the season but also on the size of your group.

3

Getting to Know Sydney

SYDNEY IS LIKE A GIANT PEOPLE-EATER AND NOW CONTAINS ABOUT TWO thirds of the population of New South Wales or one fifth of all Australians. The metropolitan area stretches inland from the South Pacific Ocean to the foot of the Blue Mountains, from Broken Bay in the north to Port Hacking in the south.

1 Orientation

Arriving

BY PLANE Kingsford Smith International Airport, the main gateway to Australia, is located in Mascot, about five miles south of the center of Sydney. *Newsweek* magazine once described it as being run "with Aussie-friendly efficiency," but alas, t'ain't no more. With an annual 24% increase in tourist arrivals, the friendliness lingers but most of the efficiency has faded. There are long overlapping lines at reservations counters and Customs checks, wild scrambles for long-delayed baggage, invisible luggage carts, and absentee porters. As a dessert, so to speak, the government charges you a $A25 departure tax when you leave. On the plus side, the airport has all the necessary facilities, from currency exchange and showers to around-the-clock cafeterias and car-rental counters. A major effort is under way to upgrade Kingsford Smith back to the pleasant facility it once was.

The excellent **Airport Express** bus service delivers you to your hotel and costs $A6. **Cab** fare is around $A18.

Tourist Information

The **NSW Travel Centre,** at 19 Castlereagh St., near Martin Place (☎ **231-4444**), spreads out a welcome mat on behalf of the state government. Very handy, very helpful, and tremendously busy, the office provides maps, brochures, and information booklets, plus an avalanche of leaflets advertising anything from antique shops to Zanzibarian restaurants. Office hours are 9am to 5pm Monday through Friday.

The privately run **Sydney Convention and Visitors Bureau** operates a small kiosk in Martin Place between Castlereagh and Elizabeth Streets (☎ **235-2424**), open Monday through Friday from 9am to 5pm.

City Layout

Much of Sydney is located on a peninsula. The city proper is minute compared with the horizon-filling vastness of suburbs reaching farther and farther inland. **Sydney Harbour** (actually Port Jackson, but nobody calls it that) divides the area into **Sydney proper** and the **North Shore.** The harbor is a wonderful jigsaw of hundreds of islands, peninsulas, coves, and inlets, many with their own miniature beaches. (The famous surfing beaches are not inside the harbor but on the open seafront to the east.) Spanning the water at the narrowest point is the unlovely but essential **Sydney Harbour Bridge,** choked with traffic at most hours, but offering magnificent views. The vast majority of tourist attractions and accommodations are clustered south of the bridge as are luxurious mansions and posh suburbs.

The focal point and the center of the city is **Martin Place,** a large pedestrian plaza fringed by outdoor cafes that bustles with office workers at lunch break. On weekdays a rock, jazz, folk, or dance ensemble usually performs in the sunken stage area. If you stand with your back to the pillars of the General Post Office (GPO), you're facing due north. That is the direction of the Harbour Bridge, of Circular Quay (terminal for ferry services), and at the tip of Bennelong Point, Sydney Opera House. Northeast and east stretch the Royal Botanic Gardens and their southward extension, the Domain. Southeast is Hyde Park, from which point William Street runs straight and rather steeply uphill to **Kings Cross,** a kind of adjunct to center city.

South of you, at the grubby end of Pitt Street, stands **Central Railway Station,** a national and intrastate rail terminal. Also in the area is **Chinatown,** crammed with Chinese eateries. Due west is **Darling Harbour,** Australia's most ambitious urban-development project. Two streets away to the northwest is **Wynyard Station,** terminal for city train and bus transportation. Extending either through Martin Place or nearby are the city's main shopping streets— George, Pitt, Castlereagh, and Elizabeth.

Sydney has no ghetto districts in the American sense. Its ethnic minorities are mostly scattered, with some concentrations. Italians are concentrated in Leichhardt, and Vietnamese in Cabramatta. A neglected and impoverished Aboriginal enclave is in Redfern, near Central Station. Sydney does have poor, disintegrating neighborhoods, some of which have been gentrified. Not long ago, for instance, Surry Hills and the dockside region of Woolloomooloo were such areas. The narrow-chested terrace rows have since been transformed into chic little town houses, driving rents up and most of the original inhabitants out.

In fact, the Sydney equivalent of the American Victorian brownstone is the formerly working-class terrace house, preferably with the proletarian frontage intact, but with the interior upgraded to art nouveau and a BMW parked outside. The curlicued wrought-iron balcony railings known as "Sydney lace," once believed worthless and sold for scrap, now fetch nice prices. If you can get a couple of brass coach lanterns, polish them to a high shine, and stick them over the entrance, you've got it made, mate.

IMPRESSIONS

The men strike you as quite ordinary but Sydney's women are probably the prettiest, shapeliest, most spirited creatures in the southern hemisphere.
—French Journalist Bertrand Dorot, 1989

It so happens that Sydney is also Australia's largest industrial center, manufacturing almost everything you can think of, including nuclear reactor equipment. However, factories are concentrated in pockets well away from the better residential and recreation areas, and tourists can spend weeks in Sydney without running across a manufacturing plant.

There is no actual wrong or right side of the tracks, but some suburbs count decidedly as top-grade, while others are merely trendy. Suburbs lie along the shorelines of lower Sydney Harbour, along the eastern oceanside from **Double Bay** to **Palm Beach** and **Vaucluse**, and in the leafy, tucked-away regions of the North Shore, where residents have fought bitter battles against the introduction of hotels, hamburger stands, and movie theaters.

NEIGHBORHOODS IN BRIEF

Sydney has hundreds of neighborhoods, though the locals hardly ever use the term. They call everything beyond the relatively small downtown area a "suburb," including districts that are simply extensions of the city. In order to clarify this for American readers— whose concept of a suburb is quite different—I have differentiated between inner and outer suburbs to convey a realistic picture. Visitors are most likely to inspect the following places.

Circular Quay   is not—and never was—circular. It's the city's waterfront with wharves from which ferries shuttle and where occasional cruise ships dock.

Chinatown,   also known as Haymarket, borders on Darling Harbour. It's a tight, crowded, and colorful mix of stalls, restaurants, and specialty stores.

Oxford Street   is Sydney's longest and most varied, but not very fashionable, shopping drag. It runs from Bondi Junction all the way to Hyde Park, changing character several times en route.

Kings Cross,   an uphill adjunct to the city. It's like Times Square and Montmartre rolled into one, but garnished with some first-class hotels and restaurants as well as charming street cafes.

Woolloomooloo,   called "The Loo," an erstwhile dockside slum adjoining the Domain. It has undergone intense gentrification and now boasts some of the finest entertainment pubs and most stylishly refurbished houses in town.

Paddington   Paddo to locals. It's a winding hilly region stretching north of Oxford Street, famous for antique shops, private art galleries, trendy cafes, interior designers, and yuppy-bohemians.

Darlinghurst   East of the city, one of Sydney's oldest neighborhoods. It's a jumble of archaic dwellings, lively pubs, and cosmopolitan restaurants.

Darling Point   Separated from Kings Cross by Rushcutters Bay Park, contains posh homes, luxury marinas, and the Cruising Yacht Club.

IMPRESSIONS
93.5 percent of the population of Sydney . . . live in suburbs outside the municipal boundaries. To paraphrase Parkinson's Law, cement tends to expand to fill the available space.
—Arthur Koestler, *The Faceless Continent,* 1969

Double Bay   Dubbed "Double Pay," the closest of the fashionable eastern suburbs. It contains the svelte Cosmopolitan Centre shopping hub with some of the "innest" boutiques and delis on the continent.

Surry Hills   East of Central Station. Once a proletarian stronghold, it is now partly gentrified and contains Belvoir Street Theatre, the pick of the avant-garde stages.

Globe and Camperdown   Two of the three inner suburbs over which the University of Sydney has sprawled (Chippendale is the other). It's crammed with students, bookstores, and good inexpensive eateries.

Bondi   Site of Australia's most celebrated and closest in surfing beach, though far from the best. It's very lively, but not particularly charming.

Watsons Bay   Panoramic peninsula jutting from the eastern suburbs. Overlooking the harbor entrance, it contains a couple wonderful oceanside restaurants and The Gap—Sydney's favorite suicide leap.

Parramatta   Western suburb 18 miles from the city. This was once the intended capital of New South Wales colony. It features historic buildings and a small-town atmosphere.

Manly   Thirty-five minutes by ferry from Circular Quay. Manly is Sydney's vacation world with four ocean beaches, a giant aquarium, promenades, and water playgrounds.

Kirribilli   Just across Harbour Bridge. Hilly and scenic, it's a suburb of engrossing views and upscale apartment blocks.

Hunters Hill   Across Gladesville Bridge, this North Shore peninsula is allegedly Sydney's snootiest enclave. It's sprinkled with charming old colonial homes, some of stone hand-hewn by convicts.

Mosman   With hills and panoramic vistas across the harbor. Mosman contains the famous Taronga Zoo, adjoining Ashton Park nature reserve.

---

2   Getting Around

Sydney's public transportation system is like the proverbial curate's egg—parts of it are excellent. The excellent portions are the electric train network, partly underground, and the ferry service. The buses have a tendency to get tangled in traffic jams, to travel in convoys, and to skip stops.

Sydney Transportation Systems

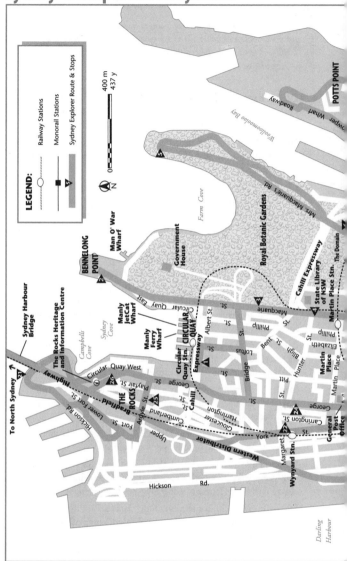

By Public Transportation

DISCOUNT PASSES You can save quite a bit of money by purchasing a **SydneyPass** that lets you travel on all buses and ferries in and around Sydney for three days. They cost $A50 for adults, $A20

TO ELIZABETH BAY

Billyard Ave.
Onslow Ave.
Roslyn Gardens
Challis Ave.
Macleay St.
Greenknowe Ave.
Elizabeth St.
El Alamein Fountain
KINGS CROSS
WOOLLOOMOOLOO
Victoria St.
South Dowling St.
Darlinghurst Rd.
Bayswater Rd.
Kings Cross Rd.
Craigend
Rd.
St.
Kings Cross Stn.
St.
Bourke St.
Cathedral St.
Palmer St.
William St.
Sir John Young Crescent
Art Gallery Rd.
The Mint
St. James Stn.
Archibald Fountain
St.
College St.
Hyde Park
Liverpool St.
Oxford St.
Burton St.
St.
St.
Crown St.
Campbell St.
Museum Stn.
Wentworth Ave.
Central Stn.
→ To Bondi Beach ↗

TNT Harborlink Monorail:
Harbourside
Convention
Haymarket
World Square
Park Plaza
City Centre

City Circle Line:
Circular Quay Station
Wynyard Station
Town Hall Station
Central Station
Museum Station
St. James Station
Martin Place Station
Kings Cross Station

City Centre
Park Plaza
Park St.
Town Hall Stn.
Elizabeth St.
Castlereagh St.
World Square
King St.
St.
Market St.
Clarence
Kent
Sussex
St.
St.
Druitt St.
Bathurst
George St.
Goulburn St.
Campbell St.
St.
Hay St.
Eddy Ave.
Railway Square
Dixon St.
CHINATOWN
DARLING HARBOUR
Pyrmont Bridge
Convention Center (Darling Harbour)
Western Distributor
Convention
Chinese Garden
Haymarket
Ultimo St.
Harris St.
Harbourside

Post Office ⊠   Information ⊕

LL16

for children under 16, and are available at the airport, the New South Wales Travel Centre, Circular Quay, and The Rocks. The SydneyPass also allows you to take three different harbor cruises, the Sydney Explorer Bus, and the Airport Express bus.

The carriages are comfortable double-deckers only slightly disfigured by graffiti. The routes are partly above, partly below ground, and they operate on eight major lines. Study the route maps displayed in all stations for destinations and connections. Trains run from 4:30am to midnight. Travel charges are by sections, starting with a short ride for $A1.20. Children under 4 travel free on the entire system, and those between 4 and 16 at half fare. A money saver here is **CityHopper,** costing $A2.10. This entitles you to unlimited, off-peak train travel for one day—after 9am weekdays and anytime weekends.

State Rail operates CityRail service and Countrylink trains, which carry passengers farther afield. These trains leave from Central Railway Station, on Eddy Avenue where George and Elizabeth streets converge. For information, call **217-8812** or **224-4744.**

BY MONORAIL   Like the underground train, the speedy monorail connecting the central business district to Darling Harbour doesn't compete with vehicular traffic. Instead, Sydney's sleek, state-of-the-art system glides over the heads of pedestrians and above congested streets. The system usually operates from 7am to 10pm Monday through Wednesday, 7am to midnight Thursday and Friday, 9am to midnight Saturday, and 9am to 8pm Sunday, but it's a good idea to check the hours on signs posted in the stations. The city center/Darling Harbour round-trip takes approximately 12 minutes. Tickets cost $A2.50; children under five are free. The monorail connects with trains at Town Hall Station. For more information call **TNT Harbourlink** (☎ **552-2288**).

BY BUS   There are two free bus routes. Route 777 takes you through the city center, and Route 666 runs from Hunter Street, at Wynyard, to the Art Gallery of New South Wales. **Long-distance buses** leave from the bus terminal at the corner of Riley and Oxford Streets (☎ **268-1881**). **Suburban buses** leave from Circular Quay for the eastern suburbs and beaches, from Carrington and York Streets at Wynyard Park for the northern suburbs and beaches. For bus information call Metrotips at **954-4422.**

Operated by State Transit, **Sydney Explorer** is a great value for tourists. The easily recognizable red buses follow a 35-kilometer (22-mile) loop around the city and pass some 26 spots of interest to visitors. Ticket holders can get off at any point in the trip and rejoin the bus whenever they like. Buses run about every 20 minutes.

Tickets, which cost $A20 for adults and $A45 per family, are good from 9am to 7pm on the day of purchase. The buses operate seven days a week and tickets are sold on board. Bus stops are marked with distinctive red-and-green Sydney Explorer signs.

BY FERRY   The terminal for all ferry services is **Circular Quay,** which isn't (and never was) circular. Ferries connect the city with the North Shore and traverse the harbor from 6am to 11:30pm. The craft in use range from racing hydrofoils to wallowing little tubs, and make delightful traveling, particularly on sunny days. Destinations

Sydney Ferries

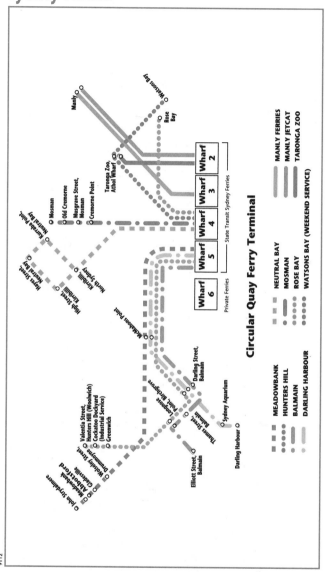

are clearly marked on the individual piers. The main services run to
Manly, Neutral Bay, Taronga Zoo, Kirribilli, Balmain, Cockatoo
Island, and Hunters Hill. Fares depend on distance. A single trip on
the inner harbor costs $A1.20 for adults, half price for children.

By Taxi

Much used and even more in demand. Sydneysiders take taxis like New Yorkers, usually hailing a cruising cab. Rates are $A1.65 at flagfall and A85¢ per kilometer thereafter. Phone bookings cost an extra A60¢. The major taxi companies are **Taxis Combined** (☎ 332-8888), **Legion** (☎ 289-9000), and **RSL** (☎ 699-0144).

WATER TAXIS   Harbour Taxis (☎555-1299) or **Taxis Afloat** (☎ 922-4252) will take you anywhere around the harbor, either to specific points or on general observations tours. The rates vary according to distance. A trip from, say, Circular Quay to Watsons Bay costs around $A30.

By Car

Before getting behind the wheel, *please* make a point of studying the rules set out below. I prefer my readers alive.

U.S., British, and Canadian driver licenses are accepted during the length of your stay.

Don't hesitate to ask for directions. Sydneysiders look busy, but they'll go out of their way to put you on the right track, frequently attaching some scraps of local lore to their instructions. The only catch is that if you get lost in a tourist area, chances are that whoever you approach will turn out to be another, equally lost, tourist. Spotting a native around Circular Quay, for instance, can be quite a task.

Note: Gasoline is called petrol here. ("Gas" refers only to what you cook with.) It sells for about A80¢ per liter (3¹/₂ liters make a gallon).

RENTALS   Sydney has many rental-car companies, but for reliability it's best to choose one of the local Big Three. All have reservation counters at Kingsford Smith airport as well as downtown: **Thrifty,** 75 William St. (☎ 380-5399); **Avis,** 214 William St. (☎ 357-2000 or 516-2877); and **Hertz,** corner of William and Riley Streets (☎ 360-6621).

While overseas driving licenses are valid for up to one year in Australia, overseas insurance coverage is *not.* Compulsory third-party insurance is automatically added to all car-rental contracts; more comprehensive coverage is optional. To rent a car you must be 21 years of age or older, and if you're under 25 you may be asked for a special reference.

Rates of all companies are in a wild state of competitive flux. Whatever figures I put down will probably be passé by the time you read this. All companies have special deals to attract customers, but these change just as often. For example, Thrifty rents medium-size, air-conditioned vehicles at $A55 a day, or $A45 a day for four or more days. The company also offers special weekend discounts. If you pick up a car anytime on Friday and return it at the same time on Monday, using it for three days, you only get charged for two.

PARKING   The situation downtown ranges from tight to impossible. For inner-city exploration it's best to use public transport or your legs.

DRIVING RULES   Sydney traffic is not quite as maniacal as that of, say, Paris or Buenos Aires. But it's heavy, fast, and at some points very badly regulated. Two glaring danger spots are the intersection where William Street runs into Kings Cross and the junction of George Street and Broadway at Central Station. Motorists are generally law-abiding (the fines are too heavy to ignore) but they have some pervasive bad habits. They insist on right-of-way, regardless of circumstances. They're very cavalier about giving signals, and count among the world's worst tailgaters, virtually crawling up your exhaust in order to make you move faster.

Traffic drives on the left-hand side of the road and cars therefore have right-hand steering. At crossings you look right-left-right. The other important points to remember are to give way to all cars at T intersections if you're approaching on the stem of the T, and to give way to cars coming from the right at intersections, unless they have traffic lights or stop signs. Wearing seat belts is *compulsory*, and failure to do so can earn you a stiff fine.

You very quickly get accustomed to right-hand steering wheels, although you'll find yourself groping for the handbrake on the wrong side. The most enduring nuisance for overseas motorists is that they continually turn on the windshield wipers when they mean to flick the indicators.

If you belong to a motoring association at home you are entitled to all services offered by the **National Roads and Motorists Association (NRMA),** 151 Clarence St. (☎ **260-9222**). They'll provide you with maps, brochures on road rules, and the best general advice on Aussie automobiling you'll get anywhere.

By Bicycle

Like New York, London, or Paris, central Sydney is *not* commendable biking territory. Streets are narrow and jammed, traffic ruthless. When possible, confine your riding to designated bike trails. Bicycles (called pushbikes in Australia) can be rented at **All Bike Hire,** corner of Canterbury Road and Gibson Avenue, Bankstown (☎ **707-1691**).

Fast Facts

American Express   The local office is at 92 Pitt St. (☎ **239-0666**), open Monday to Friday 8:30am to 5:30pm and Saturday 9am to noon.

Area Code   To call Sydney from the U.S., use the country code for Australia, **61,** and the city code for Sydney, **02.**

Babysitters   Your hotel can probably come up with a babysitter for you. Or you might try the Hyde Park Family Centre, at the corner of Park and Elizabeth Streets (☎ **265-9411**), which also provides facilities for mothers of infants and small children to change and breast-feed them, heat bottles, etc. The All Sydney Baby

Sitting Service (☎ 521-3333) comes to your hotel and charges an hourly rate plus traveling costs.

Business Hours   Most banks are open from 9:30am to 4pm Monday to Thursday and from 9:30am to 5pm on Friday. Most stores are open from 9am to 5:30pm Monday to Friday (Thursday until 9pm), on Saturday and Sunday from 9am to 4 or 5pm. Some shops stay open later on Friday, and some are open only until noon on Saturday.

In theory, pubs are open from 10am to 10pm, but in practice hours vary according to the establishment. Kings Cross drinking spots keep their own hours, serving drinks as long as they have customers. Elsewhere, it depends on whether a pub puts on live entertainers or recorded music, or poetry readings or turkey raffles, or any combination of the above.

Car Rentals   See "Getting Around" earlier in this chapter.

Climate   See "When to Go" in Chapter 2.

Crime   See "Safety," below.

Currency   See "Information, Entry Requirements, and Money" in Chapter 2.

Currency Exchange   You'll get better exchange rates for your American dollars or dollar-denominated traveler's checks at a bank than at your hotel. The Thomas Cook Currency Exchange Centre, Kingsgate Shopping Centre, Kings Cross (☎ 356-2211), is open Monday to Friday 8:45am to 5:30pm, on Saturday and Sunday from 8:45am to 1pm. The Interforex Money Exchange at no. 6 jetty, Circular Quay (☎ 247-2082), is open Monday to Friday 8am to 9pm, Saturday 8am to 8pm, and Sunday 9am to 6pm; it has several other offices as well.

While there are many Westpac banks in Sydney, one of the most convenient for tourists is located at 47 George St., The Rocks (☎ 226-2388); it's open during regular bank hours (see "Business Hours," above).

Dentist   For dental problems, contact the Dental Emergency Information Service, an official service of the Australian Dental Association (☎ 267-5919). For emergency dental services on Sunday and public holidays, phone **692-0333.**

Doctor   See "Hospitals," below.

Electricity   It's 220–240 volts AC, 50 Hertz, and plugs are flat three-pin types. North American and Japanese visitors will need both a transformer and adapter for electrical appliances. Visitors from the U.K. will require only the adapter plug. The more expensive hotels feature universal outlets that will support both 240-volt and 110-volt appliances. But check with your hotel before you plug in any small appliances you have brought with you.

Embassies and Consulates   All embassies are in the capital city of Canberra, but should you lose your passport or face some other similar problem, the following countries maintain consulates in Sydney: Canada, 50 Bridge St. (☎ **364-3000**); New Zealand, on the 25th floor of the State Bank Building, 52 Martin Place (☎ **233-8388**); United Kingdom, Level 16 Gateway, 1 Macquarie Place (☎ **247-7521**); United States, Level 59, MLC Centre, 19 Martin Place (☎ **373-9200**).

Emergencies   To call the police, ambulance, or fire brigade, dial **000** from any telephone—no coins needed.

Eyeglasses   For optical repairs or prescription work, go to the OPSM branches at 183 Macquarie St. (☎ **217-1948**) and 73 King St. (☎ **217-1885**).

Hairdressers and Barbers   These are as good as, as numerous as, and cheaper than those in the U.S., although they keep shorter hours. Try Eddie Azzi, Sky Garden, Castlereagh Street, Suite 106A (☎ **232-1116**).

Holidays   See "When to Go" in Chapter 2.

Hospitals   I hope you don't need them, but just in case, here are some of Sydney's major public hospitals: Sydney Hospital, Macquarie Street (☎ **230-2111**); Royal Prince Alfred, Missenden Road, Camperdown (☎ **516-6111**); and Prince of Wales, High Street, Randwick (☎ **399-0111**).

Hotlines   Crisis Centre (☎ **358-6577**), Gay and Lesbian Hotline (☎ **319-2799**), Life Line (☎ **264-2222**), Poison Information Centre (☎ **519-0466**); Rape Crisis Line (☎ **819-6565**).

Information   See "Tourist Information" earlier in this chapter.

Laundry and Dry Cleaning   There are hundreds of such establishments all over town. Wash on the Rocks, 9 Argyle Place, The Rocks (☎ **247-4917**), is open Monday to Friday from 7am to 6pm and Saturday from 8am to 3pm.

One-hour dry-cleaning is available at Lawrence Dry Cleaners, Wynyard Station (☎ **262-1583**), and Maurice Dry Cleaners, 11 AMP Centre (☎ **231-2498**).

Library   Visit the State Library of New South Wales, Macquarie Street (☎ **230-1414**).

Liquor Laws   See "Sydney Dining" in Chapter 5.

Lost Property   In the airport, go to the Federal Airport Corporation's administration office, second floor, International Terminal (☎ **667-9583**). If you left something in a taxi, phone the taxi company's main office. If you left something on a ferry, bus, or train, go to 490 Pitt St., near the Central Railway Station (☎ **219-2757** or **211-1176**). Each bus depot also maintains its own lost property office.

Luggage Storage/Lockers   These are located at Kingsford Smith Airport and Central Railway Station.

Newspapers and Magazines   The *Sydney Morning Herald* is the major metropolitan newspaper. The *Australian*, distributed across the country, is also widely read. *OutRage* is Australia's leading gay and lesbian monthly. The *Sydney Star Observer* is a free gay and lesbian biweekly paper.

For overseas publications try Alison's, 83 Clarence St.; Newsagency, Australia Square; Aroney's, 238 Pitt St.; or Brimar, 167 Kent St.

Photographic Needs   Nearly all chemist shops sell and process film. For camera equipment as well as repairs go to Paxton's, 285 George St. (☎ **299-2999**) or Fletcher's, 317 Pitt St.

Police   See "Emergencies," above.

Post Office   Decidedly the weak link in the Australian service chain. The General Post Office (GPO) is on Martin Place between Pitt and George Streets (☎ **230-7033**), open Monday to Friday 8:15am to 5:30pm, Saturday 8:30am to noon.

Post offices are open from 9am to 5pm Monday through Friday. Standard letters within Australia cost A45¢; overseas aerogrammes, A65¢; airletters and postcards to the U.S., A90¢.

Radio   Also known—British style—as wireless. Sydney radio depends heavily on pop music and call-in chatter of the intellectually undemanding kind. But you also get classical music on 92.9 FM, current affairs on Radio National (576 FM), and continual broadcasts of parliamentary debates on 630 AM.

Religious Services   Among Sydney's places of worship are the following: *Anglican,* St. Andrew's Cathedral, next to Sydney Town Hall (☎ **269-0642**); *Baptist,* Central Baptist Church, 619 George St. (☎ **211-1833**); *Roman Catholic,* St. Mary's Cathedral, College Street (☎ **232-3788**); *Jewish,* Great Synagogue, 166 Castlereagh St. (☎ **267-2477**); *Lutheran,* St. Paul's, 3 Stanley St., Woolloomooloo (☎ **419-5686**); *Presbyterian,* Scots Church, at York and Margaret Streets (☎ **29-1301**); *Uniting Church,* St. Stephan's, 197 Macquarie St. (☎ **221-1688**); *Seventh-Day Adventist,* 219 Edgecliff Rd., Woollahra (☎ **858-4061**).

Restrooms   Public restrooms are mostly situated in parks, although department stores, hotels, and bars will usually let you use their facilities.

Safety   There is less crime in Sydney than in large American cities, but enough to warrant caution. There are fewer muggings, robberies, and rapes, but a lot of pursue-snatchings, car thefts, hotel burglaries, and pickpocketing. Much of it is drug-related. Whenever you're traveling in an unfamiliar city or country, stay alert. Be aware of your immediate surroundings. Wear a moneybelt and don't sling your camera or purse over your shoulder. This will minimize the possibility of your becoming a victim of crime. Every society has its criminals. It's your responsibility to be aware and be alert even in the most heavily touristed areas.

Shoe Repairs   As fast as in the U.S. and about as expensive. Midtown repairers include Brice's at P60 Imperial Arcade, Pitt Street, and Sullivan's at Wynyard Station, York Street.

Taxes   The only tax that targets visitors is the departure tax levied at the airport upon your departure.

Taxis   See "Getting Around," earlier in this chapter.

Telegrams/Telex/Fax   Send them from any post office. Your hotel will also send them, but at a hefty surcharge.

Telephones   Sydney's public telephones are numerous; those in actual working order, less so. Telephone books frequently look as if an army of soldier ants had marched through the pages. The red or gold phones found in shops, bars, and hotel lobbies are better bets. A call costs A30¢ on either type. Most telephones let you make STD (long-distance) and ISD (international) calls directly. Charges vary according to distance; the maximum charge on weekdays for three minutes is A$2. All calls from hotel rooms will have an additional hefty surcharge.

Television   Sydney has television stations broadcasting four major networks: the government-run Australian Broadcasting Company (ABC), which shows no commercials, and the private stations ATN7, TCN9, and TEN10, which show a great many. ATN7 also runs a continuous program of news from the U.S. from midnight to dawn Monday through Friday. A fifth channel, SBS, presents multicultural programs in various languages and excellent foreign-language movies with English subtitles. You'll find Australian video fare very similar to American, with the ABC taking the place of PBS, except that the humor is more risqué and the commentaries more bland.

Time   Because of the international date line, Sydney is a day ahead of North America. In addition, because the seasons are reversed, when North America is on standard time, Sydney is on daylight saving time, and vice versa. Thus from roughly early March to late October, when it's noon (standard time) on Tuesday in Sydney, it's 10pm (eastern daylight time) on Monday in New York and 7pm (Pacific daylight time) in California. And from late October to early March, when it's noon (daylight saving time) on Tuesday in Sydney, it's 8pm (EST) on Monday in New York and 5pm (PST) in California.

Tipping   The outstretched palm is not symbolic of Australia, and there is less tipping here than in most countries (which makes the Aussies such lousy tippers when abroad). Neither hotels nor restaurants add service charges to their bills. However, it is customary to tip 10% to 15% in the plusher restaurants, to give about $A1 to hotel porters for carrying luggage, and to let cab drivers keep small change from the fare.

Transit Info   Call Metro Trips (☎ **954-4422**) daily from 7am to 10pm.

Useful Telephone Numbers   NSW Travel Centre (☎ **231-4444**), Tourist Information Service (8am to 6pm daily; ☎ **669-5111**), entertainment bookings (☎ **266-4800**), event enquiries (☎ **266-4848**), beach conditions (☎ **901-7996**).

Water   Sydney's water is absolutely safe, and better-tasting—because it has fewer chemicals—than in most cities in the U.S.

Weather   You can phone **1196** for a forecast, which is every inch as accurate as the one you get at home.

---

3   Networks & Resources

The **Wayside Chapel,** 29 Hughes St., Kings Cross (☎ **358-6577**), was built with voluntary labor by a freewheeling Methodist minister named Ted Noffs in 1964. Open "to all faiths and none," the chapel has since married more people than any other church in Australia, and probably helps more desperate souls as well. This is where you go when you're in trouble (it functions as a 24-hour crisis center), if you want to locate any group or association in Sydney (straight, gay, or otherwise), if you need a crash pad or a solo bed for the night, if you're sick in body or spirit, suicidal, lonely, or broke. You'll get whatever help human goodwill and know-how can bestow, and you'll get no hassles.

FOR STUDENTS   Youth Line (☎ **264-1177**); Student Christian Movement, 72 Audely St., Petersham (☎ **568-3026**); and Sydney University, Wentworth Building (☎ **660-6422**).

FOR GAY MEN & LESBIANS   Gay and Lesbian Counselling, 197 Albion St. Surry Hills (☎ **360-3063**); Lesbian and Gayline (4pm to midnight; ☎ **360-2211**); Gay What's On (☎ **361-0655**); and Gay and Lesbians Rights, 78 Oxford St., Darlinghurst (☎ **360-6650**).

FOR WOMEN   Women's Resource Centre (☎ **607-7536**).

FOR SENIORS   Senior Citizens Clubs Information, 34 Argyle Place (☎ **247-3388**).

4

Sydney Accommodations

A S AUSTRALIA'S MAIN PORT OF ENTRY AND PREMIER TOURIST CENTER, Sydney boasts an immense array of accommodations in every conceivable price and comfort category. But there is a bit of confusion about the nomenclature applied to them. This stems from the bluenose laws slammed down during the continent's "wowser" period for the sole purpose of restricting the sale of liquor.

These laws stipulated that in order to qualify for a liquor license a "public house" had to be a hotel as well—that is, it had to accept overnight guests. For most hotels, however, only the bar trade was profitable; lodgers were a dead loss. In consequence many establishments followed a system that complied with the letter of the law while letting the spirit go hang. They maintained a few guest rooms, preferably empty and purely for show. If some benighted wayfarer actually requested a bed, the rooms were always taken, usually by the proprietor's aunts or cousins. They got away with this by means of political pull and judicious palm-greasing. And the result is that even today a fair portion of "hotels" listed in the yellow pages aren't hotels at all, but simply taverns.

There is still no clear distinction between the genuine hotels and those that merely act as liquor dispensaries. To make matters worse, the Aussies call both varieties "pubs." And to confuse matters a mite more, there are the so-called private hotels, actually guesthouses, which have no liquor license, may or may not serve food, and exist *solely* for accommodation.

Australian hotel terminology takes a bit of translating as well. "Lift," for instance, means elevator, "private facilities" denotes private bathrooms and toilets, and "tray service" stands for room service. Some Sydney establishments include breakfast in their tariff; most do not (you will find this clearly indicated in the following hotel descriptions). In any case, "continental" indicates breakfast consisting of a cereal, juice, toast, and tea or coffee (bearing no resemblance to any European repast), while a "full" or "cooked" breakfast means the works, including eggs (even a mushroom omelet), bacon, or sausages.

Virtually all Aussie hostelries provide tea/coffee-making facilities in their rooms, a feature other countries should copy. This custom is so universal that I haven't listed it in individual descriptions—you can take it for granted. The only distinction is that some establishments also supply free cookies (biscuits). Soap supplies are usually generous and are at least as good as the American quality. On the other hand, few hotels will give you a washcloth, so it's wise to carry your own.

Bathrooms, as a whole, are excellent, but even in some upper-bracket hotels come equipped with showers only. If you must have a tub, you should make this clear when reserving. Nearly all moderate establishments listed below offer private bathrooms; the few that don't are clearly indicated. Many budget accommodations do not include private bathrooms, most of the buildings are somewhat elderly, and some of them lack lifts—pardon me, elevators.

Apartments are termed "flats" or "units" below, and Sydney has many apartment hotels. They are great money-savers, particularly for couples, groups, or families. The difference in expenditure between eating in restaurants and preparing your own meals can be as much as 40%. All apartment hotels below offer full-size kitchens. I haven't included any with so-called kitchenettes.

The best part about Sydney hotel bills is the absence of government taxes or service charges. A good many hotels, however, impose surcharges for certain holiday periods. This is left entirely to the discretion of the management and can apply to just a couple of days over Christmas or to the entire length of school vacations. Since these extra charges seem to change from one season to the next it's a good idea to inquire about them.

HOMESTAYS & FARMSTAYS enable overseas visitors to stay as paying guests in Australian homes, either in urban or country areas. The choices run all the way from inner Sydney suburbs to sheep and cattle ranches in the far west, the settings from mildly luxurious to modest and simple. As a general rule homestay rates include only bed and breakfast; farmstays offer full board with meals of farmer proportions.

All homes have been inspected and classified as "superior," "quality," or "economy," and are priced accordingly. In the homestays rates run from around $A48 for an economy single to $A58 for superior accommodations. Farmstays cost from $A112 to $A125—more on one of the great rural properties. The listings below give you some idea of the surroundings to expect, plus the interests of your hosts. A couple of samples for quality homestays in the Sydney area:

"Outgoing family living in town house with panoramic views over famous Bondi Beach. Many and varied restaurants nearby. Two minutes to city bus. Hosts interested in horse-racing, education."

"Newly decorated guest area in spacious home in prestigious suburb. Host retired, pioneer of early aviation, hostess in theatre. Homey atmosphere. Animal lovers."

For listings and application forms, contact **Bed & Breakfast Australia,** P.O. Box 408, Gordon, NSW 2072 (☎ **061/498-5344**; fax 061/498-6438).

A NOTE ON PRICES All prices cited are in Australian dollars. As we go to press, $A1 equals about U.S. 70¢ so a hotel room listed here at $A100 a night costs about $65 in U.S. dollars.

The price categories in this guide are governed not only by an establishment's rates but also by its level of accommodation. If the same rate gets you a room in one place but a small apartment with kitchen in another, then the second place might fall into the "moderate" bracket because it gives you more for your money. Roughly speaking the price categories for two people are **very expensive,** $A180 and up; **expensive,** $A110 to $A180; **moderate,** $A80 to $A110; and **budget,** less than $A80. Downtown accommodations are top-heavy on the expensive side, whereas in the suburbs moderate places predominate.

Don't forget that I'm just providing a broad sampling of choices. There are plenty more in each category.

1 Downtown

VERY EXPENSIVE

Hotel Nikko Darling Harbour, 161 Sussex St., at Market Street, Sydney, NSW 2000. ☎ **02/299-1231,** or reservations toll free **800/645-5687** in the U.S. Fax 02/299-3340. 649 rms and suites. A/C MINIBAR TV TEL **Train:** Town Hall.

Rates: $A240–$A300 single or double; from $A400 suite. Major credit cards. **Parking:** Available.

Rising from the spectacular Darling Harbour Project, the Nikko opened in September 1991, making it one of the most modern hotels in Sydney. A cream-colored giant, fashioned with cool—almost frigid—elegance, the Nikko has incorporated and preserved some delightful historic touches, such as the Dundee Arms sailors' pub and a Japanese department store built into the century-old Corn Exchange building.

Apart from these mellow crannies, the Nikko is the epitome of streamlined functionalism, softened by tasteful arrays of dwarf trees. The views from the bedrooms range from impressive to magnificent, the decor is discreetly soothing, the staff courteous and helpful far beyond the call of deluxe duty. The four Executive Floors resemble a hotel within a hotel, with their own lounge, roof garden, meeting rooms, and library of business publications. For guests arriving before check-in time, the Nikko provides the Early Arrivals Lounge, complete with showers, bar, and clothes-pressing service.

Dining/Entertainment: Japanese restaurant; New Pharaoh nightclub, with state-of-the-art sound and light equipment, dance floor, and several bars; pub; two bars.

Services: Round-the-clock room service, valet, babysitting.

Facilities: Rooms for disabled, shops, well-equipped business center.

⭐ **Inter-Continental Sydney,** 117 Macquarie St., Sydney, NSW 2000. ☎ **02/230-0200,** or reservations toll free **800/327-0200** in the U.S. Fax 02/240-1240. 502 rms and suites. A/C MINIBAR TV TEL **Train:** Circular Quay.

Rates: $A285–$A350 single or double; from $A530 suite. Major credit cards. **Parking:** $A15.

This modern hotel hides discreetly behind the Victorian facade of the old State Treasury (built in 1851), whose venerable sandstone walls now enclose the lobby—possibly the handsomest in the southern hemisphere—a marble-floored central cortile surrounded by three levels of vaulted arcades, sprinkled with palms, flowers, and wicker chairs, and illuminated by torchères in the evening.

The rooms and suites all have commanding views, pastel decor with Australian themes, large built-in wardrobes, and a range of free giveaways that include little baskets brimming with bath accessories. All come with in-house TV movie channels, hairdryers, music and radio systems, refrigerators, bathrobes, and superbly sprung beds.

Dining/Entertainment: Five restaurants, as well as cafes and taverns.

Services: 24-hour room service.

Facilities: Indoor rooftop swimming pool; fitness center; arcade of shops; boutiques; well-equipped business center; multilingual staff; house doctor on 24-hour call.

★ **Old Sydney Parkroyal,** 55 George St., The Rocks, Sydney, NSW 2000. ☎ **02/252-0524,** or reservations toll free **800/855-7742** in the U.S. and Canada. Fax 02/251-2093. 174 rms and suites. A/C MINIBAR TV TEL **Train:** Circular Quay.

Rates: $A270–$A295 single or double. Children under 15 free; over 15, $A20. Major credit cards. **Parking:** $A12 (valet parking).

Having opened in 1984, this hotel is actually an infant. But it stands rooted in history. The area is the site of the original settlement of Sydney, and the hotel incorporates the brick walls of warehouses built in the 1830s. Tradition is big here. Every morning and evening, at 8am and 6pm sharp, a detachment of the regular army dressed in 18th-century uniforms marches up to raise and lower the flag over the building.

The Parkroyal has an immense central atrium the size of a cathedral, overlooked by eight gallery floors containing the guest rooms. The arrangement achieves a wonderful sense of spaciousness coupled with old-world elegance and quite disguises the thoroughly modern fixtures of the hotel.

The rooms are not large, but excellently furnished, some overlooking the ocean liners berthed at Circular Quay, just across the road. All rooms have hairdryers and ironing boards.

Dining/Entertainment: Two cocktail bars, one restaurant.

Services: 24-hour room service.

Facilities: Rooftop pool, sauna, health spa, secretarial services, rooms for the disabled.

★ **The Regent, Sydney,** 199 George St., Sydney, NSW 2000. ☎ **02/238-0000,** or reservations toll free **800/545-4000** in the U.S. and Canada. Fax 02/251-2851. 596 rms and suites. A/C MINIBAR TV TEL. **Train:** Circular Quay.

Rates: $A210–345 single or double; from $A470 suite. Major credit cards. **Parking:** $A12.

If you rate a hotel by the number of movie scenes and commercials it appears in, then the Regent ranks as numero uno. Opened in 1983 and located about a minute's stroll from Circular Quay, the Regent offers panoramic vistas quite irresistible to folks with cameras. Behind a sloping beige stone frontage rises a fluted 36-story tower (actually 35, because there's no 13th floor). The foyer is vast and quietly magnificent, constructed of polished granite, with a central atrium and a skylight above. There are green shrubs, small trees, and fresh flowers wherever you look, and scarlet armchairs and settees to enfold you.

The guest rooms follow the theme of cool, understated elegance. Most of them have superb harbor or city views, and all come with bedside controls for TV, radio, and lights, and executive desks. The marble bathrooms are heaped with free first-class toiletries, and every guest gets the use of a snowy toweling robe. Few decorations, but luxurious comfort at every turn.

Dining/Entertainment: Three restaurants, including the illustrious Kables, and two cocktail bars. The hotel's famous English afternoon tea ceremony, consisting of tea served from silver samovars and watercress sandwiches and little cakes, costs around $A16.

Services: Concierge, babysitting, massage and beauty salon.

Facilities: Business center, outdoor pool, health club, gift shop.

Sydney Boulevard, 90 William St., Sydney, NSW 2000. ☎ **02/357-2277.** Fax 02/356-3786. 273 rms and suites. A/C MINIBAR TV TEL **Bus:** 324, 325, 327, 271.

Rates: $A190 single or double. Major credit cards. **Parking:** Available.

Everything is large in this massive gray stone edifice: the lobby, the social facilities, the rooms, even the elevators. The foyer, in fact, resembles a royal reception hall and could easily engulf a guard of honor. The hotel lacks a swimming pool, but has every other imaginable convenience.

The guest rooms and suites range from large to huge—no chance of anyone getting claustrophobic here. Furnished with subdued stylishness, they welcome you with enough "nibbles," soft drinks, and liquor to stock a grocery. In-house movies for the TV set, terrycloth bathrobes, refrigerators, shampoos, shoeshine equipment, and a heap of other comforts come as standard items. So do ironing boards, a rare touch. The carpeting is sinfully rich, and the lighting can be adjusted according to need or mood.

Dining/Entertainment: The 25th Floor is an intimate bistro and a panoramic restaurant.

Services: 24-hour room service.

Facilities: Shopping center, secretarial services, steambath, massage salon, multilingual staff.

Sydney Hilton, 259 Pitt St., Sydney, NSW 2000. ☎ **02/266-0610,** or reservations toll free **800/445-8667** in the U.S. Fax 02/265-6065. 585 rms and suites. A/C MINIBAR TV TEL **Train:** Town Hall.

Rates: $A220 single or double; from $A500 suite. Major credit cards **Parking:** Valet.

Towering over the city, the Hilton has everything you expect from that international luxury chain, plus a few unique local touches—for instance, the Marble Bar in the basement. This wonderful ornately curlicued piece of Victoriana was marked for demolition when the hotel was put up. But the powerful Builders' Laborers Federation refused to destroy it, and the management wisely left the bar intact and built the Hilton over it. Today this extravaganza is a municipal landmark and a gold mine for the owners.

The guest rooms are furnished in the now traditional Hilton style: soothing color schemes, huge wardrobes, blissful beds, and fingertip convenience—carefully planned—for every gadget around. Computerized door locks are coded for each individual guest.

Dining/Entertainment: Five bars, two restaurants, a cafe, and a swank disco called Juliana's.

Services: Concierge, babysitting.

Facilities: Shopping arcade, well-equipped business center, supersize swimming pool.

EXPENSIVE

Park Regis, 27 Park St. (at Castlereagh Street), Sydney, NSW 2000. ☎ **02/267-6511.** Fax 02/264-2252. 120 rms (showers only). A/C TV TEL **Train:** Town Hall.

Rates: \$A110 single or double. Major credit cards. **Parking:** On premises.

This hotel stands in a superb location between the green expanse of Hyde Park and the business district. Surrounded by duty-free shops, it occupies ten floors in a soaring high-rise that also contains a one-floor parking garage. The small lobby is on the ground floor; the actual hotel starts on the sixth. There is a rooftop swimming pool, a restaurant on the premises, fax facilities, and airport bus service. The rooms and suites are medium-size, recently and cheerfully furnished in light woods, and offer views of either the park or the thronged streets. All have pleasant rustic prints on the walls, refrigerators, and bedside and mirror lights. The wardrobes appear a little cramped for two persons. The hotel is well carpeted and has efficient elevator service.

Hyde Park Inn, 271 Elizabeth St., Sydney, NSW 2000. ☎ **02/264-6001.** Fax 02/261-8691. 85 rms (showers only). A/C TV TEL **Train:** Museum.

Rates (including light breakfast): \$A120 single; \$A135 double. Major credit cards. **Parking:** Available (limited).

Smallish, intimate, but well situated, this hotel faces Hyde Park. It has a handy wall map of Sydney showing landmarks. The inn does not take convention groups and only favors small tours. Most rooms have smart little snack kitchenettes, and all are spacious, tastefully furnished, and lavishly endowed with wardrobe space and lighting fixtures. Restaurant on the premises.

★ **Hyde Park Plaza Hotel,** 38 College St., Sydney, NSW 2000. ☎ **02/331-6933.** Fax 02/331-6022. 182 apts. A/C TV TEL **Train:** Museum.

Rates (including light breakfast): \$A140–\$A270, depending on size. Major credit cards. **Parking:** Free.

This fashionable white structure faces the green expanse of Hyde Park. Some of the greenery seems to have crept into the foyer, which has

Sydney Accommodations

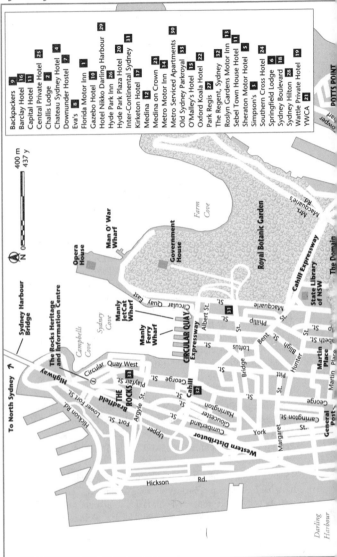

Backpackers 9
Barclay Hotel 16
Capital Hotel 11
Central Private Hotel 25
Challis Lodge 2
Chateau Sydney Hotel 4
Downunder Hostel 7
Eva's 8
Florida Motor Inn 1
Gazebo Hotel 10
Hotel Nikko Darling Harbour 29
Hyde Park Inn 26
Hyde Park Plaza Hotel 20
Inter-Continental Sydney 31
Kirketon Hotel 17
Medina 12
Medina on Crown 23
Metro Motor Inn 14
Metro Serviced Apartments 30
Old Sydney Parkroyal 33
O'Malley's Hotel 15
Oxford Koala Hotel 22
Park Regis 27
The Regent, Sydney 32
Roslyn Gardens Motor Inn 13
Sebel Town House Hotel 11
Sheraton Motor Hotel 5
Simpson's 3
Southern Cross Hotel 24
Springfield Lodge 6
Sydney Boulevard 18
Sydney Hilton 28
Wattle Private Hotel 19
YWCA 21

subdued lighting, sliding glass doors, and enough plants and shrubs to fill a small garden. The Plaza offers more than just apartments. There is a very stylish restaurant at ground level with an adjoining cocktail bar; a rooftop recreation area with swimming pool, spa, gym, and sauna; a laundromat; valet service; and fax facilities.

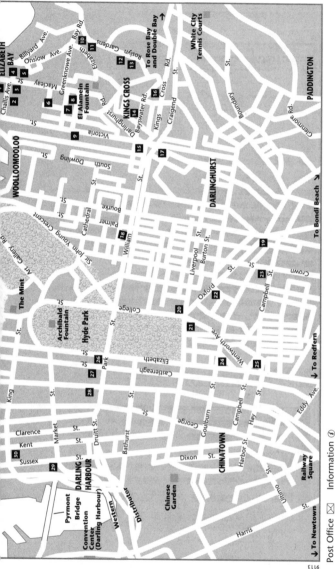

Post Office ⊠   Information ⓘ

The units vary from studios to two-bedroom and family suites.
All are equipped with full-size electric kitchens, linen, and utensils.
Some (not all) also have private terraces. Room decor is light and
charming, with elegant rattan furniture, occasional tables, and excellent modern wall decorations. The specialty here is flexi-suites that
can be rapidly converted to fit different groupings.

Metro Serviced Apartments, 132–136 Sussex St. (at King Street), Sydney, NSW 2000. ☎ **02/290-9200,** 36 apts. A/C TV TEL **Train:** Wynyard.

Rates: $A129. Major credit cards. No parking.

Located at the harbor end of King Street, this shiny new accommodation complex offers just that—accommodation, with no other facilities except excellent security. The units are split-level (the bedroom is upstairs) and completely self-contained. The rooms are not large, but are furnished in bright ultramodern style and equipped with every appliance, including private laundries. There is ample wardrobe and kitchen space, every kitchen has a microwave oven, and the apartments can sleep up to four people.

Southern Cross Hotel, at Elizabeth and Goulburn Streets, Sydney, NSW 2000. ☎ **02/282-0987,** or reservations toll free **800/223-5652** in the U.S. Fax 02/211-1806. 183 rms and suites. A/C MINIBAR TV TEL **Train:** Museum.

Rates (including breakfast): $A145 single or double. Major credit cards. **Parking:** Valet.

A converted apartment block, the Southern Cross greets you with a small, smart lobby, its ceiling studded with little lights.

The rooms and suites are of medium size, in russet and beige color schemes, and feature extra-large beds and dressing areas in front of the bathrooms. Wardrobes are not only spacious but equipped with sliding doors. A lot of other items come with the room: plush bathrobes, regular executive desks, rentable movies and videos, radio, digital alarm clock, refrigerator, and individual climate control. The hotel stands a block from Hyde Park, so there is a jogging track at your doorstep.

Dining/Entertainment: Multistar restaurant, cocktail bar.

Services: Complimentary morning paper and shoeshine, 24-hour dry cleaning, babysitting.

Facilities: Rooftop garden with pool, secretarial service, sauna.

BUDGET

Central Private Hotel, 356 Elizabeth St., Sydney, NSW 2000. ☎ **02/212-1068.** 38 rms. TV **Train:** Central Station.

Rates: $A25 single with shared bath; $A40 double with shared bath, $A45 double with private bath; $A50–$A60 family room with private bath. No credit cards.

This is an economy establishment, austerely furnished but with a lot of handy facilities. The rooms come with fridges, TVs, and washbasins, and there are laundry, drying, and ironing facilities on the premises. Room sizes range from small singles to rather spacious family units sleeping three to four adults. No restaurant is in the building, but several are in the vicinity.

$ **Wool Brokers Arms,** 22 Allen St., Pyrmont, NSW 2009. ☎ **02/552-4773.** Fax 02/552-4771. 30 rms (none with bath). TV **Monorail:** Convention Station.

Rates: $A55, single; $A75, double. AE, MC, V.

A hotel for nonsmokers only, this refurbished Victorian heritage building stands adjacent to Darling Harbour. The period bedrooms have the advantage of high ceilings and come equipped with fridge, color TV, and intercom with the front desk. Furnishings are plain, but the hotel has guest laundries and a pleasant dining room serving breakfast. Thoughtfully managed, this is also one of the few hotels in town that you can reach via Sydney's controversial monorail (see "Getting Around" in Chapter 3).

YWCA, 5–11 Wentworth Ave., Sydney, NSW 2000. ☎ **02/264-2451.** Fax 02/283-2485. 50 rms (some with bath). A/C TV TEL **Train:** Museum.

Rates: $A42 and $A60 single or double without bath; $A60 and $A85 single or double with bath. AE, BC, DC, MC, V.

This place looks like an office building, and two of its eight floors are in fact given over to offices. The others comprise the YWCA, which, despite its name, takes members of both sexes. There's good elevator service, a large and low-cost cafeteria, TV lounges, laundry facilities, and absolutely sparkling bathrooms. Bedrooms are of fair size and functional, and have nice carpeting, mirrors, spacious wardrobes, and fluorescent ceiling lights. Some (not all) are equipped with hot- and cold-water handbasins. There is a room for the disabled, and the entire building is no smoking.

Frommer's Smart Traveler: Hotels

1. Don't be too influenced by exteriors. Some of Sydney's most comfortable places look either sterile or weathered from the outside.

2. Make a point of inquiring about special weekend or family rates. They can save you up to 25% of the regular tariff.

3. Cash traveler's checks at a bank rather than a hotel. The hotel exchange rate tends to be somewhat less favorable.

4. Sydney hotels don't offer summer discounts—summer is peak season. But a number have discounts in winter (June through August).

5. Try to reserve a back room in hotels fronting a main thoroughfare. Traffic noise can play havoc with your sleep.

6. Motels or motor hotels usually offer free guest parking. For other accommodations, ask about parking charges, which can range from zero to $A15. Some smaller establishments have no parking facilities.

7. Don't depend on hotel wakeup calls when you have to catch a plane. The waking service is the weakest link of Aussie hospitality.

2 Oxford Street

This is a kind of in-between area that stitches the inner suburb of Darlinghurst to the center city. The two merge with no definable border. Oxford Street is an endlessly long thoroughfare, heavy with traffic and crammed with shops, restaurants, and pubs. It is known as a gay hangout, but not obtrusively so, and makes up in zest and variety what it lacks in chic.

MODERATE

Oxford Koala Hotel, corner of Oxford and Pelican Streets, Darlinghurst, NSW 2010. ☎ **02/269-0645,** or reservations toll free **800/528-1234** in the U.S. Fax 02/283-2741. 328 rms and suites. A/C TV TEL **Train:** Museum.

> **Rates:** $95 single or double; from $A125 suite. AE, DC, MC, V. **Parking:** On premises (free).

A huge reddish-brown structure, this handy hotel shares a shopping arcade block with the terminal of Pioneer and Greyhound bus lines. Tour groups stream in and out constantly, but the hotel staff manages crowds with remarkable ease and smoothness. The Koala caters to the business world as much as to tourists, offering secretarial services, fax, photocopying, and desktop publishing facilities. It also has an oversize, heated rooftop pool. The rooms and suites are of fair size, furbished in practical style and equipped with refrigerators, alarm clocks at bedside, individual temperature controls, and modern bathrooms. The hotel restaurant serves fast breakfast, buffet style, then switches to more leisurely table service for lunch and dinner.

★ **Wattle Private Hotel,** 108 Oxford St. (at Palmer Street), Darlinghurst, NSW 2010. ☎ **02/332-4118.** Fax 02/331-2074. 12 rms (all with bath). A/C TV TEL **Bus:** 380, 382.

> **Rates:** (including breakfast): $A60 single; $A70–80 double; from 80 twin-bedded suite. BC, MC, V.

Wattle House is like a surprise package with all the goodies hidden under plain wrapping. It has a rather cluttered little lobby and no elevator. But the rooms of the small hotel are charming, the facilities extensive, and the rates astonishingly low. The Wattle has a stylish little coffee lounge on the ground floor, serving a complimentary breakfast. The furnishings are modern, cheerful, and very comfortable; the carpeting excellent; the wardrobe space ample; and some of the rooms have private balconies.

3 Kings Cross Area

Sydney's version of Montmartre, Soho, Greenwich Village, or North Beach is different by also being the town's major hotel region. While undeniably a red-light district, the Cross also offers some of the finest accommodations in Australia. Don't be confused by the various district names in this section—Kings Cross is actually a border area between three inner divisions. If a hotel is listed here, it's in the Cross area.

VERY EXPENSIVE

⭐ **Sebel Town House Hotel,** 23 Elizabeth Bay Rd., Elizabeth Bay, NSW 2011. ☎ **02/358-3244.** Fax 02/357-1926. 166 rms and suites. A/C MINIBAR TV TEL **Train:** Kings Cross.
Rates: $A195 single or double; $A600 suite. AE, BC, DC, MC, V. **Parking:** Free.

A gleaming white structure, the Sebel acts as a magnet for visiting movie, stage, video, and concert stars from around the globe. Their often gaudy attire adds a certain casual flavor to the otherwise conservative foyer. The adjacent cocktail bar is festooned with the signed portraits of media celebrities who have graced the bar stools, and frequently the floor as well. A welcoming board in the lobby is eagerly scanned by reporters, autograph hounds, and groupies alike.

The spacious and luxurious guest rooms and suites are done in soothing brown and salmon hues and are equipped with timber-paneled walls, bathroom scales, hairdryers, baskets of toilet articles, and cleverly sited lighting fixtures.

Dining/Entertainment: Sebel has a classic Edwardian restaurant, the Encore, as well as a cocktail bar.

Services: 24-hour room service.

Facilities: Roof-deck heated swimming pool; Finnish sauna; Function Centre for weddings, banquets, and other events.

EXPENSIVE

Chateau Sydney Hotel, 14 Macleay St., Potts Point, NSW 2011. ☎ **02/358-2500,** or reservations toll free **800/624-3524** in the U.S. Fax 02/358-1959. 94 rms and suites. A/C MINIBAR TV TEL **Train:** Kings Cross.
Rates: $A160–$A180 single or double; $A350 suite. Children under 15 free. AE, BC, MC, V. **Parking:** Free.

Chateau Sydney is designed along classical French lines, the entire frontage of the green-and-white seven-story building taken up by gracefully curved little balconies. While not exactly a château, the hotel preserves touches of plush intimacy that give it an ambience all its own. Nothing mass-produced about this establishment, from the small, chic walnut-colored lobby with mirror panels along the walls to the exquisite little restaurant and the brasserie-style cocktail bar with French doors opening on a patio. Bedrooms are tastefully decorated and equipped with remote-control TV and, on the higher floors, wondrous city and harbor views. Tariffs generally depend on the view.

Dining/Entertainment: Restaurant, cocktail bar.

Services: 24-hour room service.

Facilities: Swimming pool, laundry for guest use, meeting room.

Gazebo Hotel, 2 Elizabeth Bay Rd., Elizabeth Bay, NSW 2011. ☎ **02/358-1999.** Fax 02/356-2951. 391 rms and suites. A/C MINIBAR TV TEL **Train:** Kings Cross.

Rates: $A160–$A180 single or double; from $A240 suite. Major credit cards. **Parking:** On premises.

One of the most beautiful hotels in town, the Gazebo edges close to the deluxe bracket. An eye-catching structure, consisting of an ivory-colored 17-story tower with a more conventional square addition, the hotel produces a grandiose overall effect. The lobby follows the circular shape of the tower and manages to be both vast and svelte in equal proportions, in shades of blue and ivory and sprinkled with delightfully welcoming armchairs. On the reception desk stands a huge bowl of apples, a gesture aimed at Japanese visitors who regard apples as luxury fruit.

The Gazebo has a heated rooftop pool with sauna, two restaurants (one of them a glassed-in affair that *looks* like outdoors but isn't), and a chic cocktail bar. Some of the rooms come with balconies and panoramic views, plus electronic combination lockers for valuables. All feature refrigerators, plus exceptionally handsome furnishings, vast beds, vast wardrobes, hairdryers, radios, and twin lamps at desks and bedsides.

Dining/Entertainment: Two restaurants, two cocktail bars.

Services: Room service, bed turndown.

Facilities: Business center, meeting area, outdoor pool, sauna.

⭐ **Medina,** 70 Roslyn Gardens, Elizabeth Bay, NSW 2011. ☎ **02/356-7400.** Fax 02/357-2505. 58 apts. A/C TV TEL **Train:** Kings Cross.

Rates: $A110 single; $A125 double. AE, BC, DC, MC, V.

Located on an attractive residential street, this handsome white building is fronted by balconies and a rock garden with miniature waterfall. Guests use a private entrance that avoids the lobby, which strengthens the homey atmosphere of the Medina. The apartments are of fair size, tastefully furnished, and fitted with luxurious deep-pile carpets, electric clocks, excellent illumination, large wardrobes with mirror-faced sliding doors, and (in some) balconies offering delightful views. All units have streamlined kitchens with utensils and modern bathrooms (some with showers only).

Simpsons, 8 Challis Ave., Potts Point, NSW 2011. ☎ **02/356-2572,** Fax 02/356-4476. 14 rms. A/C TV TEL **Train:** Kings Cross.

Rates: (including continental breakfast) $A135–$A200 single; $A145–$A210 double. BC, MC, V.

Parking: Free. **Closed:** Christmas–New Year's Day.

Built as a decidedly upper-crust family residence in 1892, Simpsons has retained the charm and spaciousness of its period while adding the modern innovations needed to make it sleekly comfortable. The bedrooms are large and airy, the beds regal, TV sets discreetly hidden in cupboards. The hallways are grand affairs, decorated with stained-glass windows, beautiful art prints and friezes of Australian flora. The breakfast room is a converted conservatory, glass-walled and vivid, with greenery inside and out. Guests are spoiled with arrays of toiletries, gratis newspapers, shoe-cleaning equipment, snuggly bathrobes, and power plugs that fit American shavers (a rarity). The continental breakfast includes freshly squeezed orange juice, croissants, and brioches. Furnishings include many genuine antiques, but none so fragile as to arouse trepidations when you brush past. The building has three floors, but no elevator.

MODERATE

Hotel Capital, 111 Darlinghurst Rd., Kings Cross, NSW 2011.
☎ **02/358-2755.** Fax 02/358-2888. 214 rms. A/C MINIBAR TV TEL **Train:** Kings Cross.
Rates: $A95 single or double. Major credit cards. **Parking:** Free.

The Capital Hotel rises right where the Cross crosses, at possibly the busiest junction in Sydney. Resembling an immense slab of white and dark chocolate, it adjoins the Kings Cross railway station and is surrounded by a cluster of bars, cafes, shops, and boutiques.

Equally convenient for large tour groups and business travelers, the Capital handles huge numbers of both with ease. The hotel has excellent business facilities, a sheltered swimming pool, a sun-swept restaurant, a gym, spa, and fitness center, and a pleasantly subdued bar (as distinct from the more boisterous watering holes downstairs). The bedrooms are furnished in smart beige and ivory hues, and are spacious and virtually soundproof. All have radios, refrigerators, large wardrobes, excellent lighting, and impressive city or harbor views. From way above you can watch the electric trains running to and fro like so many miniature toys.

⭐ **Florida Motor Inn**, 1 McDonald St., Potts Point, NSW 2011.
☎ **02/358-6811,** or reservations toll free **800/528-1234** in the U.S. Fax 02/358-5951. 91 apts. A/C MINIBAR TV TEL **Train:** Kings Cross.
Rates: $A109–$A120 single or double; $A117–$A128 triple; $A136 quad. AE, DC, MC, V. **Parking:** Free.

Standing at the bottom of a quiet, tree-lined dead-end street of Kings Cross, the Florida is almost hidden by a curtain of greenery. Sydney's nightlife center lies only blocks away, but none of its din reaches this oasis. The hotel has a beautiful lawn and palm-fringed swimming pool with sauna, hand tennis, table tennis, and barbecue facilities, plus a most obliging staff.

The units range from studios to one- and two-bedroom apartments, the latter comfortably sleeping six people. Some units are air-conditioned and all are spacious, with large built-in wardrobes, wide beds, bedside clock radios, and masses of cushions. The all-electric kitchens come with complete cooking and eating equipment, including wineglasses and egg cups; the bathrooms have tubs and showers. The one-bedroom units can accommodate four people.

Metro Motor Inn Kings Cross, 40 Bayswater Rd., Kings Cross, NSW 2011. ☎ **02/356-3511.** Fax 02/357-1426. 39 rms. A/C TV TEL **Train:** Kings Cross.

Rates: $A95 single or double. Major credit cards. **Parking:** On premises.

A dazzling white ultramodern structure, this motor inn features large viewing windows at street level. A small establishment, the Metro offers the advantages of intimacy and every up-to-the-minute convenience except a swimming pool. The lobby has a luxury ranch-style air, aided by flowering shrubs and russet carpeting. The bedrooms are of fair size and fitted with separate kitchenettes. No restaurant on the premises, but half a dozen are within strolling distance. Bedroom furnishings are stylish, with large mirrors, good armchairs, and bright color schemes. All bathrooms have tubs as well as showers.

$ Sheraton Motor Hotel, 40 Macleay St., Potts Point, NSW 2011. ☎ **02/358-1955.** Fax 02/356-2005. 60 rms. A/C TV TEL **Train:** Kings Cross.
Rates: $A89–$A99 single or double. Major credit cards. **Parking:** On premises.

This Sheraton offers an unusual standby rate whereby you can get any room that happens to be vacant for $A58. Blessed with a particularly attentive staff, the hotel features a coffee lounge as well as a Japanese social club and a cocktail bar. The bedrooms are smartly, though not lavishly, furnished, and have full-length bedroom mirrors and plenty of space all round. Rates depend largely on the view from the room.

BUDGET

Barclay Hotel, 17 Bayswater Rd, Kings Cross, NSW 2011.
☎ **02/358-6133.** Fax 02/358-4363. 40 rms (30 with bath). A/C TV TEL **Train:** Kings Cross.
Rates: $A40–$A50 single; $A50–$A60 double. AE BC MC V.

The Barclay is an elderly five-story building that has gone through a thorough rejuvenation process. The bedroom decor is on the functional side, but the rooms come with facilities like air-conditioning, refrigerators, spacious wardrobes, and ample lighting. You'll find a restaurant, a cafe, and a guest laundry on the premises. Bayswater Road is busy and noisy, though ideal transportation-wise: a bus stops at the front door, and the airport express stops around the corner.

Challis Lodge, 21 Challis Ave., Potts Point, NSW 2011.
☎ **02/358-5422.** Fax 02/357-4742. 62 rms (36 with bath). TV TEL **Train:** Kings Cross.
Rates: $A26–$A36 single; $A34–$A54 double. BC, MC, V.

The Challis is a peach-and-white Victorian terrace building, nicely restored, with charming period touches. The interior is a maze of well-carpeted but confusing corridors and stairways. The rooms have high ceilings, few ornamental frills, but good lighting, ample hanging space, and wood flooring polished to a high sheen. All have fridges; some also offer private balconies. The lodge stands in a quiet side street. No meals are served but plenty of restaurants are nearby. Ask about special weekend rates.

Kirketon Hotel, 229 Darlinghurst Rd., Kings Cross, NSW 2010. ☎ and fax **02/360-4333.** 64 rms (34 with bath). TV TEL **Train:** Kings Cross.

Rates: (including continental breakfast): without bath $A38.50 single, $A58 double, $A70 triple; with bath, $A51.50 single, $A68 double, $A90 triple. Major credit cards.

This exceptionally well-equipped and well-run budget house lies behind a rather plain exterior. The Kirketon lobby looks drab, but the bedrooms are excellently maintained and equipped with radios, refrigerators, and smoke alarms. You have the choice of rooms with private bathrooms and those with hot- and cold-water basins and shared bathrooms. Breakfast is served in the Thai restaurant on the premises. For those on truly tight budgets there are also two bunkrooms (accommodating four persons each) costing $A22 per sleeper.

O'Malley's Hotel, 228 William St., Kings Cross, NSW 2011. ☎ **02/357-2211.** Fax 02/357-2656. 15 rms (10 with bath). A/C TV TEL **Train:** Kings Cross.

Rates: $A50 single; $A60 double.

A landmark building and a patch of Ireland in Sydney, O'Malley's is cozily old fashioned and comfortable. Even the five technically bathless rooms have their own—just across the hallway and used by nobody except the room occupants. The bedrooms are simply furnished, but come equipped with electric hair dryers, good light fixtures, generous wardrobe space, and well-sprung beds. There's quite a lot of action in the bar downstairs, but the sounds don't penetrate the sleeping quarters. And the management ranks among the most amiable extant.

Roslyn Gardens Motor Inn, 4 Roslyn Gardens, Kings Cross, NSW 2011. ☎ **02/358-1944.** Fax 02/357-7939. 29 apts. A/C TV TEL **Train:** Kings Cross.

Rates: $A69 single; $A79 double. Major credit cards. **Parking:** On premises.

An attractive yellow-brick building fronted by balconies and waving palms, this economy establishment offers surprising quality. The lobby is unassuming, but the units have everything required for independent comfort: fully equipped all-electric kitchens of fair size, private balconies, bathrooms with tubs and showers, and ample wardrobe space. The rooms are rather small, but the beds are excellent and you get clock radios as well.

Springfield Lodge, 9 Springfield Ave., Kings Cross, NSW 2011. ☎ **02/358-3222.** Fax 02/357-4742. 72 rms (46 with bath). TV TEL **Train:** Kings Cross.

Rates: $A30–$A40 single; $A35–$A45 double. MC, V.

Resembling a Southern plantation mansion, this pillared white building is fronted by a charming terrace with wrought-iron tables and chairs. The street is a fairly sedate plazalike affair, although just off throbbing Darlinghurst Road. Bedrooms are functionally furnished, some with private facilities, and the hallways are excellently maintained. You get ample lighting and wardrobe space, and pay according to whether you want a private bathroom.

4   Surry Hills

Surry Hills is an inner district southeast of the city.

Medina On Crown, 359 Crown St., Surry Hills, NSW 2010. ☎ **02/267-1455.** Fax 02/267-1716. 65 apts. A/C MINIBAR TV TEL **Bus:** 324, 325, 327, 271.

Rates: $A180 one–bdrm apt; $A230 two–bdrm apt. **Parking:** Free. Major credit cards.

Opened in 1994, this is Sydney's newest apartment hotel and custom-tailored for the traveling executive on or off the job, with or without family. The Medina is symbolic of the gentrification process that has turned formerly blue-collar Surry Hills into a smartly cosmopolitan extension of the City.

The apartments—with one to three bedrooms—follow an elegantly open design, the decor contemporary but not sterile, with lavishly appointed kitchens, private balconies, and carefully matched color patterns throughout. Bathrooms are small, but equipped with tubs *and* showers. Each apartment comes with microwave and dishwasher, two TV sets, two telephones, video and stereo CD player, electric hair dryer, and laundry unit. There is a "formal" lounge and dining area—more relaxed than formal—and an in-house video library. The building has a rooftop tennis court and down below a heated swimming pool, gym and spa, as well as a brasserie and cafe. Babysitting service arranged on request. No-smoking apartments available.

5   Edgecliff

Edgecliff is situated just east of King's Cross.

Metro Motor Inn Edgecliff, 230 New South Head Rd., Edgecliff, NSW 2027. ☎ **02-328-7977.** Fax 902/360-1216. 34 rms. A/C TV TEL **Train:** Edgecliff.

Rates: $A85 single or double. Major credit cards. **Parking:** On premises.

Standing diagonally opposite the Edgecliff rail and bus station, the Metro is a small, glass-fronted building on a very busy road east of Sydney. Modern, convenient, and bland, the hotel has a modest lobby with adjoining breakfast lounge and a great deal of room comfort. All bedrooms have bathrooms with tubs and showers and clock radios. Furnishings and decor are good standard motel-style and the hotel conveniences include a guest laundry and video movies screened free each night. There's a rooftop garden deck with panoramic views. The staff will arrange for babysitters.

6 Double Bay

Called "Double Pay" by the locals, this is one of Sydney's poshest neighborhoods, awash with Jaguars and Volvos, a region where the delis sell beluga caviar and truffled pâté and the boutiques display no price tags. It's located north of Edgecliff.

VERY EXPENSIVE

 The Ritz-Carlton, Double Bay, 33 Cross St., Double Bay, NSW 2028. ☎ **02/362-4455,** or reservations toll free **800/241-3333** in the U.S. Fax 02/362-4744. 140 rms and suites. A/C MINIBAR TV TEL **Bus:** 324, 325, 327.

Rates: $A179–$A219 single or double; from $A425 suite. AE, BC, DC, MC, V. **Parking:** $A10.

This is the newer of Sydney's two Ritz-Carltons (the other luxuriates downtown) and had U.S. President George Bush as guest just after it opened in December 1991. Built in French provincial style and presenting a deceptively simple sandstone facade, the R-C wraps patrons in a silk cocoon of laid-back comfort and impeccable service. The bedrooms come with large marble bathrooms, executive writing desks, three telephones, remote-control TV, monogrammed toweling bathrobes, private balconies, refrigerators, and an entire shelf of European toiletries. Maid service is twice daily.

The hotel has two restaurants; one a relaxed all-day dining room; the second a more formal gourmet temple known as The Grill, specializing in tidbits such as wild forest pigeon consommé or gooseliver butter. Then there is the lobby lounge serving snacks and afternoon tea, and the Champagne and Espresso Bar, serving exactly that. Although the hotel stands surrounded by Double Bay's svelte shopping outlets, it boasts its own boutique row, the Promenade, in case you don't wish to venture outside.

There is a rooftop swimming pool with a lavishly equipped fitness center overlooking the expanse of Sydney Harbour. Also a separate kosher kitchen and the Grand Ballroom with crystal chandeliers.

Dining/Entertainment: Two restaurants, lounge, bar.

Services: 24-hour room service, secretarial service, concierge, valet, babysitting, shuttle service to the city.

Facilities: Swimming pool and fitness center, executive business center, shopping arcade, in-house movies, meeting rooms, Ritz-Carlton Club with lounge.

EXPENSIVE

 Savoy Hotel Double Bay, 41 Knox St., Double Bay, NSW 2028. ☎ **02/326-1411.** 34 rms (showers only). A/C MINIBAR TV TEL **Bus:** 324, 325, 327.

Rates (including continental breakfast): $A125–$A145 single or double. AE, BC, DC, MC, V.

The Savoy sits amid the outdoor cafes and chic shops of the area. Definitely not high-tech, the Savoy has no elevator and the reception is up two flights of stairs. But the establishment is utterly charming, the rooms furnished in all light wood and pastel hues, intimate lighting, and avant-garde prints. Guest rooms come with comfortable couches, refrigerators, clock radios, and hairdryers. The staff is as amiable as the decor. Rooms are divided into "standard" and "deluxe."

7   Bondi

The name Bondi (pronounced bon-DEYE) conjures up the most famous strip of surf and sand in Australia, and the celebrated beach is there all right, but not everywhere. This means that Bondi is a very large suburb in the east, and sprawls way inland. From Bondi Junction it's several bus stops before you catch sight of water. Most of Bondi, in fact, is a rather charmless region of red-roofed brick homes, made interesting only by its array of multinational shops and restaurants.

MODERATE

City Beach Motor Inn, 99 Curlewis St., Bondi Beach, NSW 2026. ☎ **02/365-3100.** 26 rms. A/C TV TEL **Bus:** 380.

Rates: $A95 single or double; $A115 triple. BC, MC, V. **Parking:** On premises.

This small, modern, green-roofed, red-brick motel lives up to its name as it stands near the ocean. There's a swimming pool on the premises, although in this locality you hardly need it. The units, while not lavishly furnished, are equipped with refrigerators and electric blankets for cool nights. It also has an in-house laundry and a restaurant directly opposite.

BUDGET

$ Bondi Beachside Inn, 152 Campbell Parade, Bondi Beach, NSW 2026. ☎ **02/30-5311.** 70 units. A/C TV TEL **Bus:** 380.

Rates: $A69–$A88 single or double. Major credit cards. **Parking:** Available.

Located right at the beach, this hotel shares premises with a steak house and a seafood restaurant. You may not need either because 50 units here come with fully equipped kitchens. The lobby is small and unpretentious, but the units are of fair size and decorated in appropriate ocean shadings of blue and emerald green. Wardrobes are a bit cramped (and off the floor), but lighting arrangements are excellent and some of the rooms have grand ocean vistas. All rooms come with thermostat temperature control, bathrooms with tubs and showers, and a private balcony.

$ Hotel Bondi, 178 Campbell Parade, Bondi Beach, NSW 2026. ☎ **02/30-3271.** Fax 02/30-7974. 200 rms (half with bath). TV TEL **Bus:** 380.

Rates: $A25 single without bath, $A30 single with bath; $A30–$A60 double with or without bath; from $A70 suite. Major credit cards. **Parking:** Available.

Built in what might be described as "seaside architecture," the Bondi is a landmark and social center, rising white and vast on Sydney's most celebrated surfing beach promenade. There's lots of action, with appropriate sound effects, in four bars, a beer garden, bistro, and billiard room, all running hot every weekend. The bistro meals are both excellent and cheap, and the downtown bus stops at the front door. Bedroom furnishings are not elegant, but sufficient, and every room has a refrigerator and bedside lamps.

Thelellen Lodge, 11A Consett Ave., Bondi Beach, NSW 2026.
☎ **02/30-1521.** 14 rms (none with bath). A/C TV **Bus:** 380.
Rates: $A30 single; $A39 double. AE, BC, MC, V.

Within spray distance of the beach, the Thelellen is a quiet little place with a front lawn. Homey and comfortably furnished, the rooms have good lighting, electric fans, hot- and cold-water basins, radios, and refrigerators. Light breakfast (an extra) is served in your room. A washing machine is available, as well as a guest kitchen.

8 Glebe

Glebe and adjoining Leichhardt are inner suburbs about 1½ miles west of downtown, thronged with students and garnished with intriguing restaurants and cafes.

EXPENSIVE

Haven Inn, 196 Glebe Point Rd., Glebe, NSW 2037.
☎ **02/660-6655.** Fax 02/660-6279. 55 rms. A/C MINIBAR TV TEL **Bus:** 431, 434, 459.
Rates: $A99–$A140 single or double. Major credit cards. **Parking:** Free.

Looking like a corner apartment block, Haven Inn is built around a plant-decorated inner courtyard with a swimming pool and spa. The place combines a delightfully relaxed atmosphere with maximum facilities, including VCRs in all rooms and a video library to feed them. The inn has a pleasantly rustic restaurant and cocktail bar, secretarial service, 24-hour room service, and function rooms equipped with closed-circuit TV.

Bedrooms are spacious, airy, and fitted with excellent lighting, the decor brightly modernistic but minus the usual rubber-stamped motel touches. Even the abstract prints on the walls have an individualistic flavor. Hanging space in the open closets is generous. The only item lacking in the three-story building is an elevator. The management offers courtesy bus service to Darling Harbour.

BUDGET

Pension Albergo, 5 Day St., Leichhardt, NSW 2040,
☎ **02/560-0179.** 3 rms (none with bath). TV **Bus:** 440 or 438 to Leichhardt Town Hall.

Rates: $A38 single; $A60 double. No credit cards.

A total change from the "madding" hotel crowd scenes, this small tree-fronted Victorian home offers a few guest rooms and a lot of winning hospitality. The Pension Albergo doesn't have many amenities besides a tranquil garden and a charming dining room that becomes a TV lounge after breakfast. And the breakfast here comes with fresh fruit salad, crackling croissant, hot Italian rolls, and percolated coffee.

9   Randwick

★ **Medina Executive Apartments**, 63 St. Marks Rd., Randwick, NSW 2031. ☎ **02/399-5144.** Fax 02/398-4569. 60 apts. A/C MINIBAR TV TEL **Bus:** 373, 374, 372.

Rates: $A130 single; $A150 for two to four persons. Major credit cards. **Parking:** Free.

This establishment is set in a beautifully landscaped tropical park area of an inner southeastern suburb, close to Sydney's Showground and racecourse. This Medina offers luxurious two-bedroom units, widely spaced for elbow room. The dining areas are smart enough to entertain business contacts in, and all apartments have terraces. A pool, sauna, health spa, and gym are on the premises, along with laundry and barbecues.

Peace and quiet reign supreme (except for birdcalls) and the interiors are decorator designed, the kitchens equipped for gourmet cooking. Serviced once a week. A bargain for two or more persons.

10   North Shore

MODERATE

Northside Medina, 167 Willoughby Rd., Crows Nest, NSW 2065.
☎ **02/430-1400.** Fax 02/436-2556. 20 apts. A/C TV TEL **Train:** St. Leonards.

Rates: $A110 1-bdrm apt, single or double. Major credit cards. **Parking:** Free.

Another member of the Medina apartment chain, this establishment is located just across Sydney Harbour Bridge, near St. Leonards rail station. The modern four-story building encloses a tropical green garden courtyard with a thatched-roof gazebo, good-sized swimming pool, deck chairs, and barbecue facilities. The decor of the self-contained apartments is kept in delicate shades of antique white and burgundy; the furnishings include couches and settees that are simultaneously elegant and comfortable, wall-to-wall carpeting, and built-in wardrobes with mirrored doors. Other amenities include spacious kitchens with microwave ovens, electric ranges and refrigerators, and deft little touches like videos, daily newspaper, and milk deliveries to your door. A guest laundry is on the premises, and babysitters are available on request.

11   Manly

Seven miles northeast of center city, across the harbor, Manly is best reached by either the whizzing hydrofoil (13 minutes) or the plowing ferry (35 minutes). This is a real resort with palm-fringed promenade, shopping and entertainment centers, four surfing beaches, and six calm-water harbor beaches.

VERY EXPENSIVE

Manly Pacific Parkroyal, 55 N. Steyne, Manly, NSW 2095. ☎ **02/977-7666.** Fax 02/977-7822. 169 rms. A/C MINIBAR TV TEL

Rates: $A185–$A220 single or double. AE, BC, DC, MC, V. **Parking:** Free.

This hotel fronts the very edge of Manly's finest surfing beach. From the outside the establishment looks like merely another block of modern seafront apartments, but the interior reaches international luxury standards. The Pacific Parkroyal houses Gilberts, a lavishly handsome restaurant specializing in marine delectables; an equally elegant cocktail bar; a second, more informal restaurant; and Dalleys nightclub, Manly's smartest mingling center. The Pacific has a large swimming pool and relaxation deck (despite the beach at its front door), and public rooms plush enough for society weddings. Guest rooms are beautifully furnished, the decor resembling a sunburst of amber and scarlet. Large and carpeted, they have every possible convenience. The main lobby and grand staircase are decked in greenery and fresh flowers, and at night the subdued thunder of the surf helps you sleep. Rates are the same for singles or doubles, prices depending on whether your room has an ocean view or faces west (inland).

BUDGET

Periwinkle, 18 E. Esplanade, Manly, NSW 2095. ☎ **02/977-4668.** Fax 02/977-6308. 18 rms (two with bath). TV **Rates** (including light breakfast): $A70 single; $A78 double; $A86 triple. BC, MC, V. **Parking:** Available. Free.

Built in 1895, the Periwinkle carefully preserves its 19th-century patina. A very attractive little guesthouse with wrought-iron colonial verandas overlooking an inner courtyard, the place has the high ceilings and spacious bedrooms characteristic of the period, as well as a cozy guest lounge with an open fireplace, proud staircases, a player piano, and some—not all—modern conveniences (most bathrooms, for instance, are shared). There's a sun room with color TV, a guest kitchen, laundromat, and large ceiling fans.

12 At the Airport

Remember to show your airline ticket at this hotel for the international travelers rate.

Sydney Airport Parkroyal, Bourke Road (at O'Riordan Street), Mascot NSW 2020. ☎ **02/330-0600.** Fax 02/667-4517. 248 rms. A/C MINIBAR TV TEL

Rates: $A99 single or double for arriving or departing international travelers. Normal rate $A115 single or double. AE, BC, DC, MC, V. **Parking:** Free.

This massive white giant fronted by a miniature lake is Sydney's latest airport hotel. The interior is sumptuously beautiful. The lounge could double as a fashionable private club, complete with intimate corners and a library. The restaurant spreads out a Mediterranean-style buffet as colorful as a Renoir painting. The bedroom decor has discreet elegance, and the fittings include direct fax connections, convenient work desks, and TV displays of messages and flight information. Sound-proofing is excellent (you get no jet engine howls to disturb your slumber), and you're free to use the hotel facilities even after check-out. This goes especially for the Biggles Bar, named after a beloved super-hero pilot of British boys' fiction. However, unlike its sister establishment downtown, this is very much an airport oasis; so don't look for mellow charm.

13 Hostels

Kings Cross

Backpackers, 162 Victoria St., Kings Cross, NSW 2011. ☎ 02/356-3232. Fax 02/368-1435.
Rates: $A10 dorm; $A12–$A15 per person double room, $A12 per person in a flat for two to five people. AE, MC, V.

Backpackers offers a TV room and cooking facilities.

Downunder Hostel, 25 Hughes St., Kings Cross, NSW 2011. ☎ 02/358-1143. Fax 02/357-4675. 35 rms (none with bath).
Rates: $A14 dorm; $A32 single or double. MC, V.

Facilities at Downunder Hostel include a guest kitchen and a rooftop TV lounge.

Eva's, 6 Orwell St., Kings Cross, NSW 2011. ☎ **02/358-2185.**
Fax 02/358-3259.

Rates: $A15 dorm; $A26 single; $A34 double.

A mixture of hotel and hostel with a guest laundry, Eva's also has a
guest kitchen, TV lounge, and barbecue. Guests must provide their
own soap.

Glebe

Glebe Point YHA, 262 Glebe Point Rd., Glebe, NSW 2037.
☎ **02/692-8418.** Fax 02/660-0431. 150 beds. **Bus:** No. 431 or 433.
Rates: $A16 dorm; $A20 per person in room (double). MC, V.

Glebe Point has a guest laundry, TV lounge, sun deck, and barbecue. It offers discounts for YHA members in local restaurants. No
single rooms are available.

Glebe Point Village, 256 Glebe Point Rd., Glebe, NSW 2037.
☎ **02-660-5133.** Fax 02/552-3707. **Bus:** No. 431 or 433.
Rates: $A20 per person in double room; $A15 per person in dorm. BC,
MC, V.

At Glebe Point Village facilities include a TV room, guest kitchen,
and fax machine. No singles are available.

Hereford Lodge YHA, 51 Hereford St., Glebe, NSW 2037.
☎ **02/660-5577.** Fax 02/552-1771. 250 beds. **Bus:** No. 431 or 433.
Rates: $A15–$A22 seniors (over 18), juniors half price. BC, MC, V.

Hereford Lodge YHA offers a bistro, TV lounge, rooftop pool, sauna,
and undercover parking.

14 A Pension

The following accommodation is an upscale European-style pension
(like a bed-and-breakfast). The accent is on *cordon bleu* cooking and
personalized service rather than electronic gadgetry. Newtown is a
southwestern suburb close to Sydney University.

★ **Pensione Sydney Hotel,** 27 Georgina St., Newtown, NSW
2042. ☎ **02/550-1700,** Fax 02/550-1021. TV TEL **Bus:** 422, 423,
426.

Rates: (including breakfast): $A130–$A150 single or double. AE, BC,
DC, MC, V. **Parking:** Available.

A small building with surprisingly spacious rooms and an excellent
restaurant. The house is surrounded by flowers and has an ivy-
wreathed terrace on which to eat breakfast or sip a nightcap. There
is frequent bus service to the city.

5

Sydney Dining

Sydney today is one of the world's great centers of gastronomy. Many of its eating facilities were created in a unique and rather tragic fashion. Every war and political upheaval around the globe generated a flood of refugees into Australia. They brought their culinary skills with them, and frequently that was all they brought. Thus immediately after World War II there was a mushrooming of Polish, Czech, Yugoslav, German, and Romanian establishments. A little later came Hungarians. Then Vietnamese, Cambodians, Indians, and Koreans. At present Sydney is awash with Thai eateries. A sprinkling of Italian, Greek, and Chinese restaurants had always existed. Taken together they add up to a culinary spectrum that ranges from Argentinean to Yemenite, covering just about every international nuance in between.

Restaurants fill about 1,600 column inches in the Sydney telephone books, so the listings here are a mere sampling. Some Sydney friends will fume over omissions, but that can't be helped. Even in the top price bracket, the smallest, it is quite impossible to list anywhere near the total number of establishments. It is likewise impossible to enforce strict separation between independent, hotel, and pub restaurants. Some of the best eateries are located in elderly pubs and several of the elite establishments in hotels (as well as some of the worst). What you'll find, therefore, is a mixture of all three. The plethora of new restaurants has made Sydneysiders rather faddish eaters: Certain foods are "in" at one moment, out the next.

The "innest" cuisine currently is Modern Australian, also called Pacific Rim or Fusion Food; and it takes a bit of explaining. The basis consists of native ingredients in the widest sense—including buffalo, kangaroo and crocodile meat—blended with certain Asian flavors in a harmoniously adventurous East-West marriage. Thus in one meal you may get the choicest of milk-fed lamb scorched with Malay curry and surrounded by raw Japanese marine denizens. Accompanied by Barossa Valley Riesling and followed by Thai coconut parfait.

The possibilities are endless, limited only by the chef's skill and imagination. It's cuisine that can be haute or hideous, depending on whose hand is on the skillet. Under various labels this culinary style has conquered a good part of the American and European food world—raved over by millions of diners who have no inkling that it originated Down Under.

A NOTE ON PRICES All prices cited in this guide are in Australian dollars; $A1 equals about U.S. 70¢, which means that a restaurant meal listed here at $A40 costs about U.S. $28.

Menu prices are exactly as written—no taxes are added in Sydney. Many restaurants impose a surcharge on Sunday or holidays, however, which is always stated on the menu. The BYO ("bring your own") custom lets you supply potables from a liquor store at much lower prices than you'd pay at the restaurant. Some establishments are licensed *and* BYO—meaning that the choice is yours. A minority of eateries charge a corkage fee of $A1 to $A3 for supplying the necessary glasses.

As a general rule you're not expected to tip in the lower bracket restaurants and to leave only one or two bucks in the medium establishments. Once you get into the pricier regions it's the usual 10% to 15%, though few Aussies will leave that much unless they've dined in a group that made a lot of work for the staff.

Price categories in the listings below are rather broad, with large gray areas. Dinner per person (without wine) is categorized as **very expensive** at $A40 and up; as **expensive** at $A35 to $A40; as **moderate** at $A20 to $A35; and as **budget** at less than $A20. The gray areas exist because even very expensive restaurants offer some fairly inexpensive dishes while expensive and moderate restaurants often list one or two very expensive main courses.

MENU TERMS   In Australia "entree" carries its original meaning—appetizer, not, as in the United States, main course. "Sweets" are desserts, though a few cutely Dickensian joints label them "pudding." "Biscuits" are crackers, usually served with cheese. "Pavlova" is a ubiquitous dessert concoction of meringue and passion fruit and other tropical flavors. "Flake" means shark, "swedes" are turnips, and "chips" french fries. The nebulous tag "pasty" is hung on virtually anything that comes wrapped in a crust.

Few Sydney restaurants serve water automatically. In most cases you'll have to order it. And even fewer put ice in the glasses without a specific request.

1   Downtown

Very Expensive

★ **Bilson's,** International Passenger Terminal, Circular Quay West, The Rocks. ☎ 251-5000.
Cuisine: MODERN AUSTRALIAN. **Reservations:** Recommended.
Prices: Set-price dinner $A50–$A60. Major credit cards.
Open: Lunch Mon–Sat noon–2:30pm; dinner daily 6:30–10:30pm.

This amazing establishment still carries the name of the illustrious chef (Tony Bilson) who left years ago to found a restaurant of his own (Fine Bouche). But no matter—Bilson's fame as a premier gourmet restaurant remains as firmly fixed as the splendor of its location. Set on the upper level of Sydney's main ocean-liner dock, the place features wraparound glass walls offering a permanent vista of the Opera House, the bridge, and most of the magnificent harbor. And the clientele could pass for a who's who of visiting overseas celebrities and the stars of Australia's entertainment, sports, and political firmament.

The menu changes monthly, but a characteristic selection would be smoked water buffalo salad, venison pie, roasted hare with sauce poivrade, a classic escalope of salmon less frères Troiagros, veal sweetbreads champignons, and a superlative lemon soufflé. The wine cellar is among the half-dozen best (some say *the* best) on the continent. The lunch menu, Monday through Friday, is more limited but also less costly.

Kable's, Regent Hotel, 199 George St. ☎ **238-0000.**

> **Cuisine:** MODERN AUSTRALIAN. **Reservations:** Accepted.
> **Prices:** Appetizers around \$A15; main courses around \$A28. Major credit cards.
> **Open:** Mon–Fri noon–2:30pm; dinner Tues–Sat 6:30–10:30pm.

Winner of a string of culinary awards, this hotel dining room (ironically named after a Herculean convict) presents a flawless blending of luxurious decor and Oz-style haute cuisine. The long, narrow room is exquisitely appointed in art deco style, the tables gleam softly with genuine crystal and silverware, and service is so smoothly unobtrusive that it seems to be performed by smiling shadows. Quiet and serenity reign supreme, which is passing strange since some very big financial deals are sealed here almost nightly, assisted, no doubt, by one of the most grandiose (and priciest) wine lists in the land.

The fare is simultaneously creative and delicately balanced, with the accent on regional specialties such as char-grilled Tasmanian lobster, Gippsland lamb, Victorian yabbies, and Australian farmhouse cheese. The Asian influence provides a fiery tang to the crab pancakes served with Thai dressing. And the dessert specialty is a positively symphonic finale called La Stupenda—a mousse made of passion fruit and white chocolate that tastes how I imagine heavenly Ambrosia might (if I ever get to sample it).

⭐ **Rockpool,** The Rocks, 109 George St., ☎ **252-1888.**

> **Cuisine:** MODERN AUSTRALIAN. **Reservations:** Recommended.
> **Prices:** Appetizers around \$A18; main courses around \$A28.
> **Open:** Lunch Mon–Fri noon–2:30pm; dinner Mon–Sat 6:30–10pm. Major credit cards.

Deceptively plain on the outside, the Rockpool is Sydney's Mecca for celebrity-spotters and serious gourmets alike. The interior has a post-modern 1950s look, redolent with chrome, pastel laminates, and stainless steel, plus a charmingly simple enclosed courtyard dining area. The owner/chef, Neil Perry, ranks as a celebrity himself, a kind of Jupiter figure on the culinary Olympus.

The fare here is light, highly imaginative, and eye-pleasing, the accent on seafood with Asian elements. A characteristic appetizer might be smoked oysters flavored with garlic and ginger. For a main course, a delicately seared John Dory served in Indian pastry or a pigeon glazed Chinese-style or prawns with polenta flavored with onions and mushrooms might be served. Each dish comes with so many subtly blended ingredients that the meals seem orchestrated rather than cooked. The crayfish ravioli, for instance, are served with scorched butter and yogurt, and some fish courses come with delicately spiced coconut sauce. The wine list is awe inspiring—one bottle actually sells at \$A1000, though most of them go for only two-digit prices. And out in front of the restaurant there is a moderately priced oyster bar, which has the same owner and where the offerings are *nearly* as good, though not nearly as symphonic.

EXPENSIVE

⭐ **Bennelong**, in the Sydney Opera House, Bennelong Point.
☎ 250-7578.

Cuisine: MODERN AUSTRALIAN. **Reservations:** Recommended.
Prices: Main courses $A17–$A25; set-price dinner for two $A65
(pretheater only). Major credit cards.
Open: Lunch Mon–Sat noon–2:30pm; dinner Mon–Sat 5:30–10:30pm.

Bennelong is attached to the Opera House and offers some of the
most magnificent views Sydney can boast. Every table comes with a
panorama. It takes a powerful menu to compete with these surroundings, and Bennelong has it. What's more, the service is tailored for
location. The dining process is divided into pretheater and posttheater
meals, served speedily and smoothly at the appropriate times.

Sitting smack in the center of Sydney's top tourist attraction,
Bennelong tries to please as many global palates as possible, so you
get a very mixed fare, all of it well prepared and served with flourish.
But this is decidedly a tourist spot, and locals are somewhat scarce.
Try some of the more unusual dishes, such as buffalo filets (slightly
gamey and very tasty), sugar-cured river trout, and desserts such as
the mixture of chocolate terrine and apple caramel. The wines are
choice Australians, most reasonably priced.

⭐ **Claudine's**, 151 Macquarie St. ☎ 241-1749.

Cuisine: FRENCH. **Reservations:** Recommended.
Prices: Appetizers around $A8; main courses around $A22. Major credit
cards.
Open: Lunch Mon–Fri noon–3pm; dinner Mon–Sat 5:30–9pm.

Not only is there really a Claudine, but she's French-born and the
best advertisement her hostelry could possibly get. Hard to say which
is the more charming—the restaurant or its owner. Although French
and seafood-oriented, the menu is fairly international with some
Oriental touches and includes enough veal, beef, and poultry to sat-
isfy those grown tired of marine delectables. You can order a nicely
balanced mixture of, say, seafood starters, meat for the middle course,
and for dessert—well, dessert. The fare is equally excellent in all categories, and the establishment fully licensed. At lunchtime the swank
business crowd predominates; at dinner it becomes a favored-
intimate rendezvous.

Isomura, St. Martins Tower, corner of Market and Clarence Streets.
☎ 267-4552.

Cuisine: JAPANESE. **Reservations:** Accepted.
Prices: Set dinner menu $A30–$A50. Major credit cards.
Open: Daily 11:30am–10:30pm.

A sleek, streamlined high-tech eatery, this is the local representative
of the giant Ginza chain. You don't get much atmosphere, but an
impressive array of sophisticated kitchen equipment. The house specialty is kushiage: deep-fried brochettes with countless fillings—from
asparagus to salmon—served on skewers. They are delicately battered
and quite delicious, but it takes heaps of them to still a healthy

appetite. You can also order sushi (at $A22 per platter), and eat either at tables or at the super-speedy service bar. That's the best vantage point from which to admire the complex machinery used in preparation of these tidbits. Isomura offers the sharpest contrast between lunch and dinner prices; a difference of nearly 40%. The crowds are thinner and the menu correspondingly larger at night.

Sydney Tower International Restaurant, Centrepoint, corner of Pitt and Market Streets. ☎ **233-3722.**

Cuisine: INTERNATIONAL. **Reservations:** Accepted.

Prices: Appetizers around $A14; main courses around $A26. Major credit cards.

Open: Lunch Mon–Fri 11am–3:30pm; dinner Mon–Sat 5–10pm.

Sydney has no less than three revolving restaurants, which are frequently confused. The reason is that two of them happen to be located in Sydney Tower and run by the same company. This entry focuses on Level 1, the International Restaurant. (Level 2 is a moderately priced self-service eatery.)

The catch with revolving restaurants is that the emphasis can rest on the panoramic viewing, with little left for the food. This is definitely not the case here. True, the vista below is enthralling, but so is most of the menu. For most patrons the slowly unfolding city and harbor panorama is sheer joy, and the management guarantees you a ringside seat, though not necessarily by the window. The revolving mechanism works silently and smoothly, as does the service. Menu and wine list are somewhat shorter than you would expect in a svelte establishment, but that's the only concession made to the special nature of this aerie. *Note:* Your vantage position is 1,000 feet up, so if heights interfere with your appetite, you'd better dine somewhere else.

Lunch and dinner menus are the same here, but the luncheon fare comes considerably cheaper. Among appetizers are fresh avocado pear with creamy fish mousse, and a wonderfully tangy seafood terrine with mango-yogurt sauce. Turning to the main courses, there is an unusually good smoked loin of pork in cutlet form, served with red cabbage in a delicately pungent caraway sauce, or a classic rack of lamb, floating in a red wine and mustard sauce. For dessert you couldn't do much better than to order the mascarpone with amaretto, an Italian specialty allegedly prepared from a "secret" recipe (I have no idea of the ingredients except that they are dolce, alcoholic, and ambrosial).

Sydney's third revolving restaurant is the **Summit,** on the 47th floor of Australia Square Tower, George Street (☎ 247-9777). It's slightly more expensive than the Sydney Tower, and somewhat more traditional. It has dancing six nights a week.

Wolfie's, 17 Circular Quay West, The Rocks. ☎ **241-5577.**

Cuisine: AUSTRALIAN. **Reservations:** Accepted.

Prices: Appetizers around $A10; main courses around $A22. Major credit cards.

Open: Mon–Sat noon–3pm; dinner daily 6–11pm.

This place used to be called Phantom of the Opera, but the phantom dematerialized, leaving the gorgeous views behind. There is nothing in the least ghostly about the high-tech char grill kitchen installed by the new management, nor about the briskly efficient service. But the views make al fresco dining here an enchanting experience. On a mellow evening you might sit on the open deck and find the spectacle so engrossing that you forget about food—well, temporarily. Even the old "coathanger"—Sydney Harbour Bridge—becomes a thing of beauty when seen in dimming light. All around you boats and ferries skim, the lights start to twinkle, and you can lean back and let the magic enfold you.

The menu is evenly balanced between land and marine comestibles, and naturally leans toward the char-grilled (not innovative but high quality): beef or lamb loin médaillons; lobster tails; and Queensland prawns. Some of the finest items are on the dessert list—such as the profiteroles filled with Grand Marnier and served in Swiss chocolate sauce.

Moderate

 Capitán Torres, 73 Liverpool St. ☎ 264-5574.
Cuisine: SPANISH. **Reservations:** Accepted.
Prices: Appetizers $A9; main courses around $A16. Major credit cards.
Open: Lunch daily noon–3pm; dinner daily 6–11:30pm.

Capitán Torres is as Spanish as it sounds. Even the wine is Andalusian rather than Aussie. This used to be one of Sydney's prime budget restaurants, but its fame spread and, while still prime, it's no longer budget. The feature that has remained unchanged is the hugeness of the helpings. The cuisine is spicily Iberian—and this includes Portuguese dishes, like the roast chicken in tomato-and-wine sauce. On the Spanish side you can order a platter of grilled sardines, casseroled quail, barbecued steaks, saffronhued paella, and the absolutely enormous platter of mixed, grilled seafood. Sangría comes by the carafe.

Imperial Peking, 15 Circular Quay West, The Rocks.
☎ 247-7073.
Cuisine: CHINESE. **Reservations:** Accepted.
Prices: Appetizers around $A8; main courses around $A20. Major credit cards.
Open: Lunch daily noon–3pm; dinner daily 6–11pm.

There are actually four Imperial Pekings in Sydney, all in the same gastronomic class. I picked this one because of its spectacular harbor views (ask for a window table when you make your reservations) and intriguing history. This is the dream come true of Alfred Lai, architect by training, restaurateur by inclination. Lai saw his chance when he heard of a decrepit old warehouse standing empty on Circular Quay. He put both his talent and his money to work and transformed it into an absolutely gorgeous eating palace, which today ranks as one of the top trio of Chinese restaurants in Australia. Make no mistake—what you get here is haute cuisine Mandarin style, the only fare in the world that can beat the French for sheer subtlety and variety. In case you haven't tasted it before, it resembles the ordinary Cantonese version about as much as a custom-tailored Savile Row suit resembles a pair of jeans. Chow mein is not on the menu.

Possibly because of its location, the Imperial's fare emphasizes seafood rather more than is usual in Chinese restaurants. And the wine list is vastly more extensive. If you dine here with a local, he or she will be able to point out some of the VIPs clicking chopsticks around you—the Imperial draws them like a magnet. Crabs, lobsters, and the delicious little yabbies are kept live in huge glass tanks until the moment you order them. You can also get real bird's-nest soup, not the insipid imitation. Otherwise it's a rather agonizing choice from a menu featuring more than 180 dishes (not including an auxiliary listing of daily specials). Have a stab at the abalone in mustard sauce or the salt-and-pepper mudcrab, if your palate craves something fiery. Or switch to dry-land critters, like the regal Peking duck or the beef in plum sauce.

⭐ **Machiavelli Ristorante,** 123 Clarence St. ☎ 299-3748.
Cuisine: ITALIAN. **Reservations:** Recommended.
Prices: Appetizers around $A7; main courses around $A17. Major credit cards.
Open: Lunch Mon–Fri noon–3pm; dinner Wed–Fri 6–11pm.

This place is a lunchtime institution in Sydney's business world. Begun as a side venture of the Toppi family, the ristorante captivated the local luncheon market almost overnight with its quality food, slick service, and sensible prices. The vaulted white premises have a charmingly rustic air, accentuated by a huge hanging display of bacon, hams, and sausages. The wall is graced by a portrait of cunning namesake Nicollò himself, but all around hang photos of Aussie politicos, past and present. A gentle allusion? Anyway, don't miss the antipasto here, followed, perhaps, by the delicious chicken breasts marsala. The concluding coffee will jolt you through the day.

Minar, 16 Wentworth Ave. ☎ 283-4634.
Cuisine: INDIAN/VEGETARIAN. **Reservations:** Accepted.
Prices: Appetizers around $A7; main courses around $A10. Major credit cards.
Open: Lunch Mon–Fri noon–2:30pm; dinner Mon–Sat 5:30–11pm.

This famed eatery offers an unusually wide selection of vegetarian dishes alongside traditional Indian haute cuisine—as well as a distinctly upper-crust clientele, and some of the smoothest service in town. The fare is not adventurous but very comprehensive: covering the entire range of palate pleasers from the gentle glow of crushed herbs to the fiery delight of really hot curry selections. Minar's culinary fame rests on its tandoori dishes (make sure to sample the superb bread) and its outstanding array of desserts and sweetmeats. Equally memorable is the rack of lamb served in yogurt. The Indian dancers who appear on weekend nights seem quite unnecessary; they merely distract from the food. Wine selection is expensive. BYO and licensed.

Sydney Dining

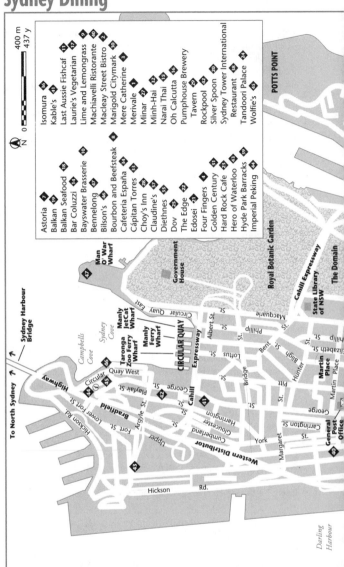

Astoria
Balkan
Balkan Seafood
Bar Coluzzi
Bayswater Brasserie
Bennelong
Bilson's
Bourbon and Beefsteak
Cafeteria España
Cápitan Torres
Choy's Inn
Claudine's
Diethnes
Dov
The Edge
Edosei
Four Fingers
Golden Century
Hard Rock Cafe
Hero of Waterloo
Hyde Park Barracks
Imperial Peking

Isomura
Kable's
Last Aussie Fishcaf
Laurie's Vegetarian
Lime and Lemongrass
Machiavelli Ristorante
Macleay Street Bistro
Marigold Citymark
Mere Catherine
Merivale
Minar
Minh-Hai
Narai Thai
Oh Calcutta
Pumphouse Brewery Tavern
Rockpool
Silver Spoon
Sydney Tower International Restaurant
Tandoori Palace
Wolfie's

Budget

$ Cafeteria España, 79 Liverpool St. No phone.
Cuisine: SPANISH. **Reservations:** Not accepted.
Prices: Soup \$A4; main courses around \$A9. No credit cards.
Open: Mon–Sat 8am–10pm.

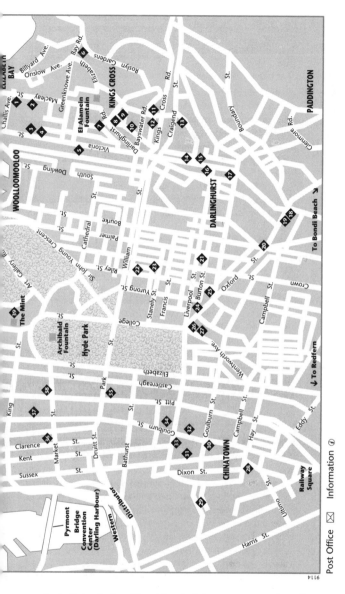

Set in Sydney's short "Spanish strip," this is an exact replica of a Barcelona or Madrid fast-food dispensary, except that it closes Sunday. You sit on bar stools along a high counter, inhale the rich aroma of bean soup, and try to make yourself heard over a happy blend of voices and music. Try the Spanish churros or the tripe—both excellent.

Diethnes, 336 Pitt St. ☎ **267-8956.**

> **Cuisine:** GREEK. **Reservations:** Recommended.
> **Prices:** Appetizers around $A5; main dishes around $A9. Major credit cards.
> **Open:** Lunch Mon–Sat noon–3:30pm; dinner Mon–Sat 5:30–10pm.

Established in 1953, Diethnes serves everybody's Hellenic favorites. Nothing remotely nouvelle here—the devoted clientele would scream blue murder at innovations. You descend a flight of stairs into a large cellarlike basement, graced with white Athenian pillars and redolent with friendly vibes. Service is fast, efficient, and smiling, and prices are happily reasonable. You order standard and excellent Greek fare (even the Australian John Dory comes with Greek salad). Otherwise it's moussaka, the great cheese-and-spinach pie called spanakopita, dolmades, calamari, and nine various and wonderful lamb dishes. The dessert array is equally solid, mostly drenched in honey and filled with crushed almonds. You could try some of the imported Greek wines to harmonize with the meal.

Skygarden, Level 3, 77 Castlereagh St. ☎ **231-1811.**

> **Cuisine:** INTERNATIONAL. **Reservations:** Not accepted.
> **Prices:** All helpings $A7–$A9. No credit cards.
> **Open:** Mon–Wed 8am–5:30pm, Thurs–Sat 9am–7pm.

The food court of a huge shopping complex, Skygardens, is surprisingly stylish, sculptured, and muraled, with comfortable seating beneath a large dome. There are four food outlets—American, Italian, Asian, and Provençal—and a very well stocked bar that even sells French champagne. The national dishes dispensed are fairly standard—no surprises—but of good quality; including the American hamburgers. The only catch is that the operations don't keep the same schedules: Some serve breakfast, some don't.

2 Chinatown

Sydney's Chinatown is located in what used to be the grimy end of the city, where the markets sprawled. Some of the markets are still there, but Chinatown has been spruced up and gentrified almost beyond recognition. Dixon Street and vicinity seem to consist of restaurants beside and on top of each other. For customers they depend mainly on the Chinese populace and only secondarily on tourism. For that reason the fare they serve is more authentic than in other parts of town, and some are polite—or condescending enough—to mark certain items "Authentic Chinese Dish" for the benefit of visiting *gweilo*. Most Chinatown restaurants are a convenient distance from the Central Station subway stop.

Moderate

Golden Century, 399 Sussex St., Haymarket. ☎ **212-3901.**

> **Cuisine:** CHINESE. **Reservations:** Recommended on weekends.

Prices: Dishes $A9–$A15. Major credit cards.
Open: Daily noon–4am.

The fare here is solidly Cantonese with just a few Mandarin dishes added for variety. The clientele is overwhelmingly Chinese—family groups and business partners—and most of them are permanent patrons. I can think of no higher recommendation. You can pick your meal from the menu or from the live denizens of the fish tank. Either way, you'll get it promptly, no matter how clamorously crowded the dining room may be. The fresh reef fish and abalone are outstanding. You can get all the standard Cantonese favorites, but, if you're feeling adventurous, try some of the more arcane delicacies, such as stewed beef tendons in oyster sauce or the "nothing chicken"—boiled in oil with onions and shredded ginger.

★ **Marigold Citymark,** 683 George St. ☎ 281-3388.
Cuisine: CHINESE. **Reservations:** Recommended.
Prices: Yum cha dishes $A3–$A5. Major credit cards.
Open: Lunch Mon–Sat 10am–3pm; dinner daily 5:30pm–midnight.

Occupying two floors, this plushly furnished, tastefully decorated restaurant is Sydney's premier yum cha haven. What's more, it's totally authentic—no concessions to Western palates. Yum cha, in case you don't know, are rolls and dumplings, either steamed or deep-fried, filled with meats, seafood, or vegetables in almost endless variety. They come to your table in trolleys and you help yourself to as many as you like. And that's the catch. They're so small and taste so scrumptious that it takes iron willpower to stop the intake.

Budget

Choy's Inn, corner of Hay and Harbour Streets. ☎ 211-4213.
Cuisine: CHINESE. **Reservations:** Accepted.
Prices: Appetizers around $A5; main courses around $A11. Major credit cards.
Open: Daily 11am–midnight.

Choy's Inn is decked out like a peasant hut. It serves delicious lemon chicken, scallops with mangoes, honey-glazed prawns, and other such specialties. Forget about the printed menu and order from the blackboard marked "specials." Licensed and BYO.

Minh-Hai, 734 George St., Haymarket. ☎ 281-1875.
Cuisine: VIETNAMESE. **Reservations:** Not accepted.
Prices: Soups around $A5; main courses around $A8. No credit cards.
Open: Mon–Sat 10am–9:30pm.

Minh-Hai is one of the few non-Chinese eateries to flourish in this region, so you know it has to be good. And cheap! It is both—sufficiently to make you forget about the shrill fluorescent lighting. The array of Vietnamese dishes available at rock-bottom rates is immense, about a dozen varieties of soups alone, not to speak of the various combination rice plates. Try the fish porridge for an unusual treat. The place is BYO.

3 Oxford Street

An amazing number of restaurants thrive along Oxford Street, which runs from the center city through Darlinghurst and Paddington all the way to Bondi Junction. Take either the 380 or 382 bus to get to this area.

Moderate

⭐ **Balkan,** 209 Oxford St., Darlinghurst. ☎ **357-4970.**

Cuisine: YUGOSLAV. **Reservations:** Not accepted.

Prices: Appetizers around $A10; main courses around $A17. Major credit cards.

Open: Tues–Sun 11am–11pm.

Balkan has one dining room downstairs, another upstairs, and needs them both to accommodate the nightly throngs. It's a long narrow premises, with plastic tables, metal chairs, sliding doors to the street, and an open-grill kitchen in front sending out aromatic signals to your taste buds. Service is fast, the tables are usually packed, the ambience relaxed. "Hearty" is the only word to describe the fare. The Serbian bean soup alone would make a meal. The other Balkan goodies are equally tasty and just as filling: *plieskavica* (a kind of hamburger), *chepavcici* (beef, veal, and pork minced together and barbecued), or *raznici* (tender chunks of pork cooked on a skewer). It takes a very hale appetite to manage more than one course here. Thick Turkish coffee is the indispensable finale. BYO.

⭐ **Balkan Seafood,** 215 Oxford St., Darlinghurst. ☎ **331-7670.**

Cuisine: SEAFOOD. **Reservations:** Not accepted.

Prices: Appetizers around $A8; main courses around $A17. BC, MC, V.

Open: Tues–Sun –11pm.

Frommer's Smart Traveler: Restaurants

1. Make lunch your main meal of the day—you get smaller selections but lower prices.
2. In BYO establishments look for the corkage charge on the menu; it can range from zero to $A3.
3. Check the wine list carefully. Some restaurants have wine prices quite out of proportion to their food prices.
4. Watch where the students eat. They have a grapevine system for finding good, inexpensive meals.
5. If you don't like froth on your coffee order a "flat white."
6. Many of Sydney's smaller restaurants don't stick to rigid hours. They'll simply close when they have no customers.
7. Don't order a set three-course meal unless you're a hearty eater. The first two courses are frequently so large that you might not manage the third.
8. Aussie beer has a higher alcohol content than American. If you want to avoid a buzz, order a "light."

Decorated and run along the same lines as the adjacent Balkan, this place is equally popular, but with the accent on marine edibles. The two places frequently pool customers—if you can't get a seat in one, you wander into the other. Portions are equally huge here, but the substance is somewhat lighter. Noisy, relaxed, and convivial, this spot is not a hideaway for an intimate rendezvous. For starters, try the baby calamari, with wonderfully tangy charcoal-grilled whiting to follow. Alternatively you can order most of the meat dishes available at the other Balkan bastion. BYO.

Bombay Tandoori, 231 Oxford St., Darlinghurst. ☎ **361-3014.**

Cuisine: INDIAN. **Reservations:** Accepted.

Prices: Appetizers around $A5; main courses around $A11. Major credit cards.

Open: Lunch Mon–Fri noon–3pm; dinner daily 6–10pm.

A handsomely colorful establishment with Indian murals adorning the mottled walls and earthy red linen decking the tables. Most of the dishes come smoke-roasted, tandoori-style, and you also get a range of vegetarian specialties. Try the Murgh shahi korma—filleted chicken breasts marinated in yoghurt and served in a creamy nut-flavored sauce with basmati rice. Or one of the huge mixed platters heaped with smoke-roasted lamb, prawns, and chicken, accompanied by traditional hot nan bread.

Odos, 175 Oxford St., at Taylor Square. ☎ **360-1963.**

Cuisine: MODERN AUSTRALIAN. **Reservations:** Accepted.

Prices: Appetizers around $A8; main courses around $A14. AE, BC, MC, V.

Open: Lunch Wed–Sun from 10am–2:30pm; dinner daily 6pm–midnight.

A newcomer to a region positively brimming with eateries and drinkeries, Odos goes in for both by turning into a bar nightly until 3am. The decor has changed somewhat since the place ceased to be the National Bank building. Now it sports black-tiled walls, brightly glowing bar stools, and an exceedingly laid-back atmosphere. Among the best offerings here are the seared kangaroo fillet with wild mushrooms and the range of fresh, crisp, tastefully arranged salads.

BUDGET

 Kim, 235 Oxford St., Darlinghurst. ☎ **357-5429.**

Cuisine: VIETNAMESE. **Reservations:** Recommended.

Prices: Appetizers around $A5; main courses around $A9. BC, MC, V.

Open: Wed–Mon 7–10:30pm.

Simple yet quite stylish, this dainty little establishment serves Vietnamese morsels. It has only 13 tables downstairs and upstairs, but wood-paneled walls, soft lanterns beneath a beamed ceiling, and the ambience produced by a mixture of Gallic finesse and Asian piquancy. The menu is printed in Vietnamese with English translations. You can go through any number of courses here. Goi tom is a starter salad of chicken, shrimp, and carrots with peanuts; mangtay is a classic asparagus soup made with chunks of crab. Main courses include sweet-and-sour squid, and bean curd stuffed with onions and vermicelli. Several unusual desserts beckon as well, such as a pudding made of sweet corn and creamed rice and a surprisingly palate-pleasing jelly of seaweed. BYO.

Silver Spoon, 203 Oxford St., Darlinghurst. ☎ **360-4669.**

Cuisine: THAI. **Reservations:** Recommended.
Prices: Appetizers around $A6; main courses around $A11. AE, BC, MC, V.
Open: Lunch daily noon–3pm; dinner daily 6–10pm.

If you enjoy the delicate heatwaves of Thai cuisine, this is the establishment to head for. It's dainty and carefully groomed—furnishings look fragile (but aren't), decorations are lovingly and artfully arranged, and even the paper napkins greet you folded into floral patterns. There is an agreeable contrast between the gently spiced appetizers and the robust heat of the curry main dishes, preparing your palate in stages, so to speak. Among the starters are plates of fish cakes and slightly sweetish coconut-cream soup. Then you have a choice of four main courses and an array of curry dishes (including a vegetarian one that really scorches). It's a good idea to follow the daily specials here, particularly in the seafood line, because they really *are* special. If you don't feel seaworthy, try the grilled chicken. BYO.

Tandoori Palace, 86 Oxford St., Darlinghurst. ☎ **331-7072.**

Cuisine: INDIAN. **Reservations:** Accepted.
Prices: Appetizers around $A6; main courses around $A11. Major credit cards.
Open: Daily 11am–11pm.

Tandoori Palace is tastefully decked out and boasts a very elegant cocktail bar—a rarity in Indian eateries. The fare offers specialties from half a dozen Indian regions, and the menu is cleverly balanced between red-hot and mildly seasoned dishes. You can order an economy meal or a somewhat expensive repast, as your exchequer permits. Among the lamb dishes, the saag gosht, cooked with spinach and spices from the proprietor's own recipe, stands out. On the mild side you have the beef badami, served in a creamy sauce with ground almonds. If you're a couple your best bet is the mixed platter for two; heaped with succulent chunks of chicken, lamb, and king prawns, roasted in a tandoor. At the finish try the homemade mango ice cream with pistachio nuts.

4   Kings Cross

Very Expensive

⭐ **Edosei,** 22 Rockwell Crescent, Potts Point. ☎ **357-3407.**
Cuisine: JAPANESE. **Reservations:** Accepted.
Prices: Appetizers $A7.50; main courses $A22; sushi $A16. Major credit cards.

Open: Lunch Mon–Sat noon–2pm; dinner Mon–Sat 6–10pm.

Edosei houses the most famous sushi bar in Sydney. You have a choice between breasting the bar or gracing a table in the dining room. There's more privacy in the latter, but you miss seeing the sushi knife-and-cleaver acrobats in action. No matter how often you witness it, it always seems a minor miracle how the chefs remain unscathed and the food emerges delicious. Among the treats here are the Tokyo-style mixed sushi called nigri, and the outstanding grilled squid. The Edosei is one of the very few places that serves Japanese wine plus a range of Japanese desserts that may surprise palates more accustomed to the whipped-cream type.

Expensive

 Bayswater Brasserie, 32 Bayswater Rd., Kings Cross.
☎ 357-2177.
   Cuisine: MODERN AUSTRALIAN. **Reservations:** Not accepted.
   Prices: Appetizers around $A9; main courses around $A18. BC, MC, V.
   Open: Mon–Sat noon–midnight, Sun 9am–11pm.

Considered by many the best of its breed in town, this gourmet spot has the distinction of also serving light snacks apart from regular repasts, as well as breakfast on Sunday. The clientele is top-heavy with wealthy business executives and the atmosphere is one of gilt-edged activity. Seating arrangements include a charming and almost secluded courtyard and a back room that's downright idyllic. The setting is part pub, part bistro—you choose one or the other according to mood. During the day the light streams in through glasshouse windows, but at night the place becomes darkly romantic.

Frommer's Cool for Kids: Restaurants

Skygarden   (p. 86) Has a variety of small food outlets, including one selling American burgers, in a marketplace setting.

Last Aussie Fishcaf   (p. 95) An old-fashioned jukebox, rock 'n' roll renditions, plus visiting jugglers, magicians, and trick cyclists are guaranteed to keep kids entertained.

Roma   (p. 101) You don't have to be Italian to bring your family here. The fabulous array of cakes has universal junior appeal.

Titina   (19 Norton St., Leichhardt; ☎ 569-2959) If your youngsters can read they'll be enthralled by the graffiti that form the decor. And perhaps contribute some.

Home Cooking   (p.108) Makes English-style children's meals at fractional prices.

Pancakes on the Rocks   (10 Hickson Rd., The Rocks: ☎ 247-6371) Provides assorted games for children and parents. Quite apart from the biggest array of pancakes in town.

There's nothing standard about the Bayswater's bill of fare. The menu is almost adventurous in its variety. Appetizers, for instance, include a plate of freshly made goose sausages served with sweet potato, thick peasant-style lima bean soup, and chickpea purée. Main courses include a veal tongue accompanied by avocado, a rare choice between pan-fried octopus and barbecued calamari, rolled stuffed loin of lamb with sweet okra, plus a vast array of pasta dishes, from meat to marine, that you won't usually find in the plusher restaurants. But this is precisely the special charm of the "BB" (as its legions of fans call it) as it can suit very nearly every palate—though not quite every purse. For dessert the BB offers possibly the richest hazelnut torte south of the equator.

Benkay, Hotel Nikko, 81 Macleay St., Kings Cross. ☎ **368-3000.**

> **Cuisine:** JAPANESE. **Reservations:** Accepted.
> **Prices:** Fixed-price dinner menus $A35–$A70. Major credit cards.
> **Open:** Daily 6:30–10pm.

A superior hotel restaurant, furnished in the same cool ultracontemporary style as the entire building. The service is impeccable, the food of the highest quality, but you'd better forget about ambience. The sushi bar has an international reputation and is usually occupied by Japanese visitors. The teppan bar offers portions much larger than the normal Japanese helpings. Your first taste of the fresh ingredients will explain the popularity of the place. The miso soup is an aromatic masterpiece, and the dessert sherbets are so delicately and originally flavored that they seem to stem from a secret recipe kept locked in a vault.

Paramount, 73 Macleay St., Kings Cross. ☎ **358-1652.**

> **Cuisine:** MODERN AUSTRALIAN. **Reservations:** Accepted.
> **Prices:** Appetizers around $A8; main courses around $A19. Major credit cards.
> **Open:** Lunch daily noon–2:30pm; dinner daily 6–10pm.

Chef-owner Christine Manfield is one of Sydney's most distinguished kitchen wizards, but her reputation was gained in other people's kitchens. Now she runs her own restaurant, and the Paramount manages to be both chic and "gemütlich"—a rare combination. Amber-hued, softly lit, and supremely comfortable, the place has none of the nervous snobbery that afflicts so many fashionable new dining spots. It doesn't have to *prove* anything.

The cuisine here has more Asian nuances than most Modern Australian fare, but highly original. Try the crab salad with mint, sliced coconut, and shallots. Then perhaps the glazed ginger duck or the ocean trout served with a mousse of prawns, followed by mango sorbet. The dishes, colorful as a painter's palette, delight the eye as much as the palate.

Moderate

Bourbon And Beefsteak, 24 Darlinghurst Rd., Kings Cross. ☎ **358-1144.**

Cuisine: AMERICAN. **Reservations:** Accepted.
Prices: Appetizers around $A10; main courses around $A18. AE, BC,
DC, MC, V.
Open: Daily 24 hours.

Only Kings Cross could produce and maintain this astonishing
multipurpose establishment. Bourbon is literally all things to all
people: breakfast in the morning (and all day), lunch at lunchtime,
dinner later, supper still later, live bands and piano music in between.
Most of the time the place is packed. The interior looks as if the
contents of a thrift shop had been spilled over two floors, with bars,
tables, and chairs added as an afterthought. But the real surprise is
that the food for all meals is excellent, the portions are more than
generous, the atmosphere is happily nonchalant, and the clientele is
half and half tourists and locals. The menu is downright encyclope-
dic, ranging from American breakfasts to an array of Mexican dinner specialties.

★ **Four Fingers,** 150 Victoria St., Kings Cross. ☎ **358-3705.**
Cuisine: MODERN AUSTRALIAN. **Reservations:** Recommended.
Prices: 2 courses for $A22.50. BC, MC, V.
Open: Lunch Mon–Fri noon–3pm; dinner Mon–Sat 6:30–11:30pm.

A small, ocher-walled eatery, intimate and crowded, with a name
derived from the four members of the crew—two in the kitchen, two
out front. The place is operated by three partners, all with high gastronomic credentials, who impart an exceptionally individualistic
imprint on the menu. You may get to choose between ravioli stuffed
with onions and Parmesan, saddle of lamb in turnip purée, or pan-
fried chicken with yams. Desserts are frequently inspired, such as
mango slices floating in crème anglaise. The only negative aspect is
the open kitchen door, which lets you admire the equipment but also
lets in a lot of heat. BYO.

★ **Lime And Lemongrass,** 42 Kellett St., Kings Cross,
☎ **358-5577.**
Cuisine: THAI. **Reservations:** Recommended on weekends.
Prices: Appetizers around $A6; main courses around $A12. Major credit
cards.
Open: Dinner and late supper daily 6pm–2am.

A dinery for late diners in a street devoted to nightbirds, this remarkable Thai restaurant competes with a whole row of establishments
that only come alive around 10pm. The Lime is a stylish two-story
affair with a cocktail bar and outdoor tables. Try and get an outdoor
seat in the late hours; the indoor portion tends to become overcrowded and drenched in theme music. The fare is Bangkok at its
best: dry chicken curry with peanuts and lime leaves; hot and sour
prawn soup; tapioca dumplings with steamed vegetables; a unique
(and quite un–New Yorkish) type of lime cheesecake. The bar operates until around 4am.

Macleay Street Bistro, 73A Macleay St., Potts Point. ☎ **358-4891.**
Cuisine: MODERN AUSTRALIAN. **Reservations:** Not Accepted.
Prices: Appetizers around $A11; main courses around $A17. Major credit cards.
Open: Lunch Tues–Sun noon–3pm; dinner Tues–Sun 6:30–11pm.

This top-rated establishment is BYO, but not cheap in other respects. The decor is light blue on white or vice versa, and kept starkly simple. The cuisine is "nouvelle Oz" in the best meaning of the term. Courses are light and versatile, enabling you to arrange your own dining pattern that doesn't have to follow the old appetizer/main course/dessert routine. Customers rave about the char-grilled lamb kidney and the delicately smoked ocean trout.

Mère Catherine, 146 Victoria St., Kings Cross. ☎ **358-3862.**
Cuisine: FRENCH. **Reservations:** Accepted.
Prices: Appetizers around $A11; main courses around $A17. BC, MC, V.
Open: Dinner only. Tues–Sat 7pm–midnight.

You gain admission by knocking on a blue-painted door, speakeasy style. But far from being one, Mère Catherine lets you bring your own liquor. A small, traditional restaurant, candle-lit and with an ancient Breughel print on the wall, this patch of French rusticality serves appetizers that can pass as meals. The onion soup gets a shot of port stirred in by the waitress in the correct manner. The menu is standard French provincial fare, lovingly prepared. But the pièce de résistance is the superlative beef chateaubriand, served with either béarnaise and cognac or garlic butter. An immense slab for two persons costs $A53.80.

Merivale, 63 Macleay, at Challis Avenue, Kings Cross. ☎ **356-4788.**
Cuisine: INTERNATIONAL. **Reservations:** Accepted.
Prices: Appetizers around $A8.50; main courses around $A12.50. Major credit cards.
Open: Daily noon–midnight.

A twin creation of restaurant and espresso bar with outdoor tables, this is as much a socializing as an eating scene, depending on where you choose to sit. The espresso enclave opens at 7:30am for breakfast (also for an array of hangover cures). The menu may offer lamb kidneys with sautéed mushrooms or filets of flathead with watercress mayonnaise. The house wine, available by the glass, is commendable, the coffee outstanding, and the general atmosphere delightfully laid-back.

Budget

$ **Astoria**, 7 Darlinghurst Rd., Kings Cross. ☎ **358-6327.**
Cuisine: AUSTRALIAN. **Reservations:** Not accepted.
Prices: Meals around $A11. No credit cards.

Open: Lunch Mon–Sat 11am–2:30pm; dinner Mon–Sat 4–8:30pm.

In the very center of Kings Cross, yet not *of* it, is the Astoria. This is an old-style Aussie diner, serving old-style food. No space is wasted on decorative touches, but everything is spick-and-span, the service fast and efficient, and the fare cooked with a minimum of alien-spice additions. A typical meal would be barley broth, Irish stew, or lamb cutlets with three veggies, and ice cream or fruit salad.

$ Cafe Pralinka, 4B Roslyn St., Kings Cross. ☎ **358-1553.**

Cuisine: CZECH. **Reservations:** Not required.
Prices: Main courses around $A7. No credit cards.
Open: Tues–Sat 11am–9pm.

This cafe is an early closer in an all-night neighborhood. A colorful miniature eatery, very Czech in flavor, including pictures of the "Good Soldier Schwejk" along the walls, the Pralinka boasts only five tables in toto. All available wall space is covered with pictures, posters, and memorabilia, and at the window table (the best in the house) potted plants tickle your neck. Helpings are huge; the fare is first rate; and the prices are as minuscule as the premises—nothing over $A7.90. Choices run between beef goulash, stuffed cabbage, roast beef with salad, and chicken paprika with rice—depending on what's chalked on the blackboard that day.

Kings Cross Steak House, 2F Roslyn St., Kings Cross.
☎ **358-5639.**

Cuisine: AUSTRALIAN. **Reservations:** Accepted.
Prices: Appetizers around $A6–$A9; main courses around $A9–$A12.50. AE, MC, V.
Open: Daily 6pm–2am.

Although the name doesn't reveal it, this BYO for beef lovers offers considerably more than steaks. The service is fast and friendly, the cuisine is hearty and cooked exactly as ordered, and the oysters that make up the appetizers are ocean fresh. Several pasta and seafood dishes are also on the menu. Bring a solid appetite.

$ Last Aussie Fishcaf, 24 Bayswater Rd., Kings Cross.
☎ **356-2911.**

Cuisine: AUSTRALIAN. **Reservations:** Accepted.
Prices: Fish-and-chips and hamburgers around $A10. Major credit cards.
Open: Dinner daily 6pm–1am.

This 1950s-era "caf" is great fun if you don't have your heart set on a quiet meal. You get a free glass of beer or wine along with your fish, burger, or pasta order, accompanied by big-band sounds from a traditional jukebox. On Sunday, Tuesday, and Wednesday nights you also get rock 'n' roll renditions by the staff, twist and limbo demonstrations by professional dancers, and—at odd times—jugglers, magicians, unicyclists, and kindred upheavals. The fare is no-frills but fresh and well prepared.

5 Darlinghurst

This district interlocks with East Sydney and Kings Cross, making it quite impossible to say where one ends and the others start. Most of these restaurants can be reached by taking the 373 or 374 bus to Taylor Square.

Moderate

The Edge, 60 Riley St., Darlinghurst, ☎ **360-1372.**

Cuisine: MODERN AUSTRALIAN. **Reservations:** Not accepted.
Prices: Appetizers and main courses around $A11. AE, BC, MC, V.
Open: Lunch Mon–Sat noon–3pm; dinner daily 6–11pm.

Currently among the trendiest eating spots in town and correspondingly packed. Apart from its mysterious name (Edge of what?) the place has several unique features. It is, to my knowledge, the only "Mod Oz" establishment that serves pizza, and it boasts a dessert selection that knocks most continental restaurants for a loop. But first try the boneless baby chicken with roast potatoes and garlic. Or the fresh-daily ocean catch, delicately charred. Or the memorable pizza from the wood-fired oven that produces the finest crust I've ever crunched. In conclusion, I'd recommend the fig tart with mascarpone. But be prepared to wait for a table. Preferably at the bar.

Hard Rock Cafe, 121 Crown St., Darlinghurst. ☎ **331-1116.**

Cuisine: AMERICAN. **Reservations:** Not accepted.
Prices: Appetizers around $A6; main courses around $A8.
AE, BC, MC, V.
Open: Daily noon–midnight.

This is the Oz version of the famed New York and London namesakes, the exterior graced by the butt end of an automobile, the interior devoted to rock memorabilia. The human traffic is tremendous, and the sound level deafening. The cafe provides good comestibles at modest prices, but drinks tend to be costly. There are hot or cold soups for starters, then either American hamburgers or English fish-and-chips, and huge, excellent desserts, all served with polish and speed.

Oh Calcutta, 251 Victoria St., Darlinghurst. ☎ **360-3650.**

Cuisine: INDIAN. **Reservations:** Accepted.
Prices: Appetizers around $A7; main courses around $A15. AE, MC, V.
Open: Lunch Thurs–Fri noon–3pm; dinner daily 6–11pm.

The Calcutta manages to be both dignified and trendy; a rare combination. Done out in black and turquoise hues, decorated with Indian artifacts, it serves lavish tandoori fare, including bread, and there's a large vegetarian selection. The outstanding meat dishes are lamb cooked in cream and spinach and the fiery beef vindaloo. BYO.

Budget

 Dov, corner of Forbes and Burton Streets, East Sydney.
☎ **360-9594.**

Cuisine: INTERNATIONAL. **Reservations:** Not accepted.
Prices: Appetizers $A6.50; main courses around $A10. No credit cards.
Open: Mon–Sat 6:30am–10pm.

Dov is a simple little cafe-restaurant with stone walls, stone floor, no
decor to speak of, but a tremendous reputation, chiefly from the
ambience. The people you share space with may be a cab driver, a
TV celebrity, a hooker, or a best-selling author. The fare is a glorious mishmash of Jewish, Italian, and Mediterranean delicacies, excellently prepared, served with flair, and amazingly cheap. Cold plates
bear chopped liver, soused herring, and Russian salad; hot dishes
range from cholent to grilled trout; desserts include a dreamy hazelnut torte with whipped cream. BYO.

Laurie's Vegetarian, corner of Victoria and Burton Streets,
Darlinghurst. ☎ **360-4915.**

Cuisine: VEGETARIAN. **Reservations:** Accepted.
Prices: Appetizers around $A4; main courses around $A10. BC, MC, V.
Open: Lunch daily noon–2pm; dinner daily 6–11pm.

Laurie's is spacious and comfortable, with distinctly leisurely service.
The main attractions (apart from modest prices) are the blackboard
specials, which really are special. Watch for the unusual and imaginative tofu dishes—such as brochettes in ginger sauce—the broccoli
schnitzel, or the spinach-and-pine-nut pockets. BYO.

Narai Thai, 346 Victoria St., Darlinghurst. ☎ **331-1390.**

Cuisine: THAI. **Reservations:** Accepted.
Prices: Appetizers around $A5; main courses around $A12. Major credit
cards.
Open: Lunch Tues–Fri noon–3pm; dinner daily 6–11pm.

Narai has several features that distinguish it from Sydney's multitude
of Thai restaurants. One is a lengthy and separate vegetarian menu,
another the mildness of the spices used, a third the outstanding service. It's a small, rather simple hostelry, with generous meals. You
can dine well on one of the satays with pungent peanut sauce, or the
vermicelli beef with mushrooms, the rice-paper rolls stuffed with
ground pork and chili, or the king prawns with garlic in pepper sauce.
Licenced and BYO.

$ No Name [Caesar's], 2 Chapel St., East Sydney. ☎ **360-4711.**
Cuisine: ITALIAN. **Reservations:** Not accepted.
Prices: Appetizers around $A5; main courses around $A8. No credit
cards.
Open: Lunch daily noon–2pm; dinner daily 6–9pm.

There's some confusion here because there are actually two places
with the same label. Neither has a name, but the one we're concerned

with is known to patrons as Caesar's. It enjoys a reputation of being *the* prime budget eatery in Sydney (though you'll get arguments). Founded many years ago as an economy diner for young single Italian immigrants, it's now a place for lining up. You queue on the stairs, then share the first vacant table with whoever was in line with you. No decorations and a basic minimum of furniture here, but the food is ample and good and astonishingly cheap. Choices range from roast veal, boiled beef, and veal scallopine to beef stew or meatballs. The No Name lies just off Crown Street. BYO.

6 Paddington

Known affectionately as "Paddo," this former working-class, now thoroughly gentrified area, lies southeast of Darlinghurst. Buses 380 and 382 go to this area.

Very Expensive

 Oasis Seros, 495 Oxford St., Paddington. ☎ **361-3377.**
Cuisine: MODERN AUSTRALIAN. **Reservations:** Recommended.
Prices: Fixed-price dinner $A55. Major credit cards.
Open: Lunch Fri only 12:30–2:30pm; dinner Tues–Sat 7–10pm.

Sydneysiders have taken to this delightfully eccentric place in a *big* way. It's a curiosity in several respects. First, because Oxford Street is generally a site for budget fare, which the Oasis is assuredly not. Second, instead of laying on the old-world chandelier decor, the owners have chosen a streamlined, starkly Scandinavian style of interior in which the most ornamental features are the crisply white table linen and gleaming cutlery. Finally, the cuisine follows no discernible style except the chef's inspiration and imagination. You might call it Aussie-Asian with Gallic touches thrown in. To give you an idea of what to expect: when I dined, there was a clear lobster soup in which floated wonton stuffed with crabmeat, roast quail with delicately spiced herb stuffing, crisply roasted duck served with Chinese ginger buns and vegetables . . . and so on, right through the equally unorthodox desserts. The wine list is *ne plus ultra* and priced accordingly.

Expensive

The Maestro, 120 Glenmore Rd., Paddington. ☎ **331-5084.**
Cuisine: FRENCH/ITALIAN. **Reservations:** Recommended.
Prices: Appetizers around $A10; main courses around $A18. Major credit cards.
Open: Lunch Mon–Fri noon–2pm; dinner Mon–Sat 6–11pm.

"Stately, velvety, and costly, imbued with old-time elegance," just about describes this establishment. You can choose to dine in the intimate courtyard or the plush interior. The house specialty is venison, superbly prepared hunter style in madeira, and the roast suckling pig, which appears to have been lifted from a Flemish still life. For something a trifle lighter there's grilled snapper stuffed with shrimp and oysters.

Budget

Siam, 383 Oxford St., Paddington. ☎ **331-2669.**

Cuisine: THAI. **Reservations:** Accepted.
Prices: Appetizers around $A4.50; main courses around $A11. Major
credit cards.
Open: Lunch Mon–Sat noon–3pm; dinner daily 6–10pm.

Next door to the famous Paddington Market, this BYO dispenses
excellent Thai edibles at a brisk pace. If you've never tasted Thai soup,
sample the prawn soup with chili. Then go on to the specials chalked
on the blackboard and frequently changed. You'll get acquainted with
ocean perch in coconut sauce, the highly spiced Thai fish cakes, and
the sweetly tangy chicken wings. There is a well-balanced, separate
vegetarian menu.

7   Surry Hills

Paddington's western neighbor, once a seedy semi-slum, now blos-
soms with smart restaurants, avant-garde theaters, and art deco
homes. These restaurants are convenient to the Central Station subway stop.

Expensive

Strelitzia, 26 Buckingham St., Surry Hills. ☎ **698-3349.**

Cuisine: INTERNATIONAL. **Reservations:** Accepted.
Prices: Fixed-price dinner $A30. Major credit cards.
Open: Lunch Mon–Fri noon–2:30pm; dinner Tues–Sat 6–10pm.

Strelitzia was converted from an 80-year-old terrace dwelling into a
small, cozy terrace restaurant containing just eight tables. The cuisine is labeled "international," but is actually a distinctive mixture of
continental and Aussie fare. You can start with baked squab stuffed
with wild rice or the country-style pâté with heavy black bread, and
then perhaps the gargantuan bowl of fish stew afloat with whole large
prawns, or filet of beef in hollandaise. There are also delicious blue-
berry tartlets to finalize proceedings. Licensed and BYO.

Moderate

Riley Street Bistro, in the Forresters Hotel, corner of Riley and
Foveaux Streets, Surry Hills. ☎ **211-0627.**

Cuisine: AUSTRALIAN. **Reservations:** Accepted.
Prices: Appetizers around $A9; main courses around $A13. Major credit
cards.
Open: Lunch Mon–Fri noon–2:30pm; dinner Wed–Sat 6–10:30pm.

The Forresters Hotel used to be just a corner pub serving characteristic pub grub across the counter. Now you follow elegant black-and-
white tiles to the upstairs bistro, which occupies the entire top floor
and consists of four dining quarters, each painted a different pastel
hue. The menu is short, but the items are long on quality. Try the
chicken filets in garlic butter or the Anglo-traditional calves' liver and

onions or the distinctly non-Anglo duck breast served in madeira, and afterward the cheese platter or some of the unusual ice cream concoctions. There's a tiny beer garden in the courtyard.

★ **212 Riley Street,** in the Cambridge Inn, 212 Riley St., Surry Hills. ☎ **212-5500.**

Cuisine: MEDITERRANEAN. **Reservations:** Accepted.

Prices: Appetizers around $A8; main courses around $A14. Major credit cards.

Open: Lunch Tues–Fri noon–3pm; dinner daily 6–10pm.

Un-ornately attractive, with sky blue ceiling, parquet floor, and a Venetian mural covering an entire wall, 212 demonstrates just how upscale Surry Hills has become in patches. The central food display, resting on columns, forms an integral part of the decor. The fare is mainly marine, but with highly original touches. Octopus, for instance, comes chargrilled and accompanied by almonds and beans. Filet of kingfish appears with green herb butter and tomato salsa. Desserts are likewise out of the usual rut—glazed apricot with fig slices or caramel apple with cinnamon cream, to quote a couple of samples. There is an extensive and expensive wine list.

Budget

★ **Cafe Elan,** 379 Crown St., Surry Hills. ☎ **332-3858.**

Cuisine: VEGETARIAN. **Reservations:** Accepted.

$ **Prices:** Appetizers around $A6; main courses around $A12. Major credit cards.

Open: Dinner only, Tues–Sat 6–11pm.

Café Elan advertises "Modern Vegetarian Cuisine," top class for all noncarnivores. The fare uses a minimum of eggs and dairy products and achieves flavor and variety by the subtle combination of Asian and Middle Eastern ingredients. Licensed as well as BYO, the Elan serves some very unusual herbal wines. Highly recommended are the spicy coconut fritters, mushroom terrine, the baked cashew tofu, and the Lebanese-style lentil bake. For an alternative starter try the tomato and ginger soup. A strict no-smoking rule is enforced between 6 and 9pm.

★ **Mohr Fish,** 202 Devonshire St., Surry Hills, ☎ **318-1326.**

Cuisine: SEAFOOD. **Reservations:** Not accepted.

Prices: Main courses around $A11. No credit cards.

Open: Daily 7am–10pm.

The name looks like a misprint but is actually that of the proprietor, Hans Mohr, a French Breton who serves what is allegedly the freshest fish in Sydney—at minimum prices and in a modicum of comfort. His premises are minuscule, holding about 20 patrons per shift, and the marine fare dished out is the reason why there are several more shifts outside happily awaiting their turn. You get steaming bowls of bouillabaisse that doesn't come any better in Marseilles, grilled sardines, and whatever is the freshest fish on the market that morning, with subtle little fruit tarts and powerful espresso in conclusion. Most of the waiting throng do so at the bar of the Shakespeare Hotel opposite. When seats become empty, one of the busy waitresses skips over and calls out the names of the next in line. It's BYO and no corkage, so you can take your drinks along.

⭐ **Roma,** 202 Elizabeth St., Surry Hills. ☎ **211-0439.**
Cuisine: ITALIAN. **Reservations:** Not accepted.
Prices: Main courses around $A12. No credit cards.
Open: Mon–Fri 8am–5:30pm, Sat 7:30am–3pm.

A cross between cafe and restaurant, Roma is an old-timer and something of a legend among Sydneysiders with either a sweet or a savory tooth. Italian to the backbone, short of elbow space and high on quality, this veteran has a blackboard menu listing simple, tasty, economy-priced vittles like cannelloni, veal, or fish of the day. But the real attraction is the immense range of superlative cakes and pastries. BYO.

8 Chippendale

An inner suburb, blue of collar and southwest of the city, sprinkled with surprisingly good eateries. Take the subway to Redfern.

Moderate

Abercrombies, 98 Abercrombie St., Chippendale. ☎ **698-7730.**
Cuisine: FRENCH. **Reservations:** Accepted.
Prices: Appetizers around $A6; main courses around $A20. Major credit cards.
Open: Lunch Mon–Fri noon–2pm; dinner Mon–Sat 6–10:30pm.

Abercrombies is a small restaurant of the kind you find in small provincial French towns. The fare is inventive as well as authentic—the blackboard menu is so closely scrawled that it takes time to decipher the dishes. Abercrombies serves outstanding quail pancakes with mushrooms, lamb's kidneys in Pernod, or pork filet with bacon and green onions. On a warm day, try the chilled cucumber soup.

Budget

Buon Gusto, 368 Abercrombie St., Chippendale. ☎ **319-4798.**
Cuisine: ITALIAN. **Reservations:** Recommended.
Prices: Appetizers around $A7; main courses around $A13. Major credit cards.
Open: Lunch Mon–Fri noon–3pm; dinner Mon–Sat 6–11pm.

Buon Gusto has a low, straw-matted roof festooned with dangling Chianti bottles, bare tiled floors, and a general air of rustic conviviality—noisy, friendly, and mostly packed. The accent is on seafood, but the homemade fettuccine is famous in its own right. As is the alla diavola (bacon in Neapolitan sauce). Conclude your meal with zabaglione, the empress of Italian desserts.

9   Newtown

An inner suburb south of the city center, Newtown is not glamorous but vibrant, and offers an abundance of good economical eateries. These restaurants are convenient to the Newtown subway stop.

Goodfellas, 111 King St., Newtown, ☎ **557-1175.**

> **Cuisine:** MODERN AUSTRALIAN. **Reservations:** Recommended weekends.
>
> **Prices:** Appetizers around $A11; main courses around $A17. Major credit cards.
>
> **Open:** Daily 6:30–10:30pm.

A relative newcomer on the Sydney culinary scene, Goodfellas has won acclaim for its decor and ambience as well as its fare. The interior, in charcoal and parchment hues, breathes an almost sévere elegance, with ornamentation at a minimum. Seating arrangements are supremely comfortable, allowing diners plenty of elbow space even when the place is packed. Service is amiably efficient, and special requests get prompt attention; the hallmark of a well-organized establishment. The menu leans toward seafood, especially in appetizers such as the excellent Yamba prawns in chili oil. If you crave terra firma fare, try the duck confit with braised lentils. Or the médaillons of kangaroo with chutney.

10   Glebe

An inner suburb and southwestern neighbor of the center city, Glebe was once mainly industrial, but is now making great strides as a restaurant region. Buses serving this area include the 431, 434, and 459.

Very Expensive

The Abbey, 156 Bridge Rd., Glebe. ☎ **660-1211.**

> **Cuisine:** ITALIAN. **Reservations:** Recommended.
>
> **Prices:** Appetizers around $A12; main courses around $A27. Major credit cards.
>
> **Open:** Lunch Mon–Fri noon–2:30pm; dinner Mon–Sat 6–11pm.

Have you ever dined, wined, and danced in a Presbyterian church? Chances are you haven't. You can catch up on that experience by going to The Abbey, located in Glebe, a student-thronged suburb adjoining the center city. The church is a Gothic edifice built in 1879 by the famous local architect Thomas Rowe. The building was restored in 1980, leaving the exterior intact. The interior now is a stunningly beautiful mixture of church and banquet hall. The high wooden rafters, stained-glass windows, and candle chandeliers blend superbly with the parquet floor and snowy table linen, giving the dining room an air of dignity, supreme comfort, and just a slight touch of austerity. There is nothing in the least austere about the food, however, among the best served in this town. Or the lengthy and impressive wine list. There is a grand piano, played later in the evening for those who wish to dance.

Expensive

Bogart, 199 Glebe Point Rd., Glebe. ☎ **692-0936.**

Cuisine: ITALIAN. **Reservations:** Accepted.
Prices: Appetizers around $A10; main courses around $A19. Major credit cards.
Open: Dinner only, daily 6–10:30pm.

Bogart has nothing to do with Humphrey or trenchcoats, but is a pleasant Italian restaurant that is both licensed and BYO. Bogart has an open fireplace for atmosphere, ceiling fans for coolness, and indoor greenery for ornamentation. While thoroughly Italian, the kitchen goes easy on the pasta dishes. Instead there's a variety of first-rate veal courses, with the veal slim and tender but not insignificant, as in some hostelries. Unusual and noteworthy are the green prawns, flavored with ginger and served on rice.

Moderate

Cafe Troppo, 175 Glebe Point Rd., Glebe, ☎ **552-1233.**

Cuisine: INTERNATIONAL. **Reservations:** Not accepted.
Prices: Appetizers around $A7; main courses around $A13. BC, MC, V.
Open: Daily 10am–1am.

A place that defies classification, as suggested by its name. For "troppo" is Oz for haywire—demented—nuts. The cafe has a hilariously fake jungle setting, tarot card readings, drop-in magicians, occasional minstrels, and breakfast service all day. It also has a wonderfully convivial atmosphere that gives you a welcome hug the moment you enter. Actually, the Troppo boasts a huge menu with offerings ranging from scrambled eggs to elaborate seafood dishes, with burgers, tortillas, and pasta plates in between and rich dark chocolate desserts at the end. You can snack or feast any time as the mood strikes you. BYO and no corkage charge.

Paganini, 43 Glebe Point Rd., Glebe, ☎ **552-1541.**

Cuisine: ITALIAN. **Reservations:** Accepted.
Prices: Appetizers around $A10; main courses around $A19. AE, BC, MC, V.
Open: Lunch Mon–Fri noon–2:30pm; dinner Mon–Sat 6–10:30pm.

A restaurant dedicated to the memory of the great violinist and the glory of Tuscan cooking. The former is part of the tasteful decor: buff, gold, and white, with violins, sheet music, Paganini's scores and concert notices acting as wall ornaments. The latter starts with the menu, which offers historical information on the origins of pesto, polenta, and tagliatelle. (Bet you didn't know the latter was invented in 1487 on the occasion of Lucrezia Borgia's wedding!) The polenta soufflé makes a fine appetizer, followed by your choice among the risotto dishes, served in the correct style from copper saucepan to plate at your table. Alternatively try the grilled breast of chicken with cannellini beans.

★ **Rasputin's,** 101 Glebe Point Rd., Glebe. ☎ **660-3906.**
Cuisine: RUSSIAN. **Reservations:** Accepted.
Prices: Appetizers around $A7; main courses around $A12. Major credit cards.
Open: Dinner only, daily 6–10pm.

It's a mystery why such a good restaurant should bear the name of a glutton who had virtually no palate and frequently wolfed down sturgeon and sweetmeats from the same plate. Anyway, *this* Rasputin is run by real gourmets. The blini here come with caviar, smoked salmon, and sour cream. The borscht has the true subtle sweet-sour tang so often missing in imitations. You could, in fact, make a sumptuous meal from the appetizers, particularly the Siberian palmein—a wonderful version of meatballs served in sharp sauce. But you'd better leave room for the chicken Kiev or the stuffed cabbage rolls.

Yak & Yeti, 41 Glebe Point Rd., Glebe, ☎ **552-1220.**
Cuisine: NEPALESE. **Reservations:** Accepted.
Prices: Appetizers around $A5; main courses around $A12. Major credit cards.
Open: Daily 6–10:30pm.

A small, unpretentiously friendly dinery, this is (currently) the only establishment to dispense Nepalese/Gurkha delicacies. Don't worry: neither yak butter nor Yeti ragout is on the menu. But you get Kathmandu sekuwa: tender chicken cubes marinated in ginger, garlic, and yoghurt or roast goat in curry sauce, plus a range of vegetarian dishes. And do try the pistachio nut ice cream flavored with cardamom. It's BYO, and cold beer goes best with the fare.

11 Balmain

Balmain is a peninsula jutting into the harbor, pleasantly hilly and close to the center city. The nicest way to get there is to take the ferry from Jetty 5, Circular Quay.

Budget ───────────────────────

$ **Berlin Cafe,** 249 Darling St., Balmain. ☎ **810-2336.**
Cuisine: GERMAN. **Reservations:** Accepted.
Prices: Appetizers around $A5; main courses around $A8. Major credit cards.
Open: Daily noon–10pm.

If seeing *Cabaret* left you intrigued with the Berlin scene of the early 1930s, head here. The atmosphere seems pretty authentic, even to the newspapers, which are free for perusal. Only the political tension is missing. But this is definitely a place in which to linger. The kitchen turns out rich German specialties, from smoked pork sausages served with possibly the finest potato salad in town to meat loaf and beef roulades and Kalbsbraten, the particular German version of roast veal. The dessert display is symphonic: apple strudel, rum cakes, superb chocolate domes filled with whipped cream, and the yellow Napfkuchen meant to be dunked messily into coffee. BYO.

Manjit's, 360 Darling St., Balmain. ☎ **818-3681.**

Cuisine: INDIAN. **Reservations:** Recommended.
Prices: Appetizers around $A6; main courses around $A10. Major credit cards.
Open: Lunch Mon–Fri noon–2:30pm; dinner daily 5:30–10:30pm.

Manjit's serves northern Indian cuisine. The decor is simple, the premises usually crowded, the service performed by brightly turbaned waiters. You can order a huge platter of appetizers, which could pass as a meal. Otherwise try the *murgh mumtaz* (buttered chicken) or the hotter *navratan korma* (vegetables in almond-curry sauce). *Roghan josh* (lamb in highly spiced gravy) is the traditional dish to be eaten with Indian bread—to dunk out the gravy. BYO.

12 Eastern Suburbs

Double Bay

Chic, trendy, and expensive, this closest of the so-called Eastern Suburbs never needed revamping of any kind. It can be reached by the 324 or 325 bus.

VERY EXPENSIVE

⭐ **Prunier's,** 65 Ocean St., Woollahra. ☎ **32-1974.**

Cuisine: FRENCH. **Reservations:** Required.
Prices: Appetizers around $A12; main courses around $A30. Major credit cards.
Open: Lunch Mon–Fri noon–3pm; dinner Mon–Sat 6–10:30pm.

A hallowed dining haven of the upper crust, Prunier's is located on one of the finest residential streets amid mansions housing foreign consulates. The setting is ultra-plush and the service, ambassadorial. The menu is unchanging, though every evening has its own "specials." As an appetizer you might select the cold crayfish soup, made of chilled fresh tomatoes with morsels of lobster meat, or the Queensland crab with sliced avocado. As a main course you might select one of the beef or poultry creations. The beef is magnificent and comes grilled exactly as ordered. I had my filet marinated in ginger and brandy, served with a green-apple salad. The ginger flavor comes through slight and subtle, just enough to impart an iota of fiery sweetness to the meat. The wine list is extensive.

EXPENSIVE

The Cleveland, 63 Bay St., Double Bay. ☎ **327-6877.**

Cuisine: CHINESE/VEGETARIAN. **Reservations:** Required.
Prices: Appetizers around $A11; main courses around $A15. Major credit cards.
Open: Lunch daily noon–3pm; dinner daily 6–11pm.

One of Sydney's most opulent Chinese restaurants, The Cleveland serves vegetarian meals downstairs, Szechuan cuisine upstairs. Both sections—actually separate restaurants—are lavishly decked out in a distinct Hong Kong style of luxury that revels in mirrors, gilt, and silken drapes. The food presented downstairs bears little resemblance to the kind of vegetarian fare you might have eaten before. This is the Buddhist brand, which delights even an inveterate carnivore like myself. I've seldom tasted anything as delicately scrumptious as the white mushrooms with crisp cashew nuts or the coconut-milk custard. Upstairs it's heartier and heavier. Try the aromatic duck smoked in camphor tea or the quite un-Gallic, gently gingered frog casserole.

MODERATE

⭐ **Hunters Lodge,** 18 Cross St., Double Bay. ☎ **363-1747.**
   Cuisine: CONTINENTAL/HUNGARIAN. **Reservations:** Accepted.
   Prices: Appetizers around $A8; main courses around $A17. Major credit cards.
   Open: Dinner only, daily 6pm–midnight.

Typical of the area's dining spots, Hunters Lodge is a beautiful, atmospheric establishment with stags' heads, antlers, and hunting arsenals on the walls but, oddly, no game on the menu. The ceilings are laced with heavy black-oak beams and hung with baskets of ferns, and there are superb 18th-century sporting prints on the walls. The award-winning cuisine is European with strong Hungarian accents. For starters there is an aromatic Hungarian fish soup called halaszle, as well as escargot or caviar frappé. As a main course a difficult choice is to be made between entrecôte chasseur with mushrooms in burgundy sauce, kidneys in port wine, or veal médaillon with paprika cream sauce.

Pepper's Bayside, 22 Knox St., Double Bay, ☎ **363-0100.**
   Cuisine: INTERNATIONAL. **Reservations:** Accepted.
   Prices: Appetizers around $A7; main courses around $A17. Major credit cards.
   Open: Daily 8am–1am.

This is one of those big, handsome, sophisticated cafe-restaurants one usually associates with Paris or Rome or Amsterdam. Half indoors, half out, and designed for seeing people and being seen. What you see are swarms of smartly garbed overseas visitors, a sprinkling of celebrities, and some of Sydney's top models. Pepper's serves anything from breakfast and light snacks to sumptuous dinners and late suppers. The savoury tartlets and sirloin steaks are outstanding, likewise the mango-parfait dessert. Take a seat on the terrace and eavesdrop on business deals and flirtations conducted in languages that *may* include English.

Watsons Bay

Perched near the tip of a magnificent Eastern Suburbs peninsula, just below Gap National Park, Watsons Bay boasts the most famous restaurant in Australia—Doyle's. This suburb can be reached on the 324 or 325 bus.

EXPENSIVE

 Doyle's On The Beach, 11 Marine Parade, Watsons Bay.
☎ 337-2007.

Cuisine: SEAFOOD. **Reservations:** Recommended.

Prices: Appetizers around $A8; main courses around $A20. BC, MC, DC, V.

Open: Lunch daily noon–3pm; dinner daily 6–9:30pm.

The sibling restaurant to this institution is **Doyle's on the Quay,** downtown (☎ **337-1572**)—neither place really needs an address. The weekend lines are equally long for both (they take reservations for only a small number of tables). You can watch the marine craft bounce by, the Windsurfers topple, the bathing beauties parade, and the seagulls thieve. This is Sydney at its absolute best. Among the amenities is a special water-taxi service from Circular Quay right to the wharf (but only till 3pm). Peter Doyle, the owner, is a celebrity in his own right.

The seafood selection is enormous, absolutely fresh, and not over-priced (but watch out for the $A3 surcharge on holidays *and* week-ends). Appetizers range from baby octopus marinated in olive oil and garlic, to jumbo prawns stuffed with bacon and calamari deep-fried in beer batter. For main courses you could pick the grand-scale plat-ter of mixed seafood, including oysters and roasted tuna; the whole grilled flounder; the pearl perch, a rarity caught only along the east-ern coast of Australia; or the sea-farmed pink filets of ocean trout. The best dessert item is the homemade brandied chocolate mousse.

Bondi

Sydney's most popular beach suburb is chockablock with restaurants and can be reached on the 380, 382, and 389 bus.

MODERATE

 Gelato Bar, 140 Campbell Parade, Bondi Beach, ☎ **30-4033.**

Cuisine: HUNGARIAN. **Reservations:** Accepted.

Prices: Appetizers around $A8; main courses around $A13. BC, MC, V.

Open: Daily 8am–midnight.

Gelato is totally misnamed. It does sell gelato, but purely as a side-line. It is, above all, one of Sydney's oldest and most respected Hun-garian restaurants. This is a brisk-service place, all bustle and effi-ciency, with no intimate corners to hide in—and the food is terrific. You get all the Magyar and Jewish favorites: chicken or liver-dumpling soup, veal or beef goulash, beef Stroganoff, wienerschnitzel, cucumber salad, and a superlative Hungarian specialty of scrambled eggs with mushrooms and fried sausages. The desserts are downright dreamy, most of them beckoning from glass showcases: Sachertorte and chestnut torte, apple strudel with a feathery-light crust, won-drously rich poppy-seed slices; plus the obligatory Hungarian sweet noodles in melted cheese sprinkled with grated walnuts. BYO.

Geronimo's, 106 Curlewis St., Bondi, ☎ **30-2756.**

> **Cuisine:** INDIAN. **Reservations:** Accepted.
> **Prices:** Appetizers around $A6; main courses around $A12. BC, V.
> **Open:** Tues–Sun 5:30–10:30pm.

Despite the name this is not an Apache establishment. Geronimo's serves *Indian*–Indian cuisine from all regions of that subcontinent, including Pakistan, Afghanistan, and Bangladesh. Furnished bistro-style and decorated with original Indian artifacts, the interior is quite stylish yet agreeably relaxed, the service both attentive and knowledgeable. The major magnet here is the thali—served nightly from 5:30 to 7:30pm—with the slogan "Eat till You're Beat." It consists of a divided tray on which customers heap as much as they want of six meat and vegetarian dishes, plus rice and condiments. The bottomless platter costs $A12.90 per glutton, children paying half. Geronimo's is BYO.

Little Snail, 96A Curlewis St., Bondi Beach. ☎ **365-4847.**

> **Cuisine:** FRENCH. **Reservations:** Recommended.
> **Prices:** 3 courses for $A20. Major credit cards.
> **Open:** Dinner only, daily 6–10pm.

Little Snail is a real rarity—a BYO that's French. But the restaurant has other claims to fame as well. By reputation it's the most romantic restaurant in Sydney, a place where couples retreat not only for dates but for silver anniversaries as well. Despite the name, snails don't loom large on the menu. They come à la bourguignonne and make a superlative appetizer. They may be followed by deliciously fragile quail or roast guinea fowl, or if you crave something heartier, pork filets poached in milk. The fare is superb.

BUDGET

$ **Home Cooking,** 292 Bondi Rd., Bondi. ☎ **30-5454.**

> **Cuisine:** ENGLISH. **Reservations:** Accepted.
> **Prices:** Appetizers around $A4; main courses around $A12. Major credit cards.
> **Open:** Dinner only. Thurs–Tues 6–10pm.

Home Cooking offers exactly what the name implies, English style. The menu is extensive, composed of solid traditionals, all well prepared, but decidedly unexotic. You get roast pork with applesauce, roast beef and Yorkshire pudding, or grilled rump steak, all properly accompanied by salad and chips. Desserts (pardon, *sweets*) follow the same homey pattern: steamed pudding with custard sauce, bread-and-butter pudding, et al. BYO.

---

13 North Shore

All the establishments mentioned so far are on the south side of Sydney's great water divide. Now we cross Sydney Harbour Bridge to the somewhat less tourist-trodden North Shore; a vast slice of territory with a very lively restaurant scene of its own. You'll find more North Shore eateries in the next sections.

The fastest way to get to the North Shore is by train, but several locations can also be reached by ferry or water taxi, and all of them by bus or cab. For route information, call the **Bus & Ferry InfoLine** 13-1315, for trains 13-1500. Your best bet is to call the restaurant you wish to go to and ask for directions.

Expensive

 Bathers Pavilion, 4 The Esplanade, Balmoral. ☎ **968-1133.**

Cuisine: MODERN AUSTRALIAN. **Reservations:** Required on weekends.

Prices: Appetizers around $A12; main courses around $A19. Major credit cards.

Open: Lunch daily noon–3pm; dinner daily 7–10pm.

A 1920s bathing pavilion with a fabulous ocean view was converted into a very upscale restaurant by Victoria Alexander, one of Sydney's foremost fashion stylists. A simple shed has become an airy sunswept charmer, irresistible for visiting camera crews. The dining room is a study in white, with traditional furniture, arched picture windows, and unobtrusively clever decorating touches. The place represents the essence of a lifestyle local pundits call "beach culture."

The Pavilion, however, is not dominated by seafood. The most intriguing appetizers are Gruyère fritters with tomato salsa or smoked quail with salad. Main courses offer difficult and slightly adventurous choices: veal cutlets with ginger-flavored sweet popato; roast duck in sauterne sauce; grilled veal liver with honey-glazed apples; chargrilled tuna and avocado slices in lemon soy sauce, to mention just a few. Unusual desserts are among the top attractions. I had a memorable pudding made of black rice, served with rhubarb. Special mention must go to the wine list.

Cafe Gueville, 105 Longeville Rd., Lane Cove. ☎ 428-1007.

Cuisine: CAJUN. **Reservations:** Accepted.

Prices: Appetizers around $A11; main courses around $A18. Major credit cards.

Open: Lunch Tues–Fri noon–2:30pm; dinner Mon–Sat 6–10:30pm.

The Gueville balances the menu with several kindred Australian dishes that harmonize amazingly well with the fiery Cajun fare. You can choose from all the New Orleans favorites—gumbo, jambalaya, and a delightfully aromatic version of blackened fish. I particularly enjoyed the mesquite chicken salad served with small onions and the Cajun pork filet piled on top of fruit-flavored salsa. BYO.

Carey Cottage, 18 Ferry St., Hunters Hill. ☎ 817-3643.

Cuisine: ENGLISH. **Reservations:** Recommended.

Prices: Fixed-price dinner $A72 for two. BC, MC, V.

Open: Lunch Wed–Fri 11am–4pm; dinner daily 7pm–midnight.

A dreamy little enclave, Hunters Hill is full of colonial mansions hand-hewn in stone by convict labor; it's one of Sydney's loveliest (and snootiest) residential areas. Carey Cottage occupies a trio of cottages grouped around a tree-shaded courtyard. The buildings date from the colonial era, have timbered walls and ceilings, and display cases filled with antique cutlery, heirloom china, and handwoven Irish linen. Because of the number of cottages, dining areas are divided into small, intimate nooks that never get crowded. Carey is BYO and concentrates on plain, wholesome, plentiful fare: steak and three "veggies," roast lamb with mint sauce, roast pork with applesauce and piles of crackling, with apple crumble and custard cream for dessert.

Le Kiosk, Shelly Beach, Marine Parade, Manly. ☎ 977-4122.

Cuisine: SEAFOOD. **Reservations:** Recommended.
Prices: Appetizers around $A11; main courses around $A26. Major credit cards.
Open: Daily noon–9:30pm.

Overlooking Manly's panoramic Shelly Beach, Le Kiosk is not a French restaurant but a good and untypical oceanfront eating spot. Housed in a 19th-century sandstone building, the place has rows of outside tables for sea-breeze dining, an extensive menu, and wondrous ocean views. The fish fare is good, reliable, and satisfying in an unimaginative fashion. Ingredients are fresh, condiments familiar, sauces unobtrusive. The dish most in demand is a perfectly enormous mixed seafood platter for two people, containing a good proportion of Australia's ocean denizens. Eating out in the garden is quite idyllic on sunny days and warm evenings. On Sunday the Kiosk puts on a famous buffet breakfast, for the sake of which many people cross the harbor.

Moderate

Amici Miei, 388 Pacific Hwy., Crows Nest. ☎ 906-7050.

Cuisine: ITALIAN. **Reservations:** Accepted.
Prices: Appetizers around $A8; main courses around $A18. Major credit cards.
Open: Lunch Tues–Fri noon–2:30pm; dinner Mon–Sat 6:30–10:30pm.

Amici Miei is so large you could easily dance between the tables. Plants, greenery, bright furniture, and crisp table linens decorated with small vases of flowers give it the right Italian air to match the shingle. The menu appears on a blackboard and changes frequently. For appetizers, you can't do better than the homemade potato dumplings called gnocchi graté, sprinkled with cheese and not at all heavy. After that, perhaps the grilled Italian sausages—spicy and succulent— or one of the special mountainous seafood platters. Licensed and BYO.

Le Petit Savoyard, 55 Ridge St., North Sydney. ☎ 923-2336.

Cuisine: SWISS. **Reservations:** Recommended.
Prices: Appetizers around $A7; main fondues around $A20. Major credit cards.
Open: Dinner only, Tues–Sat 6–10pm.

Just over the bridge, this charming oddity of Swiss-French gastronomy has an interior designed like a country auberge with candles on checkered table linen and a tree-shaded courtyard in the rear. It offers what I've always thought was a Swiss specialty—fondue. Turns out, I thunk wrong. Fondues are as native to provincial France as to Helvetia, and both come with the same customs, to wit: If a man drops his bread into the pot, he has to buy a bottle of wine; if a woman does so, she has to kiss every man at the table, including the waiter if he's standing by. Here the wine bottle would have to be brought—the place is BYO. The fondues are marvelous, come in beef, cheese, or chocolate versions, and may be supplemented by the house pâté

Budget

Mosquito Bar, Shop 5, 142 Spit Rd., Mosman. ☎ **968-1801.**
  Cuisine: AFRO-ASIAN. **Reservations:** Recommended.
  Prices: Appetizers around $A5; main courses around $A10. BC, MC, V.
  Open: Dinner only Mon–Sat 6–10pm.

Tucked away from the tourist tracks, Mosquito Bar is one of the most intriguing restaurants in all Australia. The food here is an unusual combination of Moroccan and Sri Lankan fare. The proof of this particular pudding is in the eating, and you hardly need more proof than the fact that you have to book a day in advance in order to get in. The meals taste like exotic poetry. From Morocco comes the Marrakesh brochette of lamb, from Sri Lanka the pork curry; the fish filets in Thai chili are Asian, the couscous with blue cheese and saffron African—and so the pairing goes on, right down the menu. The best thing is to mix your fare in order to get the flavor of both continents. BYO.

14   Specialty Dining

Australian Specialties

Rowntrees, 188 Pacific Hwy., Hornaby. ☎ **476-5150.**
  Cuisine: AUSTRALIAN. **Reservations:** Accepted. **Train:** Hornaby.
  Prices: Appetizers around $A12; main courses around $A22. Major credit cards.
  Open: Dinner only, daily 6–10:30pm.

Only one restaurant in all Sydney serves the food of the original Australians. Here you can sample a few items of "bush tucker," the fare of the nomadic Aborigines, but in surroundings far removed from the natural setting. Chances are you've never tasted witchety grubs (rather like salty, crunchy shrimp), water-buffalo steak (like steak with a game flavor), lillipilli, or quandongs. Other house specialties are more familiar: filet of shark, grilled barramundi (but with rainforest sour plums) or river crayfish, and Tasmanian smoked salmon. The point is that all these items, familiar or not, are sauced and seasoned with Australian spices and served up, very stylishly, with all-Australian vegetables. There is a striking contrast between the Rowntrees fare and the elegant decor that lends a certain piquancy to the setup, as does the choice all-Australian wine list (the restaurant is both licensed and BYO). The main thing, however, is the overall excellence of the fare, the imaginative use of the "wild" spices and vegetables. For a true eating adventure, Rowntrees is unmatched.

Dining Afloat

The following are Sydney's shipboard restaurants that combine dancing or shows with scenic still-water cruises around the harbor. Both weigh anchor from Circular Quay, but serve slightly different purposes. Both require advance reservations.

The *John Cadman,* no. 6 jetty, Circular Quay (☎ **922-1922**), a sleek white twin-funneled boat, beautifully illuminated, has a dance floor as busy as the dining salon (the music is *live,* not canned). Gleaming white table linen, intimate little "oil" lamps, and an array of nautical touches help the atmosphere. Dinner cruises leave daily at 7:30pm. Cost: $A72 per person.

The **Sydney Showboat,** no. 2 jetty, Circular Quay (☎ **247-5151**), is the oldest and simultaneously the newest of the floating restaurants: the oldest because there's been a showboat on the harbor for 40 years; the newest because this particular one was launched in 1987. Built to resemble the venerable paddle wheelers that used to chug around the waterfront, the *Showboat* is actually a large, 400-passenger luxury craft, elegantly fitted and elaborately equipped for different purposes. The upper deck is for observation and moonlight strolling; the three lower decks house a pretty good cabaret/vaudeville show, several bars, and the restaurants. The accent on board is on entertainment, as befits a showboat. Dinner from 7pm Tuesday to Sunday. Call ahead for show times. Dinner and show cost $A90.

Hotel & Pub Dining

Under the hand of wowser dominance, Sydney's "hotel" cuisine fell to unequaled depths. You ate plastic food off plastic tables and washed it down with beer. The result, of course, was that no one who valued his or her stomach had a meal in a pub. When the Great Culinary Revolution swept Australia, publicans became aware that they were losing a great deal of money in the upheaval; licensed and BYO restaurants were drawing off thousands of patrons who once frequented "hotels." The publicans (at least a good many of them) reacted by taking in first-rate chefs as business partners. They had the advantage of owning licensed premises, whereas restaurants had to go through the liquor rigmarole before opening their doors. The result of this belated alliance is that certain pubs today offer some of the best and most atmospheric meals extant. As a general rule they offer lunch at lower prices and serve dinner till 10pm. The survey below includes only a few of the possibilities. But any cab driver or hotel clerk will gladly add to your list.

EXPENSIVE

⭐ **Burdekin Hotel,** 2 Oxford St., Darlinghurst. ☎ **331-1046.**
Cuisine: MODERN AUSTRALIAN. **Reservations:** Recommended. **Bus:** 380, 382.
Prices: Appetizers $A12.50; main courses around $A21. Major credit cards.

Open: Lunch Mon–Fri noon–2pm; dinner Mon–Sat 7:30–10:30pm.

This is a classic example of the split personality that haunts so many Sydney watering holes…and makes them interesting. The downstairs bars are quite pedestrian, the building medium-ugly. But the fourth-floor dining room is an intimate little gem, done in art deco style, agleam with starched linen and crystal. It serves what many knowledgeable food lovers rate as the finest pub fare in town. The wine list features some of Australia's proudest vintages and the service has the friendly, assured polish of a first-class country inn. The menu is based on seafood, such as Jervis Bay mussels in saffron butter, reinforced by dry land specials like braised rabbit and roasted spatchcock.

MODERATE

⭐ **Dolphin Hotel,** 412 Crown St., Surry Hills. ☎ 380-5614.
Cuisine: AUSTRALIAN. **Reservations:** Accepted. **Train:** Central Station.
Prices: Appetizers around $A8; main courses around $A12. BC, MC, V.
Open: Lunch daily noon–2pm; dinner daily 6–10pm.

A sizable group of aficionados swear that this place serves the top "pub grub" in Sydney. It certainly does so in exceptionally pleasing surroundings. In good weather it's imperative to make reservations, because the Dolphin's tranquil and romantic garden terrace fills up fast. The salad here is famous—you can pile up as much and as often as you desire for $A7. Accompany this with seafood quiche or the exceptionally thick and juicy steak from the grill and you'll have an eminently satisfying meal.

⭐ **Hero Of Waterloo,** 81 Lower Fort St., The Rocks.
☎ 252-4441.

Cuisine: AUSTRALIAN. **Reservations:** Accepted.
Prices: Appetizers around $A6; main courses around $A12. Major credit cards.
Open: Lunch Mon–Fri 12:30–3:30pm; dinner Fri–Sat 6:30–10pm.

Built as a jailhouse in 1804, this is the oldest pub in Sydney Town. The little sandstone building was licensed as a "common and public tavern" in 1815, just after the Battle of Waterloo. It enjoyed an evil reputation during the windjammer days—drinkers would make involuntary exits through a trapdoor in the floor and wake up doing deck duty on some undermanned coffin ship sailing for China. Today this colonial relic is a *must* for visitors, and its restaurant, the Duke's Room, is full of nostalgic atmosphere with hanging gas lamps and polished brassware. It serves items such as veal in cream of mushroom sauce and chicken breasts in tarragon, alongside a good selection of Australian wines and beer. On Friday, Saturday, and Sunday there's entertainment in the form of old-time and folk music played with nostalgic fervor.

Lords', 79 Bayswater Rd., Rushcutters Bay. ☎ 331-2520.
Cuisine: AUSTRALIAN. **Reservations:** Accepted. **Train:** Kings Cross.
Prices: Main courses around $A15. Major credit cards.
Open: Daily noon–midnight.

Calling itself "The Tavern with No Peers," this establishment stands just beyond Kings Cross and serves some of Sydney's most unusual dishes. One of the house specials is crocodile steak, and a number of patrons come a long way just for that. You can also get Northern Territory buffalo steak. The hotel also features more mundane fare, like lemon sole and superb fresh rhubarb mousse with custard for dessert. On Friday night you can hear some fine live jazz here.

Pumphouse Brewery Tavern, 17 Little Pier St., Darling Harbour. ☎ 281-3967.

Cuisine: AUSTRALIAN. **Reservations:** Not accepted. **Train:** Town Hall. **Prices:** Appetizers around $A6; main courses around $A15. Major credit cards.
Open: Daily noon–11pm.

Sydneysiders have a knack of planting watering holes in the most unlikely places. This one is inside a pumping station that provided hydraulic power for the town's elevators circa 1891. Some of the antique apparatus forms part of the decor. And adjoining stands the working brewery that supplies the beer you drink with your meal. Tours of the brewery in action take place at 11am and 2pm Monday to Friday. You can dine inside the bistro or out in the garden setting, watching the streams of tourists circulating between Darling Harbour and Chinatown. Drinks include "hand crafted beers" (as distinct from the mass-produced gargle) such as a double strength wallop called Thunderbolt Ale that goes for $A6.50 per pint. Meals range from snacks to very solid three-courses. On Friday, Saturday, and Sunday nights the upstairs bar features popular bands of almost every stripe (mostly loud), starting around 10:30pm and vibrating the walls till 2am.

Royal Hotel, 237 Glenmore Rd., Fiveways, Paddington. ☎ 331-2604.

Cuisine: AUSTRALIAN. **Reservations:** Not accepted. **Bus:** 380, 382. **Prices:** Appetizers around $A6; main courses around $A13. Major credit cards.
Open: Lunch Mon–Sat noon–3pm; dinner daily 6pm–midnight.

Fiveways is the picturesque heart of "Paddo" and the Royal its historic landmark; designated as such by the National Trust. A beautifully mellow Colonial-style building, surrounded by a broad balcony, the venerable hotel is as much a social rendezvous as a food and liquor dispensary. You go there to mingle and to watch as well as to imbibe, and the trick is to get a seat on the balcony, where you can view the street scene below as comfortably as the action inside. The fare is well prepared, fresh, and solid, though not exactly innovative; eminently suited for salad/steak/seafood palates. Service is excellent at all hours and the clientele decidedly upscale.

⭐ **Spike's Brasserie,** in the Tilbury Hotel, at Nicholson and Forbes Streets, Woolloomooloo. ☎ 357-1914.

Cuisine: INTERNATIONAL. **Reservations:** Accepted. **Bus:** 324, 325. **Prices:** Appetizers around $A6; main courses around $A12. BC, MC, V.
Open: Mon–Sat noon–10pm, Sun 1–8:30pm.

Spike's is now a major draw. The reason is partly the fare, partly the entertainment. On weekdays you can get an excellent meal selecting from among marinated king prawns, house pâtés, American spareribs, quail, and quite a superlative chocolate cream pie. On Sunday it's a grand slam buffet. There's a garden for summer dining, open fireplaces for winter coziness. On Thursday, Friday, and Saturday evenings Spike's puts on "cabaret" shows—a nice, vaguely open-ended label that can cover just about anything. But every Sunday afternoon there is (or was) a not-to-be-missed chamber music ensemble called Mozart and his Mates that starts at 1pm and has music lovers flocking in from all over town.

 Tommo's Pub Brewery, 116 Victoria Rd., Rozelle.
☎ 810-7666.
Cuisine: AUSTRALIAN. **Reservations:** Accepted.
Prices: Main courses around $A10. Major credit cards.
Open: Daily noon–10pm.

The name of this place is a traditional joke around Sydney, where every kid knows that "Tommo's" denotes an illicit floating two-up game, spinning coins at a different location each night. Proprietor Rod Thomas cashed in on the tradition quite legitimately by calling his pub after himself. It attracts a lot of customers, but does lead to a certain amount of confusion because no two-up game is conducted on the premises.

But Tommo's has other claims to fame. The pub actually incorporates a brewery, separated from the splendiferous bar by a glass wall. You can watch the beer being brewed while sipping the end product. You can also ask for one of the "special" home brews, but not if you're driving. Their alcohol content is a military secret. Apart from all that, Tommo's has a leafy beer garden and a smart bistro section. The fare is good, simple, and inexpensive, built around standard favorites like steaks and salad, roast beef, and schnitzels. In case you don't wish to breast any bars, the entire boutique brewing action can be followed on the specially installed closed-circuit video system.

★ **Woolloomooloo Bay Hotel,** 2 Bourke St., Woolloomooloo.
☎ 357-1928.
Cuisine: SEAFOOD. **Reservations:** Not accepted.
Prices: Appetizers around $A9; main courses around $A13. Major credit cards.
Open: Daily 11am–9pm.

This spot is yet another symbol of how the vibes have changed in "the Loo." A decade ago this hotel bore a different name and used to raffle off girls. Now this once-infamous spot is a mecca for the upwardly mobile of all sexes and winner of the coveted 1988 Best Hotel tourism award. The pièce de résistance here is the bistro, an in- and outdoor affair with atrium roof and colored umbrellas, a view of the bay, and a celebrated pianist who tickles the baby grand at night. The bistro's blackboard menu offers stir-fried squid, chili crab, char-grilled steaks, and a mountainous mixed seafood platter. Courtesy bus to and from the city—call in advance.

Cafes

There are hundreds of cafes in Sydney, ranging from lunch spots that close in the early afternoon to all-nighters that never close at all. They may serve snacks only or offer fairly elaborate meals.

DOWNTOWN

Gumnut Tea Garden, 28 Harrington St., The Rocks, ☎ 247-9591.

A total charmer housed in an 1830s-built convict cottage, but spreading out onto a shaded brick patio. On chill days you can sit in front of the original old fireplace and count the cracks in the ancient plaster walls. The Gumnut serves breakfast, dainty lunches, and afternoon snacks daily from 9am–5pm. The traditional ham and eggs is among the best anywhere, but the homemade scones, breads, and desserts are in a class of their own. Lunch costs around $10. Unfortunately the famous scones are made only on weekends, when the place gets very crowded. **Train:** Circular Quay.

⭐ **Hyde Park Barracks,** Macquarie Street. ☎ 223-1155.

This may sound like an odd name, but this place really was the barracks of the New South Wales regiment back in the convict days. You sit in what used to be the officers' mess, overlooking the parade ground outside. A tourist landmark, often difficult to get into, the Barracks serves a set menu as well as between-meal bites. The fare is fine (sandwich platters for $A8.50–$A14), the coffee the weakest link. Better stick to tea or something stronger—the place is licensed. Open daily 10am to 4pm. **Train:** St. James.

KINGS CROSS

⭐ **Bar Coluzzi,** 322 Victoria St., Kings Cross. ☎ 380-5420.

This place is sadly misnamed since it serves no liquor, but it is one of Sydney's prime cafes. Bar Coluzzi always has a crowd spilling out on the sidewalk, always has flirtations or debates in progress, and yet has enough sheltered corner tables to let patrons read books, write letters, or just study the scene. It serves what may be the finest coffee in the southern hemisphere, as well as a limited array of scrumptious Italian pastries. Hours are 5:30am to 7:30pm daily.

⭐ **Cafe At The Fountain,** Darlinghurst Road, Kings Cross.

Directly opposite sparkling El Alamein Fountain, the heart of Kings Cross, this place offers a grandstand view of the nocturnal action all around. With a plain interior, but a vast expanse of outdoor tables and umbrellas, this is the prime rendezvous spot of the area. The iced coffee (at $A3.20 a tall glass) is the best in Sydney. Open daily 9am to 2am.

Dean's Cafe, 7 Kellett St., Kings Cross. ☎ 358-2174.

This is a coffeehouse cum BYO tailored for nightbirds and insomniacs, of which the Cross has a vast supply. The interior is so dark that you have to find a table by touch. You could spend hours in there without knowing what the decor is like. But both service and clientele are amiable, immense bowls of nachos come for $A11.50, and the homemade Cointreau cake is in a class of its own. Dean's doesn't start filling up until around 10pm. Open 9pm to 4am on weekdays, to 5am Saturday and Sunday.

GLEBE

 Badde Manors, 37A Glebe Point Rd., Glebe. ☎ **660-3797.**
Despite the dreadful pun of its name, this spot is cozy and interesting. Vegetarian by persuasion, but BYO, the Manors serves such items as eggplant cutlets and lasagne for around $A7.80 besides excellent coffee and various herbal teas. The clientele is young, mainly local, and a mixed bag of college students, journalists, and artists. Open 8am to 1am weekdays, to 5am on weekends. **Bus:** 431, 434.

PADDINGTON

Good Day Cafe, 222 Glenmore Rd., Five Ways, Paddington.
☎ **363-3834.**
This cafe overlooks a road junction with the ambience of a village square and blends in perfectly. Small, simple, with deliberately understated decor, this daytime snack shop and local rendezvous spot depends on first-rate modern art pieces—silkscreens, portraits, and still lifes—for ornamental effect. The taped background music consists mainly of jazz classics kept low enough to permit table talk. Menu offerings run from $A3.60 to $A9. For an excellent light lunch try the open focaccia with homemade pizza sauce and salad garnish followed by the fresh fruit salad. Open Monday to Friday 8am to 5:30pm, Saturday 8am to 3pm. **Bus:** 380, 382.

WOOLLOOMOOLOO

 Harry's Cafe De Wheels, 1 Cowper Wharf Rd., Woolloomooloo. ☎ **264-1843.**
This isn't a cafe at all but an institution, the scene of countless anecdotes dispensed by stand-up comics. It's a pie caravan, successor to the original Harry who fed sailors and wharf laborers for 40 years. Now the pie wagon is a magnet for night owls and visiting celebrities who wait patiently for a wedge of steaming-hot pie and a thick cuppa. Open daily 9pm to 3am. **Bus:** 324, 325.

Skandic, at Crown and Cathedral Streets, Woolloomooloo.
If you feel a craving for those open Swedish sandwiches that always make you wish for a couple more, drop in here. This rendezvous for Sydney's Scandinavians dishes up a mouthwatering selection, the concoctions piled high on white, black, or cracker bread. Combinations like herring, cucumber, tomato, and lettuce cost around $A4, but you need several for a meal. Coffee and tea are both excellent, but the hours far too brief. Open Monday to Saturday 7am to 3pm.

6

What to See & Do in Sydney

MANY OF SYDNEY'S ATTRACTIONS—LIKE ITS BEACHES—AREN'T "SIGHTS" IN the strict sense of the term. A harbor cruise, on the other hand, is very much a sight, but not in the same way as a museum. And how do you classify a colossal, multilayered, indoor/outdoor creation such as the Darling Harbour Project?

This chapter, then, is a mixed bag. Some Top Attractions are several attractions combined under one label. Others are wildlife parks located a good way out of town. You may not agree with my listing of their order of importance. However, you'll find virtually all the showpieces that make Sydney one of the world's great tourist centers. If you don't have time to enjoy them all, just pick the raisins out of the cake.

Suggested Itineraries

If You Have 1 Day

Breakfast at an outdoor cafe, either in Kings Cross or downtown, then inspect the magnificent Queen Victoria shopping complex. Next, take a guided tour through the Sydney Opera House. Follow the tour with an amble through The Rocks (see the route described in Chapter 7). In the evening, catch the Harbour Lights Cruise, departing from Circular Quay.

If You Have 2 Days

Spend the first day as above, then start your second day with a panoramic lookout from Sydney Tower and get a closeup of Sydney Harbour Bridge from Pylon Lookout. A tour of the Darling Harbour Project (an excellent location for lunch) will take most of the afternoon. Later, take the train to Kings Cross and dine at a restaurant in the area. After that . . . well, there's enough nightlife all around to keep you spinning for a week.

If You Have 3 Days

Spend the first two days as suggested above, and on your third day catch the speedy hydrofoil to Manly from Circular Quay, and swim, surf, and see the giant Oceanarium there. Later, take a leisurely ferry back to the city. Visit Chinatown for exotic displays and dinner. In the evening, join the crowds in one of the rock/jazz/folk pubs described in Chapter 9.

If You Have 5 Days or More

Spend your first three days as suggested above.

Start your fourth day with a shopping tour (window or otherwise). Take in the pedestrian malls in Martin Place and Pitt Street; nose through the chic little boutiques of the Royal, Strand, and Imperial arcades; and visit the Opal Skymine in Australia Square and watch the gems being dug out and processed. In the afternoon take the

Mosman ferry over to Taronga Zoo. In the evening you can dance at a disco or sip drinks in a piano bar. Begin your fifth day with a trip to Bondi, and enjoy Australia's most famous surfing beach. Return to the city in time to inspect the NSW Art Gallery or the Australian Museum. For a grand evening splurge, book a table at the Argyle Tavern (see Chapter 9).

If You Have More Than 5 Days

Take the train to the Blue Mountains, the city's alpine playground 50 miles to the west. . . . Visit the Featherdale Wildlife Park or the Koala Park, with more wildlife. . . . See the historic town and would-be capital of Parramatta, now simply an outer suburb. . . . Take a bus along Oxford Street to Paddington and wander among the little art galleries. . . . Join the "Sydney After Dark" tour for an organized nibble of nightlife. . . . Spend a day—or a week—exploring the string of beaches all the way out to Palm Beach.

1 The Top Attractions

⭐ **Sydney Opera House,** Bennelong Point. ☎ 250-1777.

No city ever consciously created its symbolic landmark—it just happened to become one, often in the teeth of fierce public antagonism. Most Parisians detested the Eiffel Tower when it first went up. While Sydneysiders weren't exactly opposed to the Opera House, they viewed the project with considerable cynicism.

The project was conceived in 1954 by a group of prominent citizens who selected the site, a derelict trolley depot on Bennelong Point. In 1957 the Danish architect Jörn Utzon won the international competition for a design of the building with his revolutionary sails-on-the-harbor effect, and actual work began. The projected budget of $A7.2 million was funded by means of a state lottery. But now the troubles began. The first major lottery winner became the victim of Australia's first kidnap-murder—his young son was killed by the ransom kidnapper. In 1966 Utzon, fed up with bureaucratic and union troubles, withdrew from the project and went home.

The plans he left behind were full of untried techniques and daring innovations, and the people who tried to put them into practice fell from one blunder to the next. They left out vital staircases, they left out parking lots, they forgot about fire exits, about elevators, and half a hundred other trifles. Work had to be redone, patched up, overhauled, modified. The parking garage didn't open until 1993.

For years the skeptical populace watched the skeleton that never seemed to put on flesh and coined cute little nicknames. "The Hunchback of Bennelong Point," they called it; the "New South Whale," "a haystack with a tarpaulin," and "a pack of French nuns playing football." Meanwhile the budget allocations went up and up, to $A50 million, $A110 million, and still the thing wasn't finished.

And then one day it was. People rubbed their eyes, looked again, and saw a pearl-pale sculpture, grandiose yet fragile, floating above the water against a background of blue that set it off like a painting.

It was a masterpiece, the most beautiful creation of its kind in the world. No other could match it. The *London Times* called it "the building of the century," and even the most sardonic locals realized that they had a national symbol on their foreshore. When Elizabeth II cut the ribbon in October 1973, everybody, even those who didn't give a hang about music, was aware that Sydney had entered a new era.

The Opera House is far more than simply a building housing an opera company. It's a pleasure complex in the best sense of the word. Apart from the magnificent main auditorium, the building contains three performance halls—one for concerts, one for drama, and one for more intimate recitals. You can eat and drink there as well—and very well—and during the intermissions walk out on the promenade and stroll by the water, with yachts and ocean liners sailing by. You don't have to attend a performance to admire the interior: the timber panels, the tinted glass merging into the sea beyond, the modernistic murals, the curtains woven in the bold hues of the Australian day and night.

Tours: Conducted daily 9:15am–4pm; $A9 adults, $A6 children.
Train: Circular Quay.

Sydney Tower, Centrepoint, 100 Market St., between Pitt and Castlereagh Streets. ☎ **229-7444.**

The chief landmark in the central downtown region is Sydney Tower, one of the tallest structures in the southern hemisphere. It's a giant silver needle stabbing 1,000 feet into the sky, secured by steel cables and crowned with a shining gold turret. The tower, which looks incredibly slender from a distance, rises at the Centrepoint Arcade, a maze of shops and boutiques that seems like a city of its own. The tower's observation platform offers stupendous views of the entire city area and beyond. High-speed elevators whisk you up—leaving your stomach somewhere below—and high-powered telescopes let you see still farther. The tower also contains two restaurants (one revolving) at cloud level, reached by other elevators (see Chapter 5).

Admission: $A6 adults, $A2.50 children.
Open: Daily 9:30am–9:30pm. **Train:** St. James.

Sydney Harbour Bridge, Sydney Harbour.

An immense structure, linking the downtown business district with the North Shore, this is the second-largest single-span bridge in the world. Built in 1932, the bridge is $2^3/4$ miles (2 feet shorter than San Francisco's Golden Gate Bridge) and weighs 52,800 tons. It was *the* Sydney landmark until the advent of the Opera House. Too bulky to pass as beautiful, the bridge is known affectionately as the "coathanger" among locals. The four massive stone pylons at the corners were unnecessary additions, since the bridge is supported entirely by its span girders. During World War II these pylons served as antiaircraft gun positions. Today one of them is the Pylon Lookout. If you're willing to climb up 200 steep steps, you'll have the whole magnificent expanse of the harbor at your feet.

Admission: $A1.

Open: Lookout, daily 10am–5pm.

⭐ **The Rocks**, near Sydney Harbour Bridge.

You could spend three hours or three days exploring this, the cradle of Sydney. To simplify matters, I've mapped out a walking tour that covers all salient points. See Chapter 7.

⭐ **Taronga Zoo**, Bradleys Head Road, Mosman. ☎ **969-2777.**

Located across the harbor in Mosman, Taronga Zoo probably has the most beautiful natural setting of any zoological garden in the world. Perched on a hillside 12 minutes by ferry from Circular Quay, it offers harbor panoramas together with the animals and 75 acres of bushland park. A zoo bus will meet the ferry and take you to the top of the hill—you can sightsee downhill all the way back to the ferry stop. There is also a cable train from the wharf to the top. See the koalas at their own treetop level in their specially designed enclosure. Check out the platypus house (you can watch it underwater), the rainforest aviary (where you walk through the cage and have the birds fly above and around you), and the Friendship Farm, where you can pet a lamb and stroke a wombat. In the underground building, where special lights turn day into night, you can watch the nocturnal creatures of Australia and New Guinea at their busiest (watch for the huge Queensland fruit bats called flying foxes). Plus there are the inevitable lions, tigers, elephants, chimps, bears, and monkeys.

Admission: $A13.50 adults, $A6 children.

Open: Daily 9am–5pm. **Ferry:** From no. 2 wharf at Circular Quay (adults $A2, children $A1). You can buy a special pass that combines ferry trip, cable-car ride, and zoo admission for $A17 adults, $A8.70 children.

Darling Harbour

⭐ This, the greatest urban redevelopment project in Australian history, covers the western dockside region and adds a new dimension to the downtown area. (It's reachable by monorail from downtown.) Darling Harbour used to be Sydney's tradesman's entrance, a wilderness of cranes and warehouses that fell into idle decrepitude when container shipping came in. Now the entire expanse has been transformed into a gigantic pleasure and cultural complex, with parks, gardens, and promenades thrown in as well as a monorail system to connect it with the center city.

Matters did not go altogether smoothly with this marvel; they rarely do in Sydney. It was to have contained the first *legal* gambling casino in the state (as distinct from the scores of illegal little dens now thriving). But someone discovered that the entrepreneurs involved had the wrong kind of business connections, and in the resultant uproar the casino project got shelved. It may yet reappear one day, but don't hold your breath. There are quite enough attractions to go on with in the meantime.

Harbourside Festival Marketplace is a huge, bustling, flag-fluttering marketplace, partly roofed against rain and festive with clowns, jugglers, dancers, and strolling musicians. It contains more than 200 shops and 9 restaurants and bars, as well as a disco.

The **Exhibition Centre** is a huge edifice with a great roof canopy suspended from steel masts. Seven stories high, with an enormous interior expanse free of obstructing columns, the center holds a banqueting hall designed for 5,000 guests, and has changing exhibitions.

There is also Australia's biggest **Convention Centre;** the entertainment-lined, carnival-style **Darling Walk;** and the restored, decorated, and illuminated **Pyrmont Bridge,** linking the center city with the project.

Australian National Maritime Museum, Darling Harbour. ☎ 552-7500.

Directly in front of the Harbourside Festival Marketplace is the National Maritime Museum, displaying historic ships and nautical equipment. The grandest exhibit is the 1874 vintage square-rigger *James Craig,* completely restored and equipped with a 24-projector audiovisual apparatus that gives you the thrill of a rough ocean voyage under canvas without the seasickness.

Admission: $A7 adults, $A3.50 children.

Open: Daily 10am–5pm.

Sydney Aquarium, Pier 26, Darling Harbour. ☎ 262-2300.
Largest in the southern hemisphere, the aquarium simulates a trip to the bottom of the sea by means of two floating oceanariums and 50 tanks depicting aquatic environments around Australia. You get

Frommer's Favorite Sydney Experiences

Opera in the Park   The Australian Opera gives outdoor performances each January during the Festival of Sydney.

A Jetcat Trip to Manly   It's a zooming, bouncing trip from Circular Quay to Manly.

The Final Parade of a Surf Carnival   Bands play, club flags fly, and spectators cheer as the lifesavers strut past.

Riding the Mountain Devil Railway   It's an almost vertical downhill ride on the railway at Katoomba in the Blue Mountains.

Shaking Paws with Skippy   Australia's most famous television star resides at Watarah Park.

Watching the Start of the Sydney–Hobart Yacht Race   An armada of billowing white sails streams through the Heads of Sydney Harbor.

Watching the Hand-Feeding of Giant Sharks   Divers at the Oceanarium do it daily—without losing a finger.

Sheepshearing at the Argyle Tavern   A live sheep is shorn to the exact beat of the band playing "Click Go the Shears." With the last musical "click," the last curl of wool drops.

Sydney Attractions

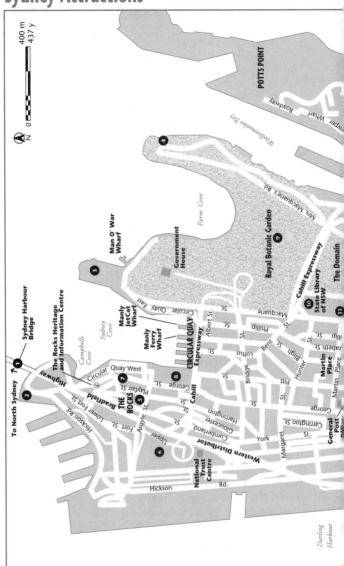

eye-to-eye encounters with sharks, stingrays, and giant eels; watch octopuses and deadly poisonous stonefish; and come within a couple of glass-partitioned inches of saltwater crocodiles grinning through barricades of teeth.

Admission: $A14.00 adults, $A7 children.
Open: Daily 9:30am–9pm.

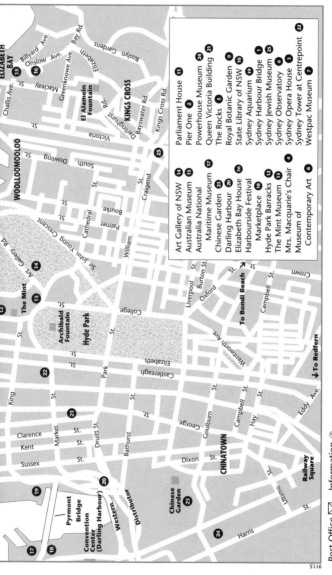

Art Gallery of NSW ⑭
Australian Museum ⑮
Australia National
  Maritime Museum ⑰
Chinese Garden ㉓
Darling Harbour ⑳
Elizabeth Bay House ⑯
Harbourside Festival
  Marketplace ⑱
Hyde Park Barracks ⑫
The Mint Museum ⑬
Mrs. Macquarie's Chair ④
Museum of
  Contemporary Art ⑧
Parliament House ⑪
Pier One ②
Powerhouse Museum ㉔
Queen Victoria Building ㉑
The Rocks ⑤
Royal Botanic Garden ⑨
State Library of NSW ⑩
Sydney Aquarium ⑲
Sydney Harbour Bridge ①
Sydney Jewish Museum ㉓
Sydney Observatory ⑥
Sydney Opera House ③
Sydney Tower at Centrepoint ㉒
Westpac Museum ⑦

Post Office ☒   Information ⓘ

5116

Powerhouse Museum, 500 Harris St., Darling Harbour.
  ☎ **217-0111.**

Powerhouse Museum has a misleading name because the exhibits are
only indirectly linked to electricity. Primarily it tells the social history of Australia by showing the machines, the buildings, tools, and
artifacts that made the country. The building is huge—large enough

to display complete aircraft, locomotives, and houses. Many of the machines and gadgets are push-button affairs that can be worked by the visitors. Others show slices of everyday life, such as an old "picture palace" from the silent days, a bush squatter's hut, and a suburban grocery. Too much to see and play with for one visit; plan on coming back to see the rest.

Admission: $A5 adults, $A2 children. Free on the first Sat of each month.

Open: Daily 10am–5pm.

Chinese Garden, Darling Harbour. ☎ 281-6863.

An exquisite piece of horticultural craftsmanship, designed by specialists from Guangdong Province, this is the largest and most elaborate such garden outside China. Linking Chinatown with Darling Harbour, the complex centers on a two-story pavilion surrounded by a pattern of interconnected little lakes and waterfalls, spanned by bridges and laced with dreamily secluded walkways.

Admission: $A2 adults, A50¢ children.

Open: Daily 9am–sunset.

2   More Attractions

Art Gallery Of New South Wales, Art Gallery Road, The Domain. ☎ 225-1700 or 225-1744.

The museum consists of two wings, one built at the turn of the century and the other in 1970, both admirably suited to their contrasting exhibits. The traditionally skylit, wine-walled galleries of the old wing contain European and Australian art dating from the Renaissance to the early 20th century. The new wing, all angled white walls and harbor-framing glass, houses impressionist and modern works, including some striking paintings by the famed Australian trailblazers Sidney Nolan, William Dobell, and Russell Drysdale. The building also features a good licensed restaurant, an excellent shop selling books, prints, and souvenir catalogs, and a small auditorium screening films on art subjects.

Admission: Gallery free; special exhibits $A12 adults, $A7 children.

Open: Mon–Sat 10am–5pm, Sun noon–5pm. **Train:** Martin Place.

Parliament House, Macquarie Street. ☎ 230-2111.

Seat of the New South Wales state legislature and the oldest legislative building in Australia, Parliament House was once the so-called Rum Hospital, origins which have given rise to countless jokes at the expense of the politicians who now occupy it. It's a beautiful piece of colonial architecture, with timber verandas and colonnades.

Open: Mon–Fri 10am–3:30pm. When Parliament is in session, visitors admitted to galleries during Question Time, Tues–Wed at 1:15pm, Thurs at 9:30am. Tours, Mon–Fri 10am–4pm. **Train:** Martin Place.

State Library Of New South Wales, Macquarie Street.
   ☎ 230-1414.

Next door to Parliament stands the NSW State Library. Impressive stone steps lead to the Dixson and Mitchell Galleries, a repository of papers, prints, paintings, and proclamations connected with the early settlement of Sydney. The galleries mount various showings of the trove. The items vary. If you're lucky you can see some of the wordless but graphic cartoons issued by colonial governors for the benefit of the Aborigines. The promises implied weren't always exactly sincere, but their meaning was clear enough.

   Open: Mon–Sat 9am–5pm, Sun 2–6pm. **Train:** St. James.

Australian Museum, corner William and College Streets.
   ☎ 339-8111.

The largest museum of natural history on the continent also houses an impressive section on Aboriginal and Pacific Islands artifacts, including reproductions of New Guinea villages. There are gigantic whale skeletons, models of sharks and other marine creatures, and hundreds of tribal weapons, artifacts, and ornaments.

   Admission: $A4 adults, $A8 families.

   Open: Daily 10am–5pm. **Train:** Museum.

Hyde Park Barracks, Queen's Square, Macquarie Street.
   ☎ 223-8922.

This is another of the beautiful Georgian-style public buildings designed by the prolific convict-architect Francis Greenway. Completed

---

Did You Know . . . ?

- The State Library of New South Wales holds the log book of Captain Bligh's ship *Bounty,* including his account of the famous mutiny.

- Inaugurated in 1829, Parliament House of New South Wales is the oldest continuously used parliamentary building in the world.

- Sydney's first hospital was built by two enterprising colonists in return for the privilege of importing 180,000 liters of rum.

- Until 1903 it was forbidden to swim publicly in Australia between the hours of 6am and 8pm.

- One square yard of Sydney is officially French soil. It's at the La Perouse monument, dedicated to the comte who sailed into the harbor just three days after the arrival of the first British fleet.

- *Il porcellino,* a bronze statue outside Sydney Hospital, on Macquarie Street, is a reproduction of the 15th-century original in Florence. "The little boar" is supposed to bring good luck if you rub its nose, but, like the original, it's also supposed to bite you if you've been unfaithful to your spouse that month.

in 1819 as a military barracks, the building is now partly a museum. The museum rooms trace the social history of Australia, starting with the convict room and concluding with the pretty dismal period style of the 1950s. Look for the special exhibitions arranged by this museum.

Admission: $A5 adults, $A3 children.

Open: Wed–Mon 10am–5pm, Tues noon–5pm. **Train:** St. James.

The Mint Museum, Queen's Square, Macquarie Street.
☎ 217-0111.

The other wing of the old Rum Hospital, partly given over to the state legislature. The colony's coins used to be minted here, but now the rooms serve as a showcase for Australian decorative arts—a good choice, because the building is itself a work of art.

Admission: $A4 adults, $A2 children.

Open: Daily 10am–5pm. **Train:** St. James.

★ **Museum Of Contemporary Art [MCA],** 132 George St., Circular Quay. ☎ 252-4033.

Sydney's newest museum is devoted to whatever passes as art in today's world. Exhibits range from oil portraits to garbage heap collages, from the works of Aborigines to those of Andy Warhol and Roy Lichtenstein. Also on view is computer-based art, modern design, sculptures, film, video, and laser creations. Some critics have remarked that the best part of the museum is its cafe, which offers superb views across Circular Quay, along with Modern Australian food.

Admission: $A6 adults, $A4 children.

Open: Daily 11am–6pm. **Train:** Circular Quay.

Sydney Observatory, Watson Road, The Rocks. ☎ 241-2478.

Standing on Observatory Hill, high above the harbor, this weathered old graystone edifice was built in 1857. It served as a timekeeper for all the ships in the harbor—at one o'clock daily the ball on its weather vane dropped and a gun was fired at Fort Denison (see below), indicating the correct time for setting marine clocks. Today the building is a museum of astronomy. Open to the public for telescope viewings Thursday to Tuesday night, with interesting daytime exhibits as well.

Admission: Free during the day. At night, $A5 adults, $2 children.

Open: Daily 2–5pm, Thurs–Tues 8pm–2am. **Bus:** 111, 431.

Pier One, Hickson Road, Walsh Bay.

Below The Rocks, underneath the southern end of Sydney Harbour Bridge, lies Pier One, a multitiered, very commercial entertainment center, not exactly stylish, but loads of fun if you're in the right mood. A kind of merry mélange of amusement park and San Francisco's Cannery, Pier One has so many attractions that you'd have to list them alphabetically. Clustered in a row of converted warehouses are bumper cars, merry-go-rounds, a movie theater, an excellent bookstore (John Cookson), market stalls, shops selling everything from jewelry to junk, a colonial village from the turn of the century, and a strange but fun amusement park ride called the Gravitron. Entertainment is supplemented by strolling minstrels, jazz musicians, folksingers, and earnest municipal bands. The fun goes on 7 days from 10am till 5 or 6pm. **Bus:** 111, 431, 433.

Royal Botanic Garden, east of Queen's Square. ☎ **231-8111.**

Stretching for miles, the Royal Botanic Garden forms the greater portion of an almost unbroken green quilt that starts at the Farm Cove, harborside in the north, and merges into **Hyde Park** to the southwest. The enormous expanse of greenery contains a glass pyramid of tropical plants, vast flower beds, duck ponds, secluded walkways, an open-air garden cafe, and a restaurant.

At the edge of the garden stands the **Art Gallery of New South Wales** and the oddly medieval-looking **Conservatorium of Music.** Inside the garden, on high ground, stands **Government House** (no, you can't get in there).

To the south, the Botanic Garden becomes the open grassy **Domain,** which was once one of Sydney's major Sunday entertainment areas. The Domain is a free-speech forum—anyone can mount a soapbox or its equivalent and bellow out orations on any subject. In prevideo times the Domain was populated by masses of leather-lunged orators declaiming on subjects ranging from industrial syndicalism to the removal of gallstones by means of prayer. Some were highly skilled in dealing with hecklers and keeping audiences amused. Nowadays their numbers have shrunk to a determined handful and most of the excitement has gone, but they still provide an intriguing interlude on a Sunday afternoon stroll.

Admission: Free.

Open: 8am to sunset.

Motor Museum, 320 Harris St., Pyrmont, ☎ **552-3375.**

Located three blocks north of the Powerhouse Museum, this is a magnet for motoring buffs from far and wide. The exhibits change constantly, but they always include an array of classic cars—those vintage aristocrats of the Rolls and Buick and MG breeds that can generate nostalgia like no other mechanical contraptions. Other cars achieved fame through famous or infamous owners, plus historic vans, motorcycles, and commercial vehicles; around 160 machines in all. The museum also houses Australia's largest slot car track, with two 8-lane tracks covering two scale kilometers on which you can test your miniature racing skills.

Admission: $A8 adults, $A4 children.

Open: Daily 10am–5pm. **Bus:** 500, 506. **Monorail:** Convention Centre station.

Sights Beyond the Inner City

Victoria Barracks, Oxford Street, Paddington. ☎ **339-3445.**
Museum ☎ **339-3330.**

A living history of Australia's military forces, Victoria Barracks, built largely by convict labor and finished in 1848, was designed to house one regiment of British infantry. British garrison troops were withdrawn in 1870, since there was no conceivable enemy that couldn't be handled by the Royal Navy. Since then, Australia's own forces have occupied the barracks, which today are the hub and command post of the Commonwealth's field and supporting units. The building is a splendid example of late Georgian architecture, crammed with military memorabilia. Every Tuesday at 10am there is a ceremonial changing of the guard, impressive to watch; following this, the premises are open to tours. The museum is also open on Sundays 10am–3:30pm.

Admission: Free.

★ **Elizabeth Bay House,** 7 Onslow Ave., Elizabeth Bay. ☎ 358-2344.

An enchanting period mansion built for the colonial secretary of New South Wales in 1838, this is Australia's finest remaining stately home. Laid out around a superb central staircase lit by an oval lantern from above, the white Grecian villa shows in what tasteful splendor the colonial upper classes dwelled at a time when Australia's lower orders were somewhat less stylishly housed. The furnishings have the typical elegant simplicity of the Georgian era (which was soon to be obliterated by the overstuffed red-brick monstrosities of the Victorians). Apart from the original furnishings, the mansion also displays changing exhibitions.

Admission: $A5 adults, $A3 children.

Open: Tues–Sun 10am–4:30pm. **Train:** Kings Cross.

★ **Sydney Agrodome,** Dalgety Centre, RAS Showground, Paddington. ☎ 331-7279.

A patch of rural Australia right in the city, located at the Showgrounds of the Royal Agricultural Society, the Agrodome introduces you to a parade of famous sheep breeds, stages shearing exhibitions, and displays the process that transforms the rough and dirty fleece into finely spun wool. The best part of the show is the wonderfully photogenic sheepdog trial, in which the highly skilled pooch keeps control over a dozen woolly charges by responding to whistle signals from its master.

The restaurant on the grounds serves traditional outback lunches, and the admission entitles you to billy tea and genuine bush dampers (unleavened strips of dough baked in campfire ashes).

Admission: $A9 adults, $A4.50 children.

Shows: 9am, noon, and 2:30pm. **Bus:** 380, 382.

Sydney Jewish Museum, 148 Darlinghurst Rd., Darlinghurst. ☎ 360-7999.

This museum fulfills a starkly contrasting dual purpose with flair, imagination, and remarkable ingenuity. It is simultaneously a showcase of Jewish life in Australia and a memorial of Jewish death in the Holocaust. Jewish history in Australia began with the first white settlement. There were Jewish convicts among those chained arrivals with the First Fleet, including the extraordinary Esther Abrahams who rose to become First Lady of the colony.

The Jewish community progressed together with the country—among its members were two Governors General and the commander of the Australian army corps in World War I, all of which makes the fate of European Jewry seem all the more tragic. The Holocaust is portrayed in a series of state-of-the-art computer interactives and visuals combined with photographic images along the walls. The effect is understated yet shattering: a chronicle of inhumanity that defies dictionary terms.

Admission: $A5 adults, $2 children.

Open: Mon–Thurs 10am–4pm, Sun noon–5pm. **Bus:** 373, 374.

Vaucluse House, Olola Avenue, Vaucluse. ☎ **337-1957.**

Another lovingly preserved stately home, Vaucluse House was formerly the property of explorer-statesman William Charles Wentworth (you'll find reminders of his name all over New South Wales). Completed in the 1830s, the house is surrounded by superbly landscaped grounds and crammed with antique furniture, somewhat gloomy oil paintings, and acres of period ornaments. There is also a costume room, a very impressive wine cellar, and a tearoom serving—what else?—afternoon tea as well as pretty-lavish picnic hampers.

Admission: $A5 adults, $A3 children.

Open: Tues–Sun 10am–4:30pm. **Bus:** 325.

★ **Fort Denison,** Sydney Harbour. ☎ **240-2111,** ext. 2036 for tour reservations.

You can't miss the little mount of rock with the round tower that looks rather like a squat submarine anchored in Sydney Harbour. Officially named Fort Denison, it was known, and dreaded, by the convicts as "Pinchgut Island," the punishment rock where you were confined on "tight rations" (meaning starved to a skeleton).

Escape from this miniature Devil's Island was virtually impossible because the harbor then was full of sharks (hunting and oil slicks have driven them away). Built and armed to protect Sydney from invasion (which never came), Fort Denison today is a tide-observation station as well as a landmark. The round martello tower still houses the six muzzle-loading cannons, which were never fired. But the "one o'clock gun" booms out from the fort every day on the dot—you can set your watch by it. The Maritime Services Board arranges tours of the island.

Tours: 1 1/2-hour tours, $A7 adults, $A3.50 children.

La Perouse Museum, Anzac Parade, La Perouse. ☎ **661-2765.**

This place commemorates the most intriguing might-have-been in Australian history. Here, at the eastern shore of Botany Bay, two French vessels commanded by Jean-François, comte de La Perouse, dropped anchor in January 1788—*three days* after the arrival of the first British fleet under Captain Phillip. The comte was a tough naval veteran; he had fought the British as an ally of George Washington's colonists during the American Revolution. But on this occasion he was not only too late, but hopelessly outgunned by the English. There is no evidence that he actually intended to raise the flag of Louis XVI and declare Australia a French possession . . . but he might well have done so had he arrived first.

As it was, the French stayed for only five weeks. Just long enough to build a stockade and drink a few frigidly polite toasts with visiting British officers. Then La Perouse sailed away—into oblivion. Neither his men nor his ships were ever seen again.

The La Perouse Museum is housed in the old cable station that once represented Sydney's only link with the overseas world. Outside stands a pillar monument erected by the French government. Inside you'll see the original charts, maps, navigation instruments, and sketches left behind by the unlucky count.

Admission: Free (donation).

Open: Mon–Fri 9am–4pm. **Bus:** 393, 394 to La Perouse.

Art Galleries

Sydney has an immense array of private galleries—some very large and beautiful, others modest little storefront affairs. Most galleries are concentrated in prosperous Paddington, north of Oxford Street, but there are some surprising treasure troves tucked in drab industrial surroundings, where rents are cheap. In all establishments admission is free, visitors welcome, and browsers encouraged.

Below are merely a few of the galleries flourishing in Sydney. If you amble through Paddington you'll come across another gallery every couple of blocks—or so it seems. Two of Sydney's leading department stores, Grace Bros. and David Jones, have small but distinguished galleries of their own. Still more galleries can be found at the University of Sydney, the Argyle Centre at the Rocks, and the City Art Institute.

Aboriginal Art and Tribal Centre, 117 George St., The Rocks. ☎ **247-9025.**

An intriguing mix of contemporary painting and traditional artifacts like body ornaments, sculptures, wooden tools, and bark designs. Strong representation of Papua New Guinea art. If you're lucky you'll catch one of the irregular didjeridoo recitals or wonderfully expressive storytelling.

Open: Daily 10am–5pm.

★ **Aboriginal Artists Gallery,** 477 Kent St. ☎ **261-2929.**

This gallery displays traditional arts and crafts by the original Australians. Exhibits include bark painting, weaponry, carved animals and religious symbols, musical instruments, mats, and ornaments— some crude, others remarkably sophisticated. The gallery also sells beautifully illustrated books on Aboriginal art.

Open: Mon–Fri 10am–5:30pm, Sat 10am–1:30pm.

Australian Centre for Photography, 257 Oxford St., Paddington. ☎ **331-6253.**

This gallery is devoted to camera artists, though it also shows an array of art posters. The exhibitions change, as do the subjects of the photographers, but the standard remains very high indeed.

Open: Wed–Sun 11am–5pm. **Bus:** 380, 382.

Australian Craftworks, 127 George St. ☎ 27-7156.

This gallery probably has the most unusual setting of any showcase in the world. The premises were originally a colonial-era police station, and the old holding cells are now used to "hold" exhibits. It displays craftworks in the widest sense, but also has specialized exhibitions for particular categories. Materials used range from leather and straw to silk and stone, and every item you see is for sale.

Open: Mon–Sat 9am–6pm.

Glass Artists' Gallery, 70 Globe Point Rd., Globe. ☎ 552-1552.

The guiding theme behind this showcase is to "challenge the traditional notion of glass." The point is driven home by the exhibits, which include some of the most unorthodox pieces ever made from such fragile material. Handcrafted and original works by Australian and New Zealand glassblowers and designers, including winners of international awards in the field. Exhibitions change frequently.

Open: Tues–Sat 10am–6pm, Sun 1–5pm. **Bus:** 431, 434.

Hogarth Galleries, Walker Lane and Liverpool Street, Paddington. ☎ 357-6839.

Here you'll find two distinct showcases under one roof, forming an intriguing contrast. One displays Aboriginal art, including bark paintings and the strangely haunting rock carvings from Arnhem Land, the wildest and least explored portion of Northern Australia. The other exhibits contemporary Australian art and features some prominent names.

Open: Tues–Sat 11am–6pm. **Bus:** 380, 382.

★ Holdsworth Galleries, 86 Holdsworth St., Woollahra. ☎ 363-1364.

Holdsworth is the largest private art gallery in the southern hemisphere and possibly the handsomest. One of the premier showcases for contemporary Australian artists, the building is so beautifully designed and laid out that it could pass as an artwork itself. The exhibitions change—sometimes three shows are displayed simultaneously in the vast hanging space available—but they invariably reflect the best efforts produced by native painters and sculptors. Names like Margaret Olley, Sidney Nolan, Sali Herman, and Arthur Boyd are regulars, with new unknowns occasionally getting their start here.

Open: Daily 10am–5pm, Sun noon–5pm. **Bus:** 324, 325, 327.

Irving Sculpture Gallery, 144A St. Johns Rd., Glebe. ☎ 692-0680.

The Irving is the only gallery in town that concentrates solely on sculpture, some from overseas artists, the majority the work of local talent. It can be realistic or abstract, symbolic or representational, depending on the exhibitions (which change every month).

Open: Tues–Sat 11am–6pm. **Bus:** 431, 434.

New Guinea Primitive Art, Dymock's Building, 428 George St. ☎ **232-4737.**

This gallery looks at first glance like an anthropological museum, since it has an immense display of art, tools, and weaponry from New Guinea and Melanesia, some of it very impressive. You wander among decorated spears, elaborate wood and stone carving, hand-woven baskets, and fierce little totem statues that would look amazingly at home on California coffee tables. Watch for the powerful works from the Trobriand Islands.

Open: Mon–Fri 9am–6pm.

Watters Gallery, 109 Riley St., East Sydney. ☎ **331-2556.**

Watters is perhaps the most widely publicized of the private galleries and therefore a magnet for modern painters who want to make it into the limelight. It has the largest collection of Australian contemporary painters in town, including some who have already achieved fame. Lots of hanging space and a very obliging staff.

Open: Tues–Sat 10am–5pm.

Nearby Attractions

★ **Ku-Ring-Gai Chase National Park**, 18 miles north of central Sydney. ☎ **457-9322.**

An idyllic escape from the urban rat race, Ku-ring-gai has everything to gladden the hearts of nature-craving city dwellers: wildflower sanctuaries, hiking trails, picnic grounds, rocks for climbing, panoramas for viewing, boats for rent, tent areas for camping. Some of the region is virgin bush, but there are also restaurants, tearooms, and kiosks for those who prefer roughing it with a knife and fork.

Admission: $A4 per car.

Open: 9am–6pm. **Transportation:** Train to Turramurra station, then connecting bus to the park entrance at Bobbin Head.

★ **Waratah Park**, Namba Road, Terry Hills. ☎ **450-2377.**

This isn't really a park but a wonderful patch of bushland carved out of the edge of Ku-ring-gai Chase, about half an hour's drive north of Sydney. Waratah is mainly an animal reserve and most of the fauna—wallabies, emus, koalas, wombats—roam around freely. Kangaroos and wombats are gentle critters, but emus—the ostrichlike flightless birds of Australia—can be ill tempered at times, so be cautious about petting any. Other Oz natives, such as dingoes and Tasmanian devils, you can watch through wire mesh. Tasmanian devils, though only the size of terriers, are ferocious carnivores that will tackle and devour game three times their size. If you watch one feeding, you'll know how it got its name. Waratah is the home of one of Australia's top television stars, Skippy the Bush Kangaroo, who loves meeting his fans and has never been known to throw star tantrums. For tourist coach reservations, call **241-1636.**

Admission: $A11.60 adults, $A5.80 children.

Open: Daily 10am–5pm.

Australian Reptile Park, Pacific Highway, Gosford.
☎ **043/28-4311.**

Here you'll get a close look at some of the less cuddly Australians: tiger snakes, taipans, death adders, crocodiles, giant pythons, and the large dinosaurian lizards called goannas. Some of these creatures are quite harmless (pythons, in fact, make good pets), but the taipans and tiger snakes count among the most venomous reptiles on earth. You can watch them being milked of their venom, which forms the basis of snakebite serums, by highly skilled keepers.

Admission: $A9.50 adults, $A4 children.

Open: Daily 9am–5:30pm. **Transportation:** Train to Gosford.

★ **Old Sydney Town,** Pacific Highway, Somersby.
☎ **043/40-1104.**

This major attraction is a fairly faithful reproduction of colonial Sydney, circa two centuries ago. Houses, workshops, taverns, barracks, churches, and government offices have been re-created as close to the originals as possible. And so have the events. You can hear a town crier bellowing out the news, watch a display of military drill, or witness a colonial magistrate's court in action. (The main historical deviation here is that all participants are stone cold sober.) The spectators (including you) take part in the action—at least in the sound effects. You see the convicted culprit marched to a public triangle and given a flogging with a cat-o'-nine-tails (not for the squeamish). After that you can take a break by attending a Colonial-era wedding.

Admission: $A14.50 adults, $A8.20 children.

Open: Wed–Sun 10am–4pm.

El Caballo Blanco, Camden Valley Way, Narellan. ☎ **606-6266.**

An area of landscaped gardens and rolling bushland, this park is filled with a happy grab bag of animal shows, thrill rides, fun vehicles, shops, and restaurants. Impossible to put under one label—there are horse-breeding paddocks and a banked race-car track, pettable wombats and kangaroos, and a shriek-inducing "twister" ride, sheepdog demonstrations, water slides, a Puffing Billy train, and an 1880s stagecoach. In the evening a superb performance by Andalusian dancing stallions ("El Caballo Blanco") takes place in a floodlit arena. There are also picnic grounds, barbecue sites, a vaguely rustic eating house, and an air-conditioned restaurant with a sumptuous spread of smörgàsbord.

Admission: $A10 adults, $A5 children.

Open: Daily 10am–5pm. **Transportation:** Train to Campbelltown station, where the special park bus departs daily from 10am. Call first for show times.

Captain Cook's Landing Place, Polo Street, Kurnell.

Surprisingly few locals know of this historic spot and museum on the tip of the Kurnell Peninsula, about 28 miles south of the center city. This was the place where Capt. James Cook first set foot on Australia (at 3pm, April 29, 1770) after anchoring his ship, the

Endeavour, in what is now Botany Bay. He and his crew stayed a week, had a brief skirmish with Aborigines, dug some pits to obtain fresh water, and sailed on. Today the area of their activities is Landing Place Park. The park has a memorial monument and the **Captain Cook Museum** (☎ **668-9923;** open daily from 10:30am to 4:30pm). It contains some of Cook's original charts and a lot of material on the voyages of the *Endeavour* and the men who sailed it.

Train: Cronulla, then **bus** 67 to Polo Street.

Featherdale Wildlife Park, 217 Kildare Rd., Doonside, ☎ **622-1644.**

Located 23 miles west of Sydney, this spread of bushland offers nearly natural habitats for a vast array of furred, scaled, and feathered denizens. There is a superb exhibit of native birds, the chance to get your photo taken cuddling a koala, or have a close—but entirely safe—encounter with a crocodile. Also on view are pettable kangaroos, wombats, fairy penguins, and decidedly unpettable Tasmanian devils.

Admission: $A8 adults, $A4 children.

Open: Daily 9am–5pm. **Transportation:** Train to Blacktown, then bus 725 to Featherdale Park.

Australia's Wonderland and Wildlife Park, Wallgrove Road, Eastern Creek. ☎ **830-9100.**

A big, colorful theme park with a strong American flavor operating alongside a ten-acre all-Aussie animal reserve. Wonderland has Yogi Bear and the Flintstones, a charming puppet theater, and dizzying rides that whirl, loop, and splash, accompanied by the joyous terror screams of the riders. The Wildlife Park offers a formidable croc named *Maniac,* giant goannas, koalas to cuddle, wallabies to feed, and a hands-on farm for kids.

Admission: Wonderland & Wildlife Park, $A26.95 adults, $A19.95 children. Wildlife Park only, $A7.50 adults, $A5.50 children.

Open: Wonderland weekends 10am–5pm; Wildlife Park daily 9am–5pm. **Transportation:** Train to Rooty Hill, then bus service (every half hour) to park.

3 Parramatta & Manly

Parramatta

Although Parramatta today is simply one of Sydney's far-western suburbs, the town was intended to be the capital of New South Wales. Most early colonial governors resided there, while Sydney Cove was used merely as a cargo port. Gradually the advantages of a coastal town became obvious, and the seat of government shifted to Sydney for good. But Parramatta remains a historic site, lovingly preserved by its citizens, and still looks and acts as if it weren't part of the metropolis at all, but an entity of its own. Which, in a fashion, it is. You get there simply by boarding a train at Central or Wynyard Station and riding some 18 miles westward.

A characteristic token of independence is the **Tourist Information Centre,** Market Street (☎ **02150/630-3703**), which will give you free maps and brochures, plus as much verbal information as you can handle. Among the city's chief attractions are the various historic houses dating from Parramatta's governmental period.

Old Government House, Parramatta Park. ☎ **02150/635-8149.**

Begun modestly in 1790, this structure was completed sumptuously in 1816. As the residence of several governors, the mansion is equipped with exquisitely crafted early colonial furniture, superb mirrors, grand staircases, and the type of representational artwork that viceroys love to surround themselves with.

Admission: $A4 adults, $A1 children.

Open: Tues–Thurs and Sun 10am–4pm.

Elizabeth Farm, 70 Alice St. ☎ **02150/635-9488.**

This is the oldest existing farmhouse in Australia, but not by any means a typical one. Built in the 1830s by one of the founders of the Australian wool industry, this was a rich man's spread and for a long time the center of the colony's social life and agricultural planning. Most of the time it was run by a woman, Elizabeth Macarthur, who furnished it tastefully and ruled with a *very* firm hand. The guided tours of the place are exceptionally informative.

Admission: $A4 adults, $A2 children.

Open: Tues–Sun 10am–4:30pm.

Linden House Museum, Smith and Darcy Streets.

☎ **02150/635-7288.**

This museum is housed in what used to be the military barracks of Parramatta. The barracks, in fact, are still occupied by soldiers, so only the museum wing of the sandstone building is open to the public. You'll see a colorful array of uniforms and many of the crude but fatally effective muskets and bayonets with which the colonial units were equipped. (Take a look at the size of those old musket balls.)

Admission: $A1 adults, A50¢ children.

Open: Sun 11am–4pm.

Notre Dame, Camden Valley Way, Narellan. ☎ **606-6266.**

The only way to describe this place is as a cross between San Simeon and Disneyland. Created as a millionaire's estate home, it contains a wild mixture of art treasures and entertainment facilities. There is a priceless collection of French antiques, a private zoo, a giant equestrian arena (with Andalusian dancing horses), a Japanese Shinto shrine, a patch of tropical rain forest, and a formal English garden. Good for a whole afternoon.

Admission: $A13.50 adults, $A7.50 children.

Open: Wed–Sun 10am–4:30pm.

Koala Park Sanctuary, 84 Castle Hill Rd., West Pennant Hills.
☎ **02/875-2777.**

One train stop north of Parramatta, this was the first private sanctuary for koalas founded in the state. The main theme here is the breeding of future koala generations. Some knowledgeable hostesses explain the animal's habits. Also present are wallabies, dingoes, wedgetailed eagles, and wombats.

Admission: $A7 adults, $A4 children.

Open: Daily 9am–5pm.

Manly

A resort area and world of its own, dedicated to surf and sun (plus tourist dollars), Manly has four ocean beaches, six calm harbor beaches, and two Marine-water swimming pools. It also offers more than 700 other attractions, including first-class restaurants, several nightclubs, hotels, shops, boutiques, seaside promenades, and funpark entertainments, as well as shady parks, gardens, and museums. Pride of place goes to the beach promenade lined with towering Norfolk Island pines along a seemingly endless boardwalk that follows the curves and indentations of the vast ocean beach.

There are two very pleasurable modes of transportation to Manly. When it's early and you're raring to go, speed the seven miles across the harbor in 13 minutes via **Jetcat** from no. 2 wharf, Circular Quay. The cost is $A4.50. Coming back, surfeited with saltwater and sun, take the leisurely **ferry** cruise. The ferries commute between Manly and no. 3 wharf, Circular Quay. It's a wonderfully scenic and relaxing chug, taking 35 minutes and costing $A3.30 for adults, $A1.60 for children.

Manly Wharf, where the ferries dock, is a mix of amusement park, shopping complex, and restaurant row. The Corso leads from there to the ocean beaches—a long and lively promenade of cafes, eateries, pubs, clubs, and typical seaside stores.

⭐ **Oceanworld,** West Esplanade, Manly. ☎ **949-2644.**

This is a unique structure, quite unlike the usual brand of marine zoo. You glide along on a moving footway inside a tunnel that runs *underneath* the immense 3.9 million-liter tank. Most people have never seen the underbellies of sharks and rays, and the sight is quite awesome. Special display windows reveal the submarine life of reef dwellers, like octopuses, poisonous stonefish, and rock eels. On top of the tank is an aquatic theater for performing seals, which you can follow above and below the surface. But the most fascinating sight is the daily feeding session, when flippered divers go below and hand-feed the sharks—the triple rows of serrated teeth snapping inches away from their fingers.

Admission: $A11 adults, $A5.50 children.

Open: Daily 10am–5:30pm.

Manly Art Gallery And Museum, West Esplanade, Manly. ☎ **949-1776.**

Here you'll find a collection of local art and memorabilia, including some intriguing old photographs of Manly in the neck-to-knee era, period swimming costumes and beach gear, seascapes by local artists, and contemporary ceramics.

Admission: $A2 adults, children free.

Open: Tues–Fri 10am–4pm, Sat–Sun noon–5pm.

Royal Australian Artillery Museum, Scenic Drive, North Head. ☎ **976-1138.**

If antique cannons are your bag, head for this museum, where you'll see rows of guns used by the Australian artillery in colonial times and later plus lots of other military equipment, ancient and contemporary.

Admission: $A3 adults, $A1 children.

Open: Sat–Sun 10am–4pm.

Manly Waterworks, West Esplanade, Manly. ☎ **949-1088.**

Located in the park across from the ferry wharf, this consists of four giant waterslides that sluice you, turning, twisting and yelling, from considerable heights into a gentle pool below. It feels pleasantly nerve-tingling but is absolutely safe, and you can vary the speed of the rides. In cool weather the water is thoughtfully heated.

Admission: $A9.95 per hour or $A14.95 all day.

Open: Weekends 10am–5pm.

Manly Horse Tram

A streetcar propelled by (live) horsepower. Dating back to 1903 and the only such vehicle still running in Australia, it can be boarded for leisurely and nostalgic sightseeing jaunts. It costs $A2 for adults, $A1 for children, and operates daily 10am–5pm.

---

4   Cool for Kids

Sydney has such a multitude of attractions for kids of all ages that it's quite impossible to squeeze them all into one segment. They would have to include all the beaches, all the boat, ferry, jetcat, and wind-jammer rides, all the excursions, and most of the parks. I have there-fore confined myself to listing the select handful that might be termed irresistible.

Sydney Tower   (p.121). The high-speed elevators up may prove more thrilling than the panorama below.

Taronga Zoo   (p. 122). The whole place enthralls kids, quite apart from their first opportunity to pat a wombat.

Sydney Aquarium   (p. 123). Eye-to-eye encounters with giant stin-grays, sharks, and immense eels.

Powerhouse Museum   (p. 125). The antique silent "picture palace" and the hands-on machine exhibits get them every time.

Sydney Agrodome   (p. 130).Watching sheepdogs keeping control over a flock of woolly and obstreperous charges.

Waratah Park   (p. 134). Australian wildlife children can mingle with—except for critters like Tasmanian devils.

Australian Reptile Park   (p. 135). Some kids become totally en-grossed by the dinosaurian lizards, the huge pythons, and the deadly taipans they can watch being milked of venom.

Old Sydney Town   (p. 135). Like a costume pageant with audience participation—for some youngsters, a trip's highlight.

El Caballo Blanco   (p. 135). The white dancing horses and thrill rides are a captivating combination.

Featherdale Wildlife Park   (p. 136). Koalas in the trees, kangaroos that nibble out of your hand on the ground.

Australia's Wonderland and Wildlife Park   (p. 136). A grand-scale amusement park, geared for child appeal, in a scenic setting

5   Organized Tours

Commercial sightseeing tours seem to be one of Sydney's major industries. Organizers show you the sights by every means of locomotion, from coaches and limousines to small cars, pedicabs, and on foot. Many sightseeing companies feature tours that include trips through the rest of New South Wales and other Australian states. In fact, you can see most of Australia with them. Get their brochures for complete listings and prices.

Sydney after Dark (☎ 252-2988), one of several nocturnal swings around the bright lights, is conducted in a scarlet double-decker bus (try to get a seat on the upper deck), narrated by a charming hostess. The tour includes a three-course dinner at the Sydney Tower Restaurant, a visit to Chinatown, a nightclub show, and a (somewhat cursory) glimpse of the night activity in Kings Cross. Courtesy pickup at your hotel. The tours—for adults only—operate Wednesday through Saturday nights, starting at 7pm, and cost either $A95 or $A79, depending on the night. You can make reservations through the Travel Centre of New South Wales or by calling directly.

AAT King's, Shop W1, 6 Circular Quay, (☎ 252-2788), has a variety of full- and half-day tours covering all of Sydney and the surrounding country. Of the half-day jaunts you can choose between morning and afternoon tours, all departing from the Day Tour Terminal at Circular Quay. One morning circuit takes in some of the famous surf beaches on the North Shore, the lookout on Sydney Harbour Bridge, Manly, and the historic Rocks area. The tour departs daily at 9:15am and costs $A32 for adults, $A28 for children.

Great Sights, Shop 2, Circular Quay West (☎ 241-2294), offers the "Grand Circle Tour," a full-day excursion. The trip takes in the Opera House, Manly, Bondi, Waratah Wildlife Park, and includes a luncheon cruise on the harbor with buffet service. The tour departs daily from Circular Quay at 9am, costing $A74 for adults, $A59 for children.

For a taste of two-wheeled adventure you can try one of the trips run by **Eastcoast Motorcycle Tours,** P.O. Box 152, Sutherland 2232 (☎ 521-4519). The machines used are classic Harley-Davidsons, the driver-guides are expert bikers with top safety records, and the runs range from two hours to full days. Helmets, jackets, and gloves are provided. One sample, the "City to Surf Tour," lasts two hours and takes in the Harbour Tunnel and Bridge, Kings Cross, The Gap, Bondi, Darling Harbour, and The Rocks. The cost is $A100 per pillion (saddle) passenger.

A change of pace is offered by the bicycle rambles organized by **Worlds Beyond,** P.O. Box 35, Balmain, 2041 (☎ **555-9653**). Bikes (muscle-powered) are supplied by the organizers, along with helmets and experienced group leaders. The jaunts run every Saturday from 8:30am to 5pm and cover around 18 miles. A gourmet lunch, morning and afternoon tea, and a ferry trip are included in the $A75 fee.

Sydney Guided Walking Tours, 15 Wigram Rd., Glebe 2037 (☎ **660-5113**), arrange possibly the most leisurely and informal of all sightseeing ventures. Their walking tour starts at the Hyde Park Barracks at 9:30am Tuesday through Saturday and ends at the Queen Victoria Building around 5:15pm. You see the State Parliament, Art Gallery, Botanical Gardens, Opera House, and other sights, take in a ferry and a jetcat ride, and imbibe local lore from a highly knowledgeable guide. Although far from strenuous, the tour does involve quite a bit of walking. Tickets include all admissions and fares and cost $A39 adults, $A26.50 children.

Dal Myles (☎ **875-3867**), is a producer of documentary films who also specializes in wildlife and bush tours. He runs eight full- or half-day ventures into the Blue Mountains or to various nature parks. One of them is a half-day excursion to a bush camp where you drink "billy tea," watch sheep being shorn, and see a boomerang-throwing demonstration. Available four days a week, the tour costs $A44 for adults, $A31 for children.

Boat Tours

CRUISES

The most economical cruises are offered by the Urban Transit Authority, which operates the harbor ferries. Their **Tourist Ferry** from no. 4 wharf, Circular Quay (☎ **247-5151**), takes you on a cruise covering five harbor islands (including Fort Denison) for $A15 per adult passenger, $A10 per child. A detailed commentary explains the sights, and refreshments are available on board. The Tourist Ferries run seven days a week, four times a day.

Captain Cook Cruises (☎ **02/247-5151;** no. 2 wharf, Circular Quay), are more elaborate. Apart from harbor tours, this company has "Coffee Cruises" (10am and 2:15pm), lasting 2¹/₂ hours, in which you take your coffee break on board a sleek white luxury cruiser and head deep into the upper reaches of the Middle Harbour. Coffee cruises sail twice a day and cost $A26 for adults, $A16 for children. The Luncheon Cruise (12:30pm) includes an excellent buffet lunch (oysters and all), lasts 1¹/₂ hours, and costs $A38, children $A29.

The **Sydney Harbour Explorer** is the water equivalent of the Explorer bus. You buy a two-hour cruise ticket, disembark at any attraction you like, then catch the next Explorer to go on. The cruises operate four times daily, and the stopping points are The Rocks, the Opera House, Watson's Bay, Taronga Zoo, and Darling Harbour. Adults pay $A16, children $A10.

If you prefer to cruise under sail, there's Matilda Cruises' *Solway Lass,* Aquarium Wharf, Pier 26, Darling Harbour (☎ **264-7377**).

A 125-foot topsail schooner, this black-hulled beauty has ten working sails, a dining saloon upholstered in leather, and a formidable wine cellar—excuse me, hold. Each canvas cruise features an appropriate repast. The daily "Luncheon Sail" of 1¹/₂ hours includes a buffet lunch and costs $A40 for adults, $A28 for children. The "Afternoon Sail" serves tea or coffee, lasts 2 hours, and costs $A22 for adults, $A15 for children. Every Friday and Saturday you can "Dine Under Canvas" and take 3 hours to do it. This is a deluxe event departing at 7pm and including a splendid carvery dinner prepared by international-standard chefs. Adults only, and the tab is $A50.

You can also get the choice of sailing either on an old windjammer or a modern catamaran. (The cats are sleeker, the jammers more romantic.) On either vessel you go on a midday lunch cruise for $A38 or a dinner cruise for $A55, taking 3¹/₂ hours. Both ventures pick up and disembark at the Man O' War steps (Opera House) and operate seven days a week.

For folks with a historical bent, the choice would be HMS *Bounty,* or at least the replica of the famous ship, which starred in the 1960s film *Mutiny on the Bounty.* Built as an exact copy of the 18th-century two-master, it is a beautiful vessel of 363 tons, unfurling 8,000 square feet of canvas, equipped with a dining salon and bar, and holding 49 passengers and a crew of 20. The modern *Bounty* sails twice daily, and the passage rates include lunch or a lavish buffet meal with wine. Adults pay $A25 or $A45, children half price. Book your berth by writing The Bounty, GPO Box 4480, Sydney, NSW 2001, or by calling **247-5151**.

Olympic Preview. Visitors can catch an advance view of the Sydney 2000 Olympic site at Homebush Bay. This will be the scene of most of the games as well as the site of the Olympic Village, which will accommodate all the competing athletes in one central area. Guided tours lead you over the Athletic and Aquatic Centres, Bicentennial Park, and the sites of the Olympic Stadium and Village and the facilities for archery, tennis, and baseball. The tours go Monday through Friday, starting from the north side of Strathfield Train Station. They cost $A5 for adults, $A2.50 for children, and advance reservations are recommended. Book by calling **735-4800.**

Air Adventures

There are several options for seeing Sydney from the bird's-eye view: executive plane, seaplane, helicopter, biplane, or hot-air balloon.

The most popular is the **Sydney Scenic Flight** (☎ **247-5151**). This is a 2-hour helicopter jaunt that hovers over the harbor and skims over the city's environs. The bird's-eye panorama unfolding below is unforgettable, taking in the Harbour Bridge, Opera House, the beaches, and colorful sailing boats on the blue Pacific. The choppers carry four to six passengers, and the flights cost $A135 for adults, $A95 for children.

Balloon Aloft (☎ **607-2255**) has a fleet of hot-air balloons based in the Camden Valley, outside Sydney. Piloted by skilled balloonists, these silent pear-shaped bulbs waft over the rolling hills with the breeze, enabling passengers to take some memorable pictures of the landscape below. Special midweek flights for visitors to Sydney include transportation to Camden from your hotel early in the morning and back in the evening. Also includes a champagne brunch after the flight. The cost is around $A170.

Red Baron Flights (☎ 709-5943) is the most unusual of all. You're not exactly in a World War I Fokker triplane, but a fair facsimile—a bright-red Tiger Moth of one world war later. You get a leather helmet and goggles before climbing into the open passenger cockpit. Only the twin machine guns are missing. You can choose the kind of flight you want—a "patrol" over Sydney or a more daring hop involving some mild acrobatics, for which this prop trainer is ideally suited. It's not for delicate stomachs, though. Flights cost around $A160 for one hour and operate seven days a week.

6   Sports & Recreation

Sport in Australia is not so much a passion as an obsession. Those who can't play, watch. Those who can't watch, listen. And all of them argue about it.

Spectator Sports

CRICKET   The rules of cricket present as much mystery to the uninitiated as does, say, baseball. Cricket has certain similarities with baseball, but is a much more leisurely game; players wear formal whites and decisions come—well, any hour. The mystery of the sport is the incredible devotion it inspires in those brought up with it. This embraces the entire fifth of the globe that was once the British Empire. Cricket is the eternal heritage Britain left to people who have long severed all other ties. Cricket's crowning glory, the "Ashes," are taken even more seriously than Americans take the World Series. The closest Australia ever came to leaving the Commonwealth was during the historic "bodyline" cricket bowling row of the 1930s. (Bodyline was the nefarious trick of aiming balls at the batsman instead of the wicket, thus knocking over the players instead of the stumps.)

The cricket season runs from October to March. For information about the games, call the **New South Wales Cricket Association** (☎ 27-4053).

FOOTBALL   Football is a winter game, played from April to August or thereabouts, and frequently on the same fields devoted to cricket in summer. "Footy," as it's called, comes in three main varieties: rugby league, rugby union, and soccer. League and union are fairly similar, but soccer differs sharply insofar as the players don't carry the ball but use only their feet and heads to propel the leather. All three draw immense crowds of partisan fans (known as "barrackers"), wearing club scarves, munching hot meat pies, and yelling their lungs out. While crowd demeanor isn't quite as homicidal as in European matches, it can be bad enough to necessitate large contingents of police and first-aid staff.

Sydney's newest and costliest sporting arena is the $A60 million **Football Stadium,** located next to the Sydney Cricket Ground in Moore Park. Apart from league, union, and soccer matches, the stadium, which comfortably seats 40,000 people, also presents rock concerts and kindred crowd feasts. Take the Clovelly, Coogee, Maroubra, or La Perouse bus from Circular Quay or Central Railway.

HORSE RACING   Sydney has four racecourses, open year-round: **Randwick** (☎ **663-8400**), **Rosehill** (☎ **637-2123**), **Canterbury** (☎ **799-8000**), and **Warwick Farm** (☎ **602-6199**). Admission to any of them costs $A6 or $A8. The premier course is on Allison Road, Randwick, which also happens to be the handiest—only three miles from downtown and easily reached by special bus services going from Circular Quay and Central Railway. Randwick is a pretty plush affair, carries the prefix "Royal," and is the home of the venerable Australian Jockey Club. The Queen Elizabeth Stand has a panoramic vista room and offers a choice of smörgåsbord or formal dining.

Recreation

ABSEILING   This, in case your Swiss isn't up to par, means rock climbing while being roped together for safety and mutual moral support. Definitely a pastime for the fit, and one that Sydneysiders have taken to in remarkable numbers. The best places for the sport are in the Blue Mountains (see Chapter 10) where an outfit called **Abseil Experience** offers lessons for beginners that start with a few feet and advance to ten stories in one day. All equipment supplied, along with experienced instructors, but you can bring your own stomachful of butterflies. The experience costs $A60 a day; pickup and return to Sydney is an extra $A15. If you prefer to go by train, the return trip from Central Station to Katoomba is $A10.60. Call **439-5581** for bookings and information.

BEACHES   There are 34 glorious ocean beaches within Sydney's city limits. No other place on earth can boast anything like that number. They form golden dashes along an undulating path stretching from Port Hacking, 30 miles south of Sydney, to Palm Beach, 20 miles north. The average annual water temperature is 68° Fahrenheit, the sand is as fine as powder, and the surf ranges from fair to spectacular. All the beaches are shark-netted and regularly patrolled (there hasn't been a shark attack since netting started some 30 years ago). The beaches are Sydney's most popular summer form of mass entertainment, but there are so many and they're so large that all you have to do is venture a bit farther out to find some relatively uncrowded ones.

Sydneysiders worship their beaches—surfing, swimming, or just roasting their skins for entire weekends. With the exception of certain Pacific Islanders, probably no one spends so much time just lying on sand with their eyes closed. The only difference the skin-cancer scare has made to this habit is that they now spray themselves with protective lotion beforehand.

The most popular beaches are the closest: **Bondi, Coogee, Maroubra, Bronte,** and **Cronulla,** all easily reached by public transport from downtown. **Manly** follows close behind, although it involves a ferry ride (see "Parramatta and Manly," above). **Whale Beach, Avalon,** and **Bilgoia** are somewhat less crowded because they lie farther out. To survey the northern shore beaches, you can catch bus 190 behind Wynyard Station to **Palm Beach,** which skirts approximately 26 miles of shoreline.

Note: All of Sydney's beaches are topless by custom and general consent.

The Lifesavers   If Australia has produced a folk-hero image equivalent to the American cowboy's, it is those bronzed young men in swimsuits who look as if they had leaped from the Olympics onto the beaches. They are members of the **Surf Lifesaving Association,** the most prestigious bunch of volunteers in the country. Oz people consider it downright decadent to hire paid lifeguards, as most other countries do. Here the task of safeguarding the beaches is performed by the 60,000 volunteer lifesavers who not only rescue swimmers in distress but perform duties left to the police elsewhere. The lifesavers are the main reason why Australia gets so little of the beach violence and vandalism that troubles America. The lifesavers are *big* guys and they settle outbursts of hooliganism very quickly.

BOATING   "Messing around in boats" ranks as one of the favorite occupations of the locals. For the best boat-rental services (as distinct from cruises) you should go to the region of **Ku-ring-gai Chase National Park,** a 40-minute bus ride or drive from downtown. The national park is a peninsula between the estuaries of the Hawkesbury River and Pittwater, dotted all around with tranquil coves, beaches, lagoons, and waterfalls. The water here is still and deep blue, sheltered from gales, and alive with fish. The hundreds of square miles of waterway constitute an inland sea, protected on all sides by the steep forested hills of the Ku-ring-gai. It's considered one of the finest boating areas in the world, made more so by the vicinity of some excellent shoreline restaurants. The craft for hire here range from simple little aluminum boats to deluxe cabin cruisers, with corresponding price ranges. You don't need a boat license for any of them, though with the larger ones you get a short briefing lesson before hoisting anchor.

The most luxurious outfit is **Skipper a Clipper,** Coal and Candle Creek, Akuna Bay (☎ **450-1888**). You get a choice of three types of cruisers, all capable of carrying eight to ten people in various degrees of comfort. All come with fully equipped galleys (kitchens, to you landlubbers), refrigerators, electric anchor winches, ship-to-shore radios, fresh linen and towels, life jackets, and first-aid kits. Also unlimited diesel fuel, a dinghy, fresh water, gas stoves, and bags of crushed ice. Rates depend on what you rent, when you rent, and for how long—between $A40 and $A110 per person per day. A refundable deposit of $A100 is required before you depart.

Halvorsen Boats, P.O. Box 21, Turramurra (☎ 457-9011), has motor cruisers on the Hawkesbury River capable of accommodating eight people. The ideal number is four, and a weekend of cruising for such a group would cost around $A500 (prices depend on the time of year).

For something smaller, simpler, and intended mainly for fishing, try **Bait 'n' Boats,** 83 Brooklyn Rd., Brooklyn (☎ 455-1206). This company has handy little aluminum craft, light yet sturdy, that rent for around $A48 a day. These boats are open and you'd be well advised to pay a bit extra for a protective canopy.

For a wonderfully lazy and relaxing day on the Hawkesbury, you can also rent a mobile houseboat—as distinct from the permanently moored breed. **Fenwick's River Houseboats,** P.O. Box 55, Brooklyn (☎ 455-1633), has these floating homes suitable for up to six people. They cruise slowly, are child's play to handle, and make ideal tanning, fishing, and just plain loafing bases. Prices on request.

BOOMERANG THROWING   This is definitely not a national sport. In fact, few Aussies have ever handled a boomerang. But Duncan MacLennan, the man who runs the **Boomerang School,** 138 William St., Kings Cross (☎ 357-1142), gives free lessons in the art to anyone who buys a boomerang from him. They proceed every Sunday morning from 10am to noon at Yarranabbe Park, since no such place as a public boomerang range exists as yet. Apart from being an expert thrower (it's all in the wrist), MacLennan is a drawling encyclopedia on the subject of these throwing sticks.

CYCLING   Australians call bicycles "push bikes" to distinguish them from motorbikes. Sydney is fairly well equipped with bicycling paths, mostly around park areas, though not as well as other Australian cities. I'd suggest you stick to these paths for your pedal-pushing. Biking among downtown traffic—on the left—can be rather hazardous (Sydney's motorists are not known for their consideration toward the pedalers). One of the prime central cycling regions is Centennial Park (which was opened to celebrate the country's first centenary in 1888), along Oxford Street, Paddington. You can rent the metal steeds from **Centennial Park Cycles,** 50 Clovelly Rd., Randwick (☎ 398-5027). They rent half a dozen types of bikes, including tandems, at rates starting at $A6 per hour.

GOLF   Although Sydney is well supplied with public golf courses, the game is not as popular as in the United States. The top Sydney golfing event is the New South Wales Open. You can contact the **NSW Golf Association** (☎ 264-8433) for details.

Public golf courses charge between $A8 and $A14 for 18 holes. Some of the closest are **Moore Park Golf Course,** Anzac Parade, Moore Park (☎ 633-3960), and **Bondi Golf Links,** Military Road, North Bondi (☎ 30-1981).

Golfers Overseas Australia (☎ **440-8449**) arranges golf tours tailored for visiting American and Japanese business executives. Run by former Qantas airline captain David Skinner, a top-grade golfer, this venture has acquired a big reputation in Japan. Skinner not only arranges the tours, but also helps players on the links.

GRASS SKIING   Probably the most unexpected sport you'll find in Sydney—and it goes right through summer—is grass skiing. It is like the snow version, except that the skis are short, the surface nonslippery, and the weather usually hot. The **Kurrajong Heights Grass Ski Park** operates an uphill tow, rents out all equipment, runs a ski school, and organizes prize contests like egg-and-spoon races on skis. Located at the top of Kurrajong Mountain (with a beautiful view of the Hawkesbury Valley) the park is open Saturday and Sunday 9am to 5pm. The fee for equipment, uphill tow, and ski lessons is $A11 for 2 hours, $A17 per full day. Call **045/677-184** for bookings. You get there by taking the train to Richmond, then the bus to Kurrajong Heights.

HORSEBACK RIDING   You can rent horses for around $A15 an hour from **Centennial Park Horse Hire**; RAS Showground, Driver Avenue, Moore Park (☎ **332-2770**).

PAINTBALL   The latest arrival on the Sydney sports scene: a combat game in which nobody gets hurt and teams can number anywhere from 5 to 50. Paintball is a high-tech—well, middling-tech—version of cops and robbers in which the teams snuff each other with harmless paint bullets fired from special CO_2-powered pistols that look rather like the ray guns wielded in the old sci-fi serials. Games are played on different terrains, last 15 minutes, and are supervised by "battle referees." Players wear goggles and jungle greens, making it quite impossible to tell who's male or female. You pay $A18 for 12 games. Paintballs are extra, so the cost of the game depends partly on how trigger-happy you get. The games are organized by **Adventure Quest** (☎ **867-4000**) and start at 7:30am daily. Bookings are essential.

PARAFLYING   As safe as it is thrilling, this sport entails being towed by a speedboat while harnessed to a parachute. The procedure looks quite daredevilish, but you could actually do it garbed in a business suit. Neither the suit nor your feet will get wet. The chute—already open—gently wafts you aloft as the paracruiser picks up speed. The cable attached to your harness can let you fly to a height of 300 feet and winch you down anytime. **Sydney Harbour Paraflying** (☎ **018/405-454**) runs breakfast, lunchtime, and twilight flights from Manly wharf, costing $A39 per flyer. This is a "weather permitting" sport, so check on conditions on the morning of your booking.

SAILING   In Australia, sailing can hardly be described as a spectator sport—not with an estimated 200,000 canvas craft out on the water on any given weekend. The real yachting set, of course, has its clubs—the **Royal Sydney Yacht Squadron** at Kirribilli and the **Cruising Yacht Club** at Rushcutters Bay—surrounded by a halo of exclusivity. But one sailing event is a true spectacle: the Sydney–Hobart Yacht Race, which takes place on December 26th every year. This is the grandest marine shindig of the season. The sight of this yachting armada streaming out through The Heads en route to Tasmania is a sight you'll never forget. If you can't be out on a boat to witness the start, pack a picnic and find a position at Lady Macquarie's Chair in the Botanic Gardens—it's the next best vantage point.

The big yachts may dominate the open sea, but Sydney Harbour belongs to the 18-footers, perhaps the most exciting sailing boats in the world. For sheer speed and exhilaration they are rivaled only by the ice yachts of North America. The sailing season runs from September through March, and during that period 18-footer races are held every Sunday. The competitors are semiprofessionals and the races fought out like miniature Americas Cups. Spectator ferries follow the boats from Commissioners Steps, Circular Quay, departing at 1:45pm. Passengers pay $A10. You're not supposed to bet on these events, but just about everybody does. For information call **363-2995.**

If you want to do a bit of sailing yourself, you can rent dinghies at the **Balmoral Sailing Club,** The Esplanade, Balmoral Beach (☎ **969-8782**).

For a more luxurious canvas cruise, try **Aristocrat Charters,** Akuna Bay (☎ **018/22-4310**). This is a white, elaborately equipped 60-foot catamaran sailing the beautiful Pittwater region, serving buffet lunches (included in the price) and drinks from a well-stocked bar on board. The *Aristocrat* sails from Newport Inn wharf at 11am every Tuesday, Thursday, Saturday, and Sunday. They send a courtesy minibus to pick up passengers at the Manly ferry terminal and return them at around 4pm (depending on wind conditions). Prices start at $A40 per cruise and advance reservations are essential.

More catamarans, *The Edge* and *The Edge Too,* sail morning, afternoon, and evening from Catamaran Cove, The Rocks, Monday to Saturday. These small craft hold around 20 people each and tack around Sydney harbor for 3 hours. You bring your own snacks, but sailing instructions come gratis with the hire. Bookings are essential. Call **018/278-511.** The cruises cost $A20.

TENNIS   Tennis is the game that has earned the Aussies their international sporting fame and the one you see them practice most often, from dawn till long after dusk. (Sydney is dotted with lighted tennis courts.) Boys and girls start playing tennis in school and stay more or less wedded to their rackets thereafter. All of which makes renting court space easy, but winning a game rather more difficult. The major tournaments are held at White City in Rushcutters Bay, and at the Entertainment Centre, Darling Harbour. These top-money events are usually scheduled between October and February and attract top-class tennis stars, male and female.

Court rentals cost somewhere between $A7 and $A17 an hour, depending on where and when you want to play. While you can always get a public court, renting tennis gear may prove elusive. Not all the courts have rackets for rent at all times, so it's best to inquire beforehand.

Some of the handy suburban courts are the following: **Trumper Park,** Quarry Street, Paddington (☎ **32-4055**); **Tennis Factory,** Prince Alfred Park, Chalmers Street, Surry Hills (☎ **698-9451**); **Moore Park Tennis Centre,** Anzac Parade, Paddington (☎ **662-7005**); and **Lyne Park Tennis Centre,** New South Head Road, Rose Bay (☎ **371-6048**).

TENPIN BOWLING   An indoor sport that never made it really big in Sydney, despite some determined media campaigns to popularize it. The closest center is the **Rushcutter Bowl,** 110 Bayswater Rd., Rushcutters Bay, which is one train stop after Kings Cross (☎ **361-0558**). The cost per game is around $A5.

WINDSURFING   Throughout Australia "wind wankers" and "surfies" are locked in a fierce debate as to which of their respective passions is the "purer"—meaning at one with nature. The debate is unlikely to be won by either side, since both use artificial equipment and motor vehicles to haul it about. In practice, however, the windsurfers have a distinct advantage, since their sport doesn't require an ocean. You can windsurf just as well on a lake, a river or a pond.

You can rent Windsurfers at the same places you learn to ride them. Hiring fees range from $A14 to $A26 an hour. The outfits listed are open all week during summer: **Rose Bay Hire,** 1 Vickery Ave., Rose Bay (☎ **371-7036**), and **Balmoral Sailboard Centre,** 2 The Esplanade, Balmoral Beach (☎ **960-1111**).

7

Strolling Around Sydney

Walking tours are among the very best ways of seeing Sydney. You can set your own pace, pick your own points of interest, stray in any direction you fancy, and linger wherever you feel like lingering. All they require is a sturdy pair of shoes and feet that match them. Parts of Sydney are ideal for strolling but in between lie fairly steep hills, overcrowded streets, and vast patches of nondescript commercial cityscapes. **Note:** Additional information on some attractions in the tours below can be found in Chapter 6.

Walking Tour 1
Downtown

Start   Martin Place.
End   Mint Museum.
Duration   About 2 hours.
Best Time   Weekend afternoons.
Worst Time   Weekday rush hours.

Start in Martin Place, which is the center of downtown Sydney as well as a pedestrian mall. You can pick up an excellent map at the:

1. **NSW Travel Centre.** The most striking feature of the flower-filled mall is:
2. **The Cenotaph,** a memorial to Australia's fallen servicemen and women. Every Thursday at 12:30pm the army stages a ceremony at the Cenotaph, then marches to the Anzac Memorial in nearby Hyde Park. At the corner of George Street stands the huge:
3. **General Post Office,** built in a kind of ersatz Venetian Renaissance style, but with inviting cool colonnades. Turn right on George Street and walk two blocks to:
4. **Australia Square.** Part of the Sydney skyline since 1967, the 50-floor (three below ground) Australia Square Tower is a circular cement, aluminum, and glass structure presently noted as the third-tallest building in the southern hemisphere. Take the fastest elevators in the southern hemisphere to the **Summit,** the largest revolving restaurant in the world, where prices are yet another Australia Square superlative.

   Level 4, the Shopping Circle, is a colorful arcade of stores and services. Note the tapestries in the main entrance, which were woven at Aubusson in France from designs by Le Corbusier and Vasarely. A massive Calder sculpture squats on the George Street plaza. (Modesty forbids me to print what the locals call it.) Continue on George Street, where you next come to:
5. **Regent Hotel.** A fluted 36-story tower (actually 35, because there is no 13th floor) behind a sloping beige stone front, the Regent is possibly Sydney's poshest hotel. It certainly is the most filmed. An immense amount of movie

footage has been expended on its foyer constructed of polished marble, with a central atrium warmed by diffused sunshine filtering through the skylight above. You could take afternoon tea in this photogenic oasis, but I'd advise you to choose a somewhat more economical refreshment break farther on. Turn right and walk into:

6. **Circular Quay.** Today the busy site of the ferry wharves and Overseas Passenger Shipping Terminal, this horseshoe-shaped quay embraces Sydney Cove, "the cradle of Australian history." It was here that Capt. Arthur Phillip put in 1788 with his flock of 1,500 to begin building a colony. It was he who honored the cove—and by extension the city—with its name, after Viscount Sydney. Sydney's past, present, and future converge on this quay. Stand facing the harbor. To your right, jutting into the froth-tipped waves, is Australia's fabulous futuristic Sydney Opera House. To your left arches **Sydney Harbour Bridge,** linking the business district to the northern suburbs. Too massive and fussy for beauty, the bridge has been dubbed the "Coathanger" by realistic Sydneysiders, who are nevertheless prompt to point out to foreign detractors that, while not the longest single span in the world, falling two feet short of the Golden Gate Bridge, it's the heaviest! A full 52,800 tons of steel went into its $2^3/_4$-mile length. The Harbour Bridge grows on you quickly. You become as affectionate toward that graceless structure as toward a floppy mutt with overgrown feet and a willing nature.

   On Circular Quay, pass the ferry wharves and food stands on your left and continue around the quay to Bennelong Point, where perches the gloriously controversial:

7. **Sydney Opera House,** which actor Robert Morley described as "looking like something that has crawled out of the sea and is up to no good." Cross the Forecourt and the lawns beyond and you'll pass the sandstone keep and turrets of:

8. **Government House,** residence of the governor of New South Wales. No, you can't drop in unless you're a visiting dignitary, and even then by invitation only. Continue on and you come to the:

9. **Conservatorium of Music,** which, for reasons unknown, was built to resemble a Tudor castle. To your left stretches the lush greenery of the:

10. **Royal Botanic Garden,** with rolled lawns, labeled shrubs, a pyramid glasshouse filled with orchids and ferns, and a restaurant kiosk. Turn right on Art Gallery Road, and you come to the:

11. **Art Gallery of New South Wales.** There's a restaurant on the second floor, serving afternoon tea and light meals,

Walking Tour—Downtown

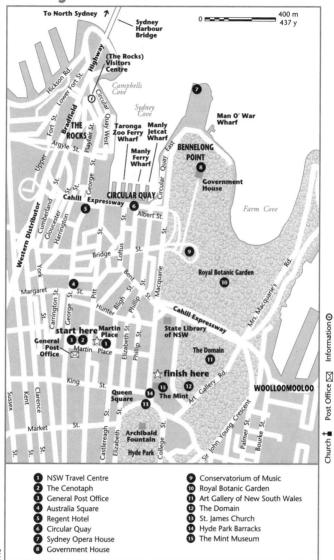

To North Sydney ↑

Sydney Harbour Bridge

(The Rocks) Visitors Centre

Campbells Cove

Sydney Cove

Man O' War Wharf

THE ROCKS

Taronga Zoo Ferry Wharf

Manly Jetcat Wharf

Manly Ferry Wharf

BENNELONG POINT

Government House

Farm Cove

CIRCULAR QUAY

Cahill Expressway

Royal Botanic Garden

Cahill Expressway

State Library of NSW

The Domain

start here

General Post Office

Martin Place

finish here

WOOLLOOMOOLOO

Queen Square

The Mint

Archibald Fountain

Hyde Park

① NSW Travel Centre
② The Cenotaph
③ General Post Office
④ Australia Square
⑤ Regent Hotel
⑥ Circular Quay
⑦ Sydney Opera House
⑧ Government House

⑨ Conservatorium of Music
⑩ Royal Botanic Garden
⑪ Art Gallery of New South Wales
⑫ The Domain
⑬ St. James Church
⑭ Hyde Park Barracks
⑮ The Mint Museum

Church ✝ Post Office ⊠ Information ℹ

which makes an inexpensive **refueling stop.** Otherwise wander south across:

12. **The Domain.** During the week this is just a vast and pleasant expanse of lawn and trees, but on Sunday it becomes populated with self-described saviors—political and religious—proclaiming their creeds from the rungs of stepladders to mildly amused audiences. Listen and remain uninformed.

Art Gallery Road becomes Prince Albert, facing Queen's Square. You are now in the architecturally most impressive part of Sydney, with handsome Georgian-colonial structures all around you. To your left on the square rises the graceful copper-sheathed spire of:

13. **St. James Church,** elegantly designed by the convict-architect Francis Greenway, completed in 1819. On your right are the Law Courts, another Greenway design, and one that so delighted Governor Macquarie that he granted the convicted forger a full pardon. Now straight ahead into Macquarie Street where, on the right, stand the:

14. **Hyde Park Barracks.** Yes, you guessed it, likewise by Greenway, but intended as a dormitory for male con-victs. It was actually used to house the New South Wales Regiment. Today parts of the building are a museum, each room devoted to a different aspect of social life from the colonial period to the 1950s. Also on the premises is an excellent **refueling stop,** the Hyde Park Barracks Café (see Chapter 5), located in what used to be the officers mess, overlooking the parade ground. You can get a set menu as well as sandwich snacks here, and drink tea or something stronger; the place is licensed.

Duly refreshed, step out on Macquarie Street and walk the few steps to the:

15. **Mint Museum.** This was originally a wing of the Rum Hospital, but today harbors a permanent collection of decorative arts, coins, flags, and stamps.

You now have a choice, probably depending on the state of your puppies, of either walking the length of Macquarie Street to the State Parliament or turning left into Martin Place; back where you started from.

Walking Tour 2
The Rocks

Start   Visitors Centre.
End   Sailors Home.
Duration   About 2 hours.

Before you start, picture the land in The Rocks district as it was in 1788, when Captain Phillip ordered his motley cargo to pitch tents and hoist the Union Jack. Here it all began, with 736 bedraggled human beings and a few rows of wooden huts and leaking tents. The immense sprawl that is contemporary Sydney, over the hills behind you, along the coves in every direction as far as the eye can see, grew from this minute patch.

The rocks today are part of a large-scale development scheme that has altered the face of Sydney while lovingly preserving its pictur-esque wrinkles. For a long time this area was the roughest, toughest scene in the southern hemisphere; a place for cheap liquor and women, notorious taverns, and nightly knifeplay, where the infamous "Sydney Ducks" reigned supreme and the garrison soldiers collected a few lifeless bodies every morning.

The old buildings have been restored, but the thug element has vanished. Today The Rocks include one of Sydney's smartest hotels, the Old Sydney Parkroyal, trendy cafes, arts and crafts studios—and a steady stream of tourists. Enjoy your walk through history.

Although I mention a particular refreshment place on your walk, The Rocks is so honeycombed with cafes, bars, restaurants, tearooms, and snackshops—indoors and out—that you could refresh yourself every 50 yards or so.

Start at the:

1. **Visitors Centre,** at 104 George St. (☎ **247-4972**), where you can find maps, books, pamphlets, and brochures pertaining to Old Sydney, and watch a free audiovisual show on the history of the area.

   Turn right from the center and walk to Circular Quay West, where you'll see:

2. **Campbells Storehouse,** dating from 1839 and today crammed with restaurants instead of cargo goods. From there you can catch one of the most spectacular harbor views Sydney has to offer.

   Turn left and come to the:

3. **Earth Exchange,** at 18 Hickson Rd. (☎ **251-2422**), a museum about the ground we live on and its development across a billion years. Exhibits include gold, gems, minerals and opals, a simulated earthquake, and an impressive volcano eruption, complete with flowing lava and sulfur aroma.

   Turn right, take the climb up through the Metcalfe Stores, then left on George Street. In a small side street you'll find the:

4. **Westpac Banking Museum** at 6 Playfair St. Westpac was once known as Bank of New South Wales, the oldest such establishment on the continent, founded in 1817. The money exhibited includes the doughnutlike "holey dollars" of 1812, and other features depict the bank's running fight against bushrangers, the gold rush era, and a re-created (and fully working) bank branch of the 1890s.

   Return to George Street and bear left. You'll pass a row of small terrace houses known as Sergeant Majors Row—which was the original name of the entire street before King George got into it. Pass the Mercantile Hotel, a hallowed Irish pub, and turn right to walk under the mighty Sydney Harbour Bridge.

   You'll come to a patch called:

5. **Dawes Point Park.** This was the first fortified position in Australia, and the guns are still standing there, waiting for

a French fleet or czarist Russian raider that never came. Today they are used chiefly as climbing trees by the local kids; quite a useful occupation for cannon.

Back under the bridge, turn left, march past Foundation Park, and down to the:

6. **Argyle Cut,** one of the early colony's major engineering feats, a 300-foot tunnel hollowed out of the solid stone to give direct access to Millers Point from Circular Quay. It was begun with convict labor in 1843, and you can still see the prisoners' marks on the granite. This used to be the riskiest spot in perhaps the toughest area of the southern hemisphere. For in its mid-history the Rocks was the gathering ground for a truly choice mob of convicts, soldiers, sailors, whalers, sealers, thugs, and prostitutes, and produced its personal species of gangsters—the larrikins. A bit later San Francisco's Barbary Coast played host to some of these same gents and ladies, with the transplanted "Sydney Ducks" acquiring the reputation of being the most vicious mob in California.

Cross Cumberland Street into Gloucester Street:

7. **Susannah Place,** at no. 58, is a colonial working class terrace that has been preserved as a kind of museum house, possibly to give an idea of just how uncomfortably blue collar city dwellers once dwelled.

Cross into Harrington Street, where just by the Harbour Rocks Hotel there is a little alley called Suez Canal. This was once the riskiest passage in Sydney Town—after dark a sure invitation to a knock on the head and an emptied pocket. Walk through and turn right into:

8. **Nurses Walk.** This stretch is dedicated to Australia's first working nurses—all deported female convicts without a nursing certificate among them.

Take the next alley into George Street:

9. **The former Police Station,** at no. 127, is still proudly marked by a stone lion's head with a night stick in its jaws. Today the place is an interesting crafts gallery and workshop.

Left on George Street, then left on Argyle Street brings you to the:

10. **Argyle Centre.** Formerly a bond warehouse, the building is now a complex of galleries and shops selling art, crafts, gifts, and souvenirs, the objects ranging from delightful to deplorable.

Refueling Stop

For refreshments at Argyle Centre is **Mary Reibey's Café** on the ground floor (☎ **247-1480**). The cafe serves Devonshire tea ($A5.20) or quiches ($A8), but the original Mary prospered by selling stronger refreshments. She was transported at the age of 13 for stealing a horse (and mighty

Walking Tour—The Rocks

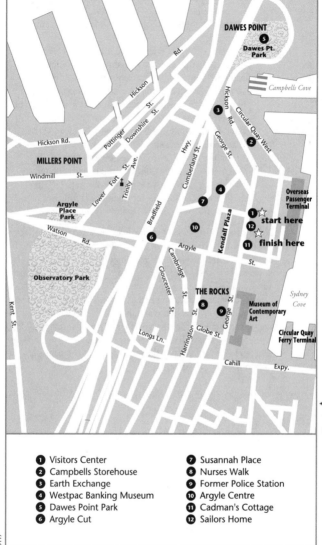

❶ Visitors Center	❼ Susannah Place
❷ Campbells Storehouse	❽ Nurses Walk
❸ Earth Exchange	❾ Former Police Station
❹ Westpac Banking Museum	❿ Argyle Centre
❺ Dawes Point Park	⓫ Cadman's Cottage
❻ Argyle Cut	⓬ Sailors Home

lucky not to be hanged for it). She died 60 years later, richer by seven children and £120,000 sterling—an immense fortune at the time, most of which she acquired by trading in the rum stored in the cellars below.

Now walk into Playfair Street, turn left, past the sculpture called *First Impressions,* down the stairs to Mill Lane and right into cobbled Kendall Lane. Then enter George Street:

11. **Cadman's Cottage** is at no. 110. Built in 1815, this is the oldest remaining dwelling in Sydney. John Cadman was a pardoned convict who became superintendent of the governor's boats; an impressive title for a former "lag." His humble abode now serves as headquarters of the Parks and Wildlife Service. Overlooking the cottage is a statue of Captain Bligh, arms folded and iron-browed, in his best "hang you from the masthead" pose.

On the same side of George Street stands the:

12. **Sailors Home,** at no. 108. This was built in 1864 to provide "clean, wholesome lodgings for seafarers," to lure them away from the temptations of brothels and rum taverns. With, sad to report, very limited success.

Note: The official Rocks Walking Tour takes 1¹/₄ hours and starts five times daily from 39 Argyle St. (☎ **247-6678**). It costs $A7 for adults, $A4.50 for children. If you don't feel like tramping up and down the hilly Rocks, you can ride in correct period style. The Horse and Carriage Company, with a rank at 101 George St. (outside the Old Police Station), operates a fleet of enclosed hansom cabs and open wagons, drawn by fine horses and piloted by nattily dressed coachmen (and women). Hansom cabs (for two persons) cost $A20 for a tour of the region, with the same charge for four in an open wagon. You can rent a carriage from the stand or call the company's reservations office (☎ **27-3181**).

8

Sydney Shopping

SYDNEY IS NOT A BARGAIN BASEMENT. PRICES FOR MEN'S AND WOMEN'S clothing are about the same as in the United States, except for beachwear,
which is slightly cheaper. Books, toys, and any kind of gadgetry are
more expensive, even if there's a favorable dollar exchange rate. You
can utilize tourist status by buying at the legion of duty-free stores
all over town and at the airport, but you can use what you buy only
after you leave the country. The most widely accepted **credit cards**
throughout Australia are American Express, MasterCard, and VISA.
If you just can't carry home your prized purchases, most shops listed
below will arrange for packing and shipping them home for you. Since
policies differ from store to store, ask about shipping before you buy.

1 The Shopping Scene

What most visitors want are not utility bargains, but distinctly Australian objects, things that symbolize the continent. And here I'd like
to sound a warning note. Sydney is inundated with stores selling
tourist souvenirs, frequently advertised in half a dozen languages.
They offer row upon row of plastic boomerangs, tin Harbour Bridges,
mulga-wood pipe stands, stuffed koalas, kangaroo-hide belts and
wallets, Opera House paperweights, rubber crocodiles, ad infinitum.
Not only are most of these fabrications pure junk, but many aren't
even made in Australia.

Genuine Australiana   You should look to certain specific goods
which, while not necessarily cheap, are excellent buys. On top of the
list go **wool products**—such as knitwear and scarves—the winners
of every quality award the world can offer. The Rolls-Royce of Aussie
knitwear (and correspondingly priced) is the Merino Gold sweater,
made from the finest wool of 17 micron thinness (finer than cash-
mere) and rather scarce, since only 200 bales of this material are
auctioned each year. The going price is roughly $A200. The Austra-
lian Wool Corporation has devised a special swing ticket that is attached to products to ensure tourists can tell the real homegrown stuff
from inferior imports. The ticket shows a sheepishly smiling lamb
against a navy background and carries explanatory texts in English,
German, and Japanese.

In the same category you can get the wonderful **sheepskin coats**
worn by outback riders in frosty weather, and sheepskin car-seat
covers; **Digger hats,** probably the most attractive military headgear
ever devised, and equally so on men and women (the upturned brim,
by the way, was for parade purposes only, enabling troops to shoulder
arms; in action Diggers wore the brim down); and **Akubra hats,** their
civilian derivations. These bush hats, worn by sartorial-minded
"bushies" of either sex, are so much part of the Oz scene that they
were featured in a recent comic strip entitled "The Life-cycle of the
Akubra." The hats, pictured as zoological species, were described
"perching happily on tree branches or hat stands, living in relative
harmony with their native cousin, the drizabone. . . . They remain

faithful to their wearer, and are often buried with them—The end of a neatly symbiotic relationship."

The **drizabone** referred to is another prized Aussie garment. Originally tailored to keep horsemen dry in tropical downpours, they have evolved into the favored rainwear for city slickers as well. They look elegant despite their length and bulk, have a dashing cape effect and actually do keep their wearers dry-as-a-bone.

For Australian **art prints** and **travel posters,** try to get hold of reproductions of works by Russell Drysdale and Sir Sidney Nolan. No one has captured the essence of the great outback and its people like these two.

Australian **folk-music records** can be remarkably good. You might even discover one with the *original* version of "Waltzing Matilda" instead of the hackneyed derivation that's been thumped to death.

ABORIGINAL ARTS & CRAFTS   These are uniquely Australian, a blending of forms and colors reflecting the immense, haunting bushland that inspired them. Their artistry conveys mood and impression rather than detail. There are an awful lot of imitations floating around, but in Section 2 I'll give you outlets that sell the genuine articles only. Following are hints of what to look for.

Bark paintings are executed on sheets of prepared bark with a feather or twig brush. A red ground color is applied first, then rubbed over with orchid juice to provide a firm surface. Only recognized artists may paint sacred subjects, like totems or rituals, but any person may render secular scenes.

Clap sticks are musical implements beaten against each other to provide rhythm backing for the ritual chanting at corroborees.

Pointing bones are rather sinister devices made of kangaroo shinbones sharpened at one end. They are used by witch doctors and elders to "point a curse" on members who have broken laws or taboos.

Woomeras are simple yet ingenious hunting and fighting implements. The woomera is attached to a spear as an extension of a man's throwing arm. Both are carefully balanced with each other and the woomera imparts additional thrust to the throw as well as a spin to the hurtling spear, making it fly farther and more accurately.

Bullroarers, used to summon men for sacred ceremonies, are made of an oval length of wood with a hole at one end to which long strings of human hair are attached. When one is swung around rapidly it produces a roaring sound that can be heard for long distances in the silent bushland, and simultaneously scares off evil spirits.

Mook mooks are small carved amulets in the shape of spirit beings that are worn around the neck as lucky charms.

You may have heard the sounds of **didgeridoos** in an Australian film or concert—an eerie melodious hum that seems to linger in the air. These musical instruments are made from small hollowed tree trunks, picked for resonance. They can be plain or richly painted, but the peculiar haunting drope they emit takes a lot of practice.

OPALS   Opals are Australia's national gemstones: The country produces over 90% of the global supply. The beauty of the stone lies in its individuality. The combination of colors and their intensity vary so greatly that no two gems are exactly alike. These hydrated silica (if you want to be scientific about them) consist of minute particles of closely packed spherical aggregates. The varying arrangements of these aggregates cause reflected light to be split into the full range of colors.

Opals range from the famous incandescent black stones to the flashing fire opals with a light-greenish base, from solid light crystal opals to rainbow-hued rocks. You get opals worth a fortune, like the 1,560-carat Empress of Glengarry (a so-called black stone that is actually azure blue), and you also get very cheap, loose rough specimens you can polish up yourself. In between these extremes you find every gradation in price and size. There are also mounted stones called doublets and triplets, which possess some of the richness of the full gems but come considerably less expensive. Furthermore, overseas visitors pay no duty or purchase tax on opals destined for export.

Most opals are found at Lightning Ridge in New South Wales and Coober Pedy in South Australia, scorched and arid regions that seem to guard their treasures by sheer harshness of environment. You can go and try a bit of fossicking there yourself, if you don't mind back-breaking toil under a scorching sun. You might even recoup your trip expenses.

World opal prices are governed by supply and demand, and Australia's major gem fields are slowly petering out. Therefore, international demand for opals will probably outstrip supply, and the stones will rise in value. If you spend at least $A500 for a small stone and hang on to it for a minimum of five years, your investment can bring good return. The kind of stone to buy for investment is a "solid" opal, which is also the most expensive. Doublets and triplets, which are artificially pieced together, look very attractive but aren't likely to increase in value.

Whatever your reason for buying, the main attribute to look for is color play—there should be no "dead" or colorless spots on a stone. So-called black opals usually are more valuable than lighter ones, and the rarest show clear red or violet-purple hues. A really fine opal with a dark body, high transparency, and maximum color brilliance, including a large proportion of red, would sell at over $A1,000 per carat.

MAJOR SHOPPING AREAS   The main attractions of a Sydney shopping spree are the locations and nature of the retailers. Few cities in the world offer such charming and unorthodox shopping environments. There are, of course, thousands of ordinary and mundane stores such as you'll find anywhere else. But I will concentrate on the more original aspects of the retail trade. Chief among them are the **shopping arcades,** which existed in Australia long before they were introduced to America—some of them were built in the 1890s. These arcades range from baroque Victorians to air-conditioned streamliners. Most of them have side passages and split levels, so that a simple walk-through can turn into a voyage of exploration. Since arcade rents are high, the accent is usually on the glamour trade, though you'll find a sprinkling of bargain outlets if you explore long enough.

The heart of Sydney's shopping world is a relatively small area stretching from Park to King Streets and between Elizabeth and George Streets. Crammed into these few blocks are an awesome number of retail stores—not to speak of hotels, restaurants, and theaters. It contains the **Pitt Street Mall,** not as attractive as the mall in Martin Place, but boasting far more shops. Here you'll also find both of Sydney's main department stores, most of the shopping arcades, all of the central shopping centers, and some very snazzy fashion outlets. Practically speaking, you don't have to stir out of this region to buy whatever you wish.

DUTY-FREE SHOPPING   You'll find duty-free stores all over Sydney and in most of the inner suburbs and at the airport. You can make your purchases long before departure, but you'll have to show your airline ticket and frequently your passport as well. It's a sensible idea not to leave your buying till the last moment but to give yourself time for some comparison-shopping. Following are a few of the many duty-free retailers.

Hardy Brothers, 74 Castlereagh St. (☎ **235-0083**), offers leather goods, watches, jewelry.

Angus & Coote, 496 George St. (☎ **267-1363**), specializes in a wide range of jewelry, diamonds, and watches.

Le Classique, 33 Bligh St. (☎ **233-1455**), is a new showroom displaying perfumes, camera gear, radios and other audio equipment, and video.

Downtown Duty Free, 20 Hunter St. and 84 Pitt St. (☎ **232-2566**), has one of the largest selections of mixed merchandise, including liquor and leather.

Grace Bros. Duty Free, 436 George St. (☎ **238-9542**). Sydney's biggest department store has a special duty-free department on the lower ground floor. Combines a vast range of goods with a convenient downtown location.

Le Mouton, 5 Bridge St. (☎ **252-4321**), carries a large selection of leather goods, souvenirs, sun glasses, cameras, perfumes, liquor, plus audio, video, and electronic equipment.

2   Shopping A to Z

ABORIGINAL ARTIFACTS

Aboriginal And Oceanic Art Gallery, 98 Oxford St., Paddington. ☎ **332-1544.**

This is both a gallery and a shop for a vast range of Australian and Melanesian artifacts, clothing, jewelry, ceramics, and weaponry as well as books and music tapes from the regions. Some of the carved animal figures and bark and sand paintings are artistic gems. Joe

Croft, a partner in this enterprise, is an "urban elder" who retired from government service and now organizes Aboriginal art exhibitions, craft fairs, and dances.

Coo-Ee Australian Emporium, Strand Arcade, Pitt and George Streets. ☎ 221-5616.

The name of this store, located on the first floor, is derived from the traditional Aussie bush cry. The emporium stocks both Western and Aboriginal handmade goods, each unique in its own way, plus pottery, wooden utensils, and a range of scarves, sarongs, and covering fabrics with Australian designs. Closed Saturday afternoon and Sunday.

ART PRINTS

Strokes, 308 Oxford St., Paddington. ☎ 360-4646.

A cross between a store and an art gallery, Strokes offers an outstanding selection of limited-edition etchings, woodcuts, lithographs, silk screens, and prints by Australian artists. Also display posters that are worth taking home. Closed Sunday.

BOOKS

Clay's Bookstore, 103 Macleay St., Kings Cross. ☎ 358-2908.

This store boasts a huge stock—half hardcover, half paperback, and what they haven't got they can get. Open Monday 9am to 6pm, Tuesday to Saturday 9am to 9pm, Sunday noon to 4pm.

Dymocks Book Department Store, 424 George St.
☎ 235-0155.

The largest bookshop in Australia and among the biggest anywhere, Dymocks has specialized sections on matters Australian, artistic, and audio, plus an outstanding map department, and features a computerized customer-service system that gets very fast results. Open daily.

DEPARTMENT STORES

David Jones, Elizabeth and Market Streets. ☎ 266-5544.

One of Sydney's largest department stores, David Jones offers art galleries, restaurants, ticket outlets, travel agencies, and beauty parlors—it sells virtually every commodity you can think of. David Jones is somewhat British in its choice of merchandise, in that it emphasizes luxury items. This is particularly noticeable in the famous food hall in the store's branch at the corner of Market and Castlereagh Streets.

Grace Bros., 436 George St. ☎ 238-9111.

This giant, classed as a "family store," sells all sorts of merchandise and also contains restaurants, art galleries, beauty parlors, travel agencies, and ticket outlets.

FASHIONS

Flamingo Park, Strand Arcade, Pitt and George Streets.
☎ 231-3027.

On the second floor, this shop is not a park and has no flamingos. The odd name hides the outlet of Australian fashion designer Jenny Kee. She has made an international reputation with her handknitted sweaters bearing koalas, kangaroos, parrots, and other Oz motifs. (I didn't see any with flamingos.)

Morrisons, 105 George St., The Rocks. ☎ 27-1596.

A decidedly masculine store, Aussie style, Morrisons sells all the garments associated with the outback male, except swagman's hats with corks dangling from the brim. You get the inimitable bush hats, moleskins, riding breeches, sheepskin coats, hacking jackets, and all other requisites of Oz male country attire. The only thing you have to supply yourself is the suntan. Open daily till 6pm.

Sydney Harbour Shop, 123 George St., The Rocks. ☎ 27-2737.

Chances are that you'll recognize the work of Ken Done even if you don't know the name. His explosively cheerful creations are now selling almost as fast in America as in Oz. Done paints designs that are both simple and evocative. His work appears on anything wearable or hangable, from T-shirts to tapestries. This is his shop (he has a studio somewhere else) and you get an idea of the amazing range of his materials. Prices go from around $A30 for a sweatshirt and $A25 for a poster to $A4,000 for one of his joyful tapestries. In between are coasters, place mats, greeting cards, and bumper stickers. Open daily.

R. M. Williams, 71 Castlereagh St. ☎ 233-1347.

Bushwear for both genders is sold here. It has a big range of very smart-looking belts, the kind of oilskin rainslickers you wear in the outback "wet," elastic-sided boots, etc., all with its own company label. Closed Sunday.

JEWELRY

Gems Of The Earth, Shop 11, Argyle Centre, The Rocks. ☎ 27-7087.

This family business has close connections with opal miners in the fields. The shop is part of the historic Rocks scene and a tourist attraction in its own right. Open daily 9am to 5:30pm.

George Olah, Darlinghurst and Bayswater Roads, Kings Cross. ☎ 358-6208.

Adjoining the Hyatt Kingsgate is this friendly family-owned operation with an enormous range of opals and other gemstones. The opals can be bought either as solids or in the form of doublets or triplets. The Olah family guarantees all the precious stones on their premises.

Costello's, 280 George St. ☎ 232-1011.

Step into the combination shop/museum/theater and you walk into a cleverly simulated and animated opal mine (with the heat, grime, and claustrophobia left out). It does, however, give you an idea of the cramped conditions and precarious earth walls that make real fossicking such devilish toil.

Continuous color films show life in the Andamooka opal fields, and gem cutters and polishers at work, honing out the stones as you finally get to see them. It drives home the fact that you probably wouldn't recognize a high-grade gem if you found one. Long counters

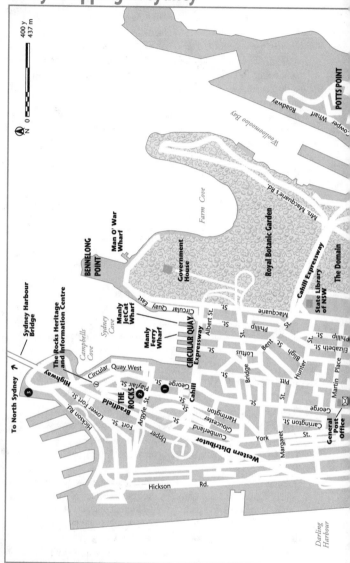

of opals are for sale, ranging from around $A15 to upward of
$A50,000. Expert advice is given free of charge, and so is admission
to the showroom and exhibition. Open daily 9am to 5:30pm.

MALLS/SHOPPING CENTERS

Centrepoint, Market and Pitt Streets.

The sky-jutting Sydney Tower rises from the top of this merry maze
of 160 specialty shops. All the stores are connected by walkways to

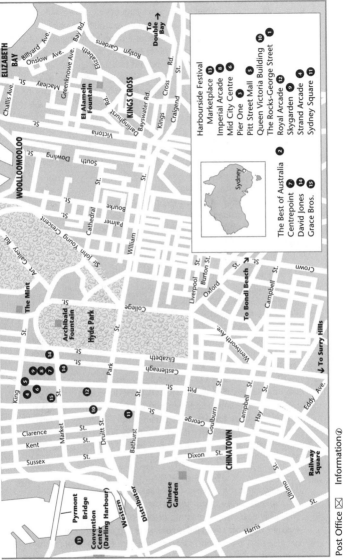

the two department store biggies. You can choose among 60 or so retailers dealing in women's clothing that runs the gamut from haute couture to outrageous.

Cosmopolitan Centre, Double Bay.

Only a section of this outstanding shopping hub is actually an arcade. But the streets and alleys around it are so compactly grouped that the whole area must be regarded as one—very fashionable—unit.

Post Office ⊠   Information ⓘ

Focal point is the Cosmopolitan Hotel, with its chic cafe-restaurant, adjoining the actual arcade. Outside run Knox Street, Knox Lane, Cross Street, and half a dozen little lanes and yards housing some of the most glamorous shopping Sydney has to offer.

You get items from old prints to hand-loomed table linen, little fashion boutiques with one or two original (and untagged) garments in the window, a Swiss deli, a restaurant specializing in venison, toys for kids, a duty-free store with designer jewelry, magnificent flower baskets, Scandinavian furniture, rare books, a French charcuterie.… I'm sure you've grasped the general tenor of the region. Double Bay is an inner eastern suburb, a few bus stops past Kings Cross. Even if you purchase nothing but an espresso, you'll have a memorable shopping stroll.

Imperial Arcade, 83 Castlereagh St.

Connecting Pitt and Castlereagh Streets, this complex concentrates on men's and women's fashions. The 114 shops are small in size, big in taste, and include bridal wear, furs, shoes, sports outfits, and designer-label jeans.

Queen Victoria Building, George Street.

This shopping complex, between Town Hall and Market Street, is the most glamorous in Australia, magnificently restored and modernized. For several decades it housed the Municipal Library and the rumor went that the fumes from the wine cellars in the basement had been harnessed to drive the elevators. Inside, under a stained-glass dome, the building looks like a cathedral of commerce. Unlike most cathedrals, it's open 24 hours a day, seven days a week, and is air-conditioned. There is a grand central staircase with wrought-iron balustrades, wheel-arched stained-glass windows, and timber shopfronts. As a centerpiece the Royal Clock, 18 feet long and weighing over a ton, shows animated pageant scenes from history. QVB houses 200 shops, boutiques, restaurants, and cafes, mostly for what is known as the "executive market"—that is, expensive. The shops range from high-fashion lingerie to duty-free (stuffed) koalas; the bistros, from English afternoon tea to sushi.

Strand Arcade, Pitt and George Streets.

The oldest arcade in Sydney, Strand has a distinctly Victorian look, rather like an ultra-refined railroad station (it opened for business in 1892). The 82 shops are small, distinctive, and one-of-a-kind, a welcome throwback from today's overwhelming standardization. You can also sip a gracious afternoon tea and invest in a reading of the tarot cards.

Skygarden, Pitt Street Mall to 77 Castlereagh St.

A highly innovative retailing concept combining a glasshouse effect and topiary trees with mosaic murals, painted "sky" ceilings and terrazzo artwork. You enter through an archway made of Venetian glass tiles and walk on hardwood parquetry flooring with inlaid animal designs. The complex is crowned by a huge crystal dome sheltering a mix of restaurants, bars, cafes, and take-out outlets. The overall impression is quite stunning and decidedly *up*market. Shops and services include a hairdresser, Eddi Azzi, who is on 24-hour call; jewelry and giftware from international outfits like Hunting World, Hermès of Paris, and Platina Opals; and rows of fashion labels like Ken Done, Country Road, and Sportsgirl.

Harbourside, Darling Harbour.

Rising on the western foreshore of Darling Harbour and reflected in the water below, this festively adorned shopping carnival contains some 200 stores, 8 regular restaurants, and 30 fast-food stands. The shops sell souvenirs, beachwear, designer togs, arts and crafts, bazaar goods, high fashion, and household gadgets, and outdo each other in decorations; some tasteful, some woeful. Strolling entertainers drift in and out to keep the atmosphere sparkling to the musical accompaniment of cash registers. Open seven days from 10am to 9pm, while the restaurants dish out meals until two in the morning.

MARKETS

Glebe Sunday Market, Corner of Derby Place and Glebe Point Road.

Held every Sunday in the playground of Glebe Public School, this is an entertainment and social as much as a shopping event. The 200 plus stalls sell "preloved treasures" alongside quite unlovable items as well as new clothes, crafted objects, handmade jewelry, homemade edibles, belts, books, baskets, unusual toys, and unabashed junk. Entertainment comes in the form of street musicians, local bands, mimes, jugglers, clowns, and tarot readers—no telling who or what will turn up. Glebe natives meet, mingle, and frequently depart with visitors from all over. Wondrous fun as long as the weather stays reasonably friendly. Runs from 10am to 5pm.

Paddington Village Bazaar, Village Church, Oxford Street, Paddington.

This highly original market has a medieval European touch. It consists of about 200 stalls, many devoted to handcrafts and folk art, but you also find very smart clothing by upcoming young designers, beautiful Australian woven products, unusual toys, and jewelry and antiquarian books that may turn out to be treasures. Among the special attractions here are the street buskers—roving minstrels, jugglers, jazz musicians, folk guitarists, balladeers, and the like, who keep the market throngs entertained. Open Saturday 8am to 5pm.

Paddy's Market.

This market, a part of Sydney's history for over 150 years, lures both locals and tourists. It was arbitrarily evicted from its traditional home in the Haymarket downtown, and for a while it seemed as if Paddy's had joined the dodo in extinction. Luckily it has been resurrected in its former glory. Paddy's functions Saturday and Sunday in Haymarket, alongside Chinatown. The action goes from 9am to 4:30pm. It features more than 1,000 stalls and requires a lot of footwork. You'll find almost everything there, mostly at bargain prices, but with no guarantees for either quality or longevity. Goods offered (loudly) run from food to footwear, from pottery to pets, from T-shirts to toys, from woollies to watches. Take your time browsing, because many of the stalls sell identical wares at wildly different prices.

MUSIC

Folkways, 282 Oxford St., Paddington. ☎ **33-3980.**

A record label as well as a music store of unusual quality, Folkways has international offerings from Berlioz to Buddhist chants, but with special emphasis on Australian music of every ilk: symphonic, ballet, bush, folk, political, jazz, and Aboriginal. Among the most intriguing buys are 19th-century convict songs and the musical scores of Australian films. Open daily.

NOVELTIES

Remo, Corner of Crown and Oxford Streets, Darlinghurst.
☎ **331-5544.**

Impossible to apply a label to this store, which not only sells whims and fancies but does a worldwide mail-order business with them. What can you buy there? Well, everything and nothing, depending which way you look at it. The mix of goods runs from deluxe leather items to birdcall whistles, from bookshelves and wooden stepladders to toothpicks made from echidna quills, from schoolroom wall charts and desk organizers to kitchenware and tobacco pipes. You might call it a museum of trivia, except that most of the trivia is also highly practical and some of it sells in the $A700 range. Browsing here is an adventure, a scouting expedition for objects you may never have heard of . . . but suddenly want.

WINE

Australian Wine Centre, Shop 3, 1 Alfred St., ☎ **247-2755.**

Located in Goldfields House, across George Street from the Regent Hotel, the Centre is a showcase of the noble Aussie grape. The place stocks more than 1000 wines from 300 vineyards, ranging from vintage to current releases. Of particular interest are the "Pick of the Month" features, such as the "Best from the West" event, introducing new releases from the Leeuwin Estate in Western Australia. You can taste the featured wines every Friday and Saturday. The staff is both enthusiastic and knowledgeable, and will expertly pack purchases to be carried with luggage according to airline standards or shipped directly to your home. Open Monday through Saturday from 9:30am to 6:30pm, and on Sunday from 11am to 5pm.

9

Sydney Nights

SYDNEY HAS FAR AND AWAY THE MOST HECTIC NIGHTLIFE OF ANY Australian city. The bulk of the nightspots are concentrated downtown and in Kings Cross; the rest scattered all over the inner suburbs. Because of Australia's hideously complicated liquor laws—and entrepreneurial methods of getting around them—the labeling of nightspots is ambiguous, to put it mildly. A great many nightclubs, for instance, call themselves restaurants; which is true insofar as they do serve food but false insofar as food is not the reason for anyone going there. A "club" may be the genuine article with regular membership lists or it may simply be a tag stuck on a drinking joint. A "disco" may have a DJ, or live bands, or both, or neither.

In consequence, the categories dividing this chapter tend to be rather hazy. A lot of the places mentioned simply defy strict classification. So, unfortunately, do their prices. As a general rule most establishments will charge whatever they think the traffic will bear. Which means they'll let you in gratis one night but sting you $A7 or $A10 the next, when they're featuring some popular group or entertainer.

Two aspects of Sydney's entertainment world have drawn heavy fire in recent times. One is the plethora of so-called "tribute" or "concept" bands that is spreading like a rash over the local pub scene. These are groups that blatantly mimic international celebrities, copying their style, repertoire, even their names, in a way that absolutely infuriates the purist among rock fans. You get performers like Elton Jack (Elton John), the Beatnix (Beatles), Dynissty (Kiss), and a couple of dozen more.

The majority of pub audiences love 'em and shrug off the barbs of outraged music critics. The mimics themselves have a ready answer, as supplied by the lead singer of one of the tribute bands: "Don't they know the best musicians play covers of Beethoven and Mozart every night at places like the Opera House without a word uttered against them?"

The second controversy sputters around karaoke, which some folks regard as the "ne plus ultra" of nightlife. Others call it Japan's revenge for Midway. Karaoke literally means "empty orchestra," and the joy it generates stems from supplying a full orchestral accompaniment to whomever wishes to warble along with it. The effect, therefore, depends on the vocal cords of the warbler. The results can be fairly devastating if the performer is (a) drunk or (b) singing in skeleton key. Karaoke has swept Sydney like a syrupy deluge, infiltrating hotel bars, cafes, social clubs, and discos, nightly transforming legions of frogs into temporary princes.

WHAT'S ON WHERE For programs, locations, and performance times of most entertainments, check the "Time Out" section of the *Daily Telegraph Mirror* on Thursday or the "Metro" section of the *Sydney Morning Herald* on Friday. A special publication called *This Week in Sydney,* available in most hotel lobbies, offers a roundup of highlights.

Periodicals specializing in the music and club scene are *Drum Media, On The Street,* and *3D World,* which you can find in music stores, some of the larger news agencies, and a number of cafes.

You can get current entertainment information by telephoning **00555-0090** for movies; **00555-0091** for theaters; and **00555-0092** for performing arts.

BARGAIN TICKETS   **Half-tix** is a small booth in the middle of Martin Place that sells theater tickets at half price between noon and 6pm Monday to Saturday. Not the best seats, and available only on the days of performance. You have to pay cash and you can't book by telephone.

1 The Performing Arts

Major Concert Halls & All-Purpose Auditoriums

★ **Sydney Opera House,** Bennelong Point. ☎ 250-7777.

Because this is an entire cultural complex, you get a large variety of offerings in its auditoriums. Standard are the **Australian Opera,** the **Australian Ballet,** the **Sydney Dance Company,** the **Sydney Symphony Orchestra,** and **Musica Viva.** Other groups divide their appearances between the Opera House and their own (more modest) premises. See also Chapter 6.

Tickets: $A26–$A125.

Sydney Entertainment Centre, Harbour St., Haymarket. ☎ 211-2222.

Well, a thing of beauty it ain't, made no more so by the gigantic and tasteless billboard across the road. But this is Australia's largest auditorium and, though it looks like an airport terminal, a marvel of interior flexibility. Four different layouts allow the center to be used for solo performers, theatrical productions, or big sporting events. It can hold from 3,500 to 12,000 people.

Tickets: $A20–$A50.

Sydney Convention Centre, Darling Harbour. ☎ 266-4800.

Although built mainly as a stamping ground for conventioneers, the center serves other purposes just as well. The place is one of the largest exhibition halls in town and frequently hosts top-ranking entertainers, solo or in groups. What it lacks in intimate charm it makes up for in state-of-the-art electronics.

Tickets: $A25–$A78.

State Theatre, Market St. ☎ 266-4030.

This campy theater was one of the grand-slam "picture palaces" of the 1930s. A cross between a McDonald's and the Taj Mahal, it has marble staircases, Moorish columns, artificial stars twinkling on azure ceilings, and a "Butterfly Room" for ladies to powder their noses in. Now it features a totally unpredictable mix of movies and musicals, hosts the Sydney Film Festival, and presents visiting dance groups like the celebrated "Africa Oye" ensemble.

Tickets: $A15–$A39.

Theaters

Australia in general, and Sydney in particular, has a thespian tradition covering some 180 years, dating back to the performances of deported convicts—who included a good proportion of "actors, vagabonds, and other paupers." From these planks-over-rumbarrels stages emerged a large and vigorous crop of legitimate theaters and music halls, flourishing in every large town of the continent.

They were driven to the verge of extinction by the combined effects of the Great Depression, rampant wowserism, managerial myopia, and chains of cheap movie houses. After World War II, when Sydney had a population of 1.5 million, it boasted exactly two regular theaters, both presenting moldy English drawing-room farces and passé American musicals. The work of Australian playwrights was considered box-office poison.

The only lights on the greasepaint horizon were a troupe of North Shore players, led by a courageous female martinet named Doris Fitton, who dared to put on some mildly nonconformist pieces, and an even braver bunch of leftist radicals—all unpaid—who enacted message plays in drafty city halls.

The cultural revolution that swept Australia in the 1960s brought about an astonishing surge of live theater—doubly amazing since the same period also ushered in television. The reason for the turnabout: Australian theater had found its own voice, and people flocked to hear it. The cycle had started with a few locally written plays like *The One Day of the Year*, which dealt with a specifically Australian and contemporary theme. But it took the applause earned abroad by *Summer of the Seventeenth Doll* and the ballet *Corroboree* to convince managers at home that they wouldn't court bankruptcy by putting on their own country's products.

Today Sydney has 27 live theaters, not counting the dozens of amateur stages functioning all over town. The city's professional companies put on more than 200 plays and musicals annually, and this doesn't include the revues performed in pubs and supper clubs as part of the nightlife scene. Contents and themes vary tremendously, but the general level of quality is very high, occasionally superlative.

Sydney, however, suffers from a geographical handicap: it has no "Broadway" and therefore no "off-Broadway" definition. All the grand old playhouses stood in the path of some urban development or other and were consequently wrecked. The town, therefore, has no theater district, and the major showcases are scattered all over the place. It's even difficult to define the term "major" except in size. The best I can do is state that the big, lavishly equipped theaters charge between $A30 and $A39 per ticket and the smaller ones between $A12 and $A25. You can buy tickets at the box offices or through the **Mitchells Bass Agency** by calling **266-4800.**

★ **Belvoir Street Theatre,** 25 Belvoir St., Surry Hills.
☎ **699-3444.**

One of the best, most original, and most variegated showcases in Australia offers an upstairs and a downstairs stage. Housed in a distinctly drab portion of town, with decor badly in need of cosmetic surgery, the theater generates originality. It features Australian works on the widest scale—including Aboriginal themes—mixed with satire, topical revues, and children's shows. The Belvoir Street has a near-fanatical local following, but is also a magnet for overseas visitors with artistic curiosity.

Tickets: $A15–$A20.

Ensemble Theatre, 78 McDougall St., Milsons Point. ☎ **929-0644.**
Located on the North Shore harborfront, this charming playhouse operates in conjunction with a pier restaurant serving precurtain buffet-style meals—a highly practical combination. **Train:** Milsons Point.

Tickets: From $A21.

Footbridge Theatre, Sydney University, Parramatta Road.
☎ **692-9955.**
This theater actually stands behind a footbridge spanning the road in front. As part of the university it naturally attracts a strong student clientele and caters to the tastes of young academia—meaning satirical, off-the-wall, and generally lighthearted fare, comfortably mocking the establishment.

Tickets: $A39.90.

Kent Street Theatre, 420 Kent St. ☎ **267-6646.**
Located in a former church, this theater presents English, Irish, and Australian plays, and occasionally very ribald Restoration comedies. The actors are members of a cooperative, but their offerings do not by any means reflect religious themes.

Tickets: $A16.

Her Majesty's, 107 Quay St. ☎ **212-3411.**
Seating 1,500, Her Majesty's offers grand-slam musicals and ballets, Christmas pantomimes, and historical epics. It has several bars and a cafe, and audiences that dress up for their night out.

Tickets: $A30–$A36.

★ **New Theatre,** 542 King St., Newtown. ☎ **519-3403.**
This theater was an offspring of the Great Depression, founded in 1932 as a platform for social protest and commentary. Originally housed above a wholesale grocery, it frequently changed premises in the course of a very stormy career, playing in private homes, on street corners, in union halls, and once even in the pit of a striking coal mine. Success has mellowed the troupe, but only to a degree. Its most famous production was Australia's first authentic musical, *Reedy River* in 1953, with a score woven around real and wonderfully catchy old bush ballads. It gets resurrected at intervals and if it's on, don't miss it. You'll come out humming "Click Go the Shears." Now comfortably settled in solid premises, the group still maintains its sharp cutting edge on social issues, but is somewhat more laid-back than in the old days. **Bus:** 422, 423, 426.

Tickets: $A10–$A15.

⭐ **Opera House Drama Theatre,** Bennelong Point.
☎ **250-7111.**

This is the main nonoperatic auditorium of Sydney Opera House (see above). It is given over in turns to the Sydney Theatre Company and the Sydney Dance Company. The range, therefore, is anything from classical ballet to very broad bedroom farces interspersed with occasional children's plays and avant-garde dance productions.

Tickets: $A34.

The Rep, 1 Brown Lane, Newtown. ☎ **565-1482.**

The Rep serves primarily as a showcase for Australian talent, but doesn't follow the American pattern of repertory theater. You can expect almost anything here—for instance, a stage adaptation of Kafka's *Trial* done as a comedy. It's a good place to observe theatrical trends before they become trendy.

Tickets: $A12.

Glen Street Theatre, Glen Street, French's Forest. ☎ **413-4488.**

Located on the North Shore, across Sydney Harbour Bridge, this theater puts on slick, sophisticated fare, usually avoiding deep "problem plays." Best to make a complete evening of a visit there. An excellent restaurant, Sorlies, is next door.

Tickets: $A19.50.

Q Theatre, corner of Railway and Belmore Streets, Penrith.
☎ **047/21-5735.**

The Q began life as a lunchtime theater on Circular Quay, but has graduated to being the only fully professional stage in the far-western region of Sydney. It performs mostly Australian plays and does them brilliantly, with clever innovative touches. Audiences don't mind the hour's drive from Sydney to see them. For visitors, the ideal time to catch a performance there is when you're on your way to or from the Blue Mountains area. **Train:** Penrith.

Tickets: $A20–$A22.

⭐ **Seymour Centre,** City Road and Cleveland Street, Chippendale.
☎ **692-0555.**

This complex features three separate theaters under one roof. For good measure, the center also features periodic chamber-music recitals, as well as modern dance performances. The trio of stages makes for a fascinatingly mixed bag—you frequently get a choice of straight drama, offbeat comedy, and surrealistic experiments on the same evening.

Tickets: $A16–$A19.

⭐ **Stables Theatre,** 10 Nimrod St., Kings Cross. ☎ **361-3817.**

Placed in a region largely known for strip shows, this little theater holds its own. With a minute stage and minimal foyer space, the Stables has acquired a great reputation for quality performances of Australian works, famous or obscure, and for a pungent line of comedy. You sit on wooden tiers, but enjoy excellent bar service during intermissions.

Tickets: $A20.

Theatre Royal, in the MLC Centre, King Street ☎ **231-6111.**

Large and lavish, the Royal is the top showcase for imported smash-hit musicals, staged splendiferously. A bar on the premises helps keep the audience happy.

Tickets: $A34–$A39.

★ **Wharf Theatre,** Pier 4, Hickson Road, Walsh Bay.
☎ **250-1777.**

The Sydney Theatre Company is an outstanding ensemble that performs intimate or esoteric fare here, and uses Sydney Opera House for broadly popular big-stage shows. This group has a splendid reputation for handling Australian dramatic themes. Half the theater is actually on a wharf above the water.

Tickets: $A27–$A36.

Dinner Theater

This form of entertainment is having a renaissance in contemporary Sydney. The food is mostly standard and uninspiring, the theater anything from slapstick farce and "mellerdrammer" to straight plays or music-hall variety. These amusements tend to be on the pricey side, but usually highly satisfying.

★ **Argyle Tavern,** 12 Argyle St., The Rocks. ☎ **27-7782.**

Decidedly tourist-oriented and filled with coachloads of visitors, this famous theater is wonderful fun, and often the happiest memory patrons take home with them. Occupying the basement of a restored warehouse, the tavern has a huge, table-filled auditorium and exudes early-Aussie atmosphere, complete with convict-hewn rock walls. Waitresses in calico gowns hand out souvenir menus with the texts of the Oz ballads to be sung printed on them, so at least you'll get to know the lyrics of "Tie Me Kangaroo Down" and "Waltzing Matilda," complete with explanatory footnotes. The courses start arriving at 8pm—good, solid fare like roast lamb and beef, meat pies, and strawberries with whipped cream. At 9:30pm the band strikes up and leads the assembled guests in a sing-along. Then comes the *Jolly Swagman Show,* a musical cavalcade that crams chunks of popularized Australiana into a few colorful hours. It's all there—the convict and the bushranger, the swagman and the barmaid, the trooper, the Aborigine playing the didgeridoo, the campfire poet, the squatter, and "Crocodile Cooce" complete with a rubber croc. The songs are jaunty, sentimental, melancholy, and defiant in turn, wildly funny in parts, climaxed with a rendering of "Click Go the Shears" during which a live sheep is shorn on stage.

Prices: Dinner and show $A59.50.

★ **Blue Gum Theatre,** 220 Railway Parade, Kogarah.
☎ **588-6266.**

Located in a southern suburb, this showcase-restaurant puts on original Oz productions, mostly short plays, delightfully accompanied by a master of ceremonies who has the right audience touch. The humor is broad ranging to mid-raunchy, but not so "in" that it can't be comprehended by benighted foreigners. The drinks start flowing at 7pm, the show starts at 8pm, and the cost includes a three-course repast. **Train:** Kogarah.

> **Prices:** $A37–$A40.

⭐ **Harbourside Brasserie,** Pier 1, Hickson Road, Millers Point. ☎ **252-3000.**

Situated exactly as the name indicates, this plush venue presents a happy mixture of theater, cabaret, and dance club, combined with excellent supper fare. New shows every week; comical, musical, or both. After the show (around midnight) you dance to live bands until after 3am. The panoramic harbor view adds to the atmosphere. The fun runs from Tuesday to Saturday.

> **Prices:** $A12–$A40.

Kaos, corner of Alfred Street and Ramsgate Road, Ramsgate. ☎ **583-1177.**

Located ten miles south of the airport and devoted to nightly nuttiness, the Kaos combines a fair menu with a full theatrical stage. Guests are greeted by some of the most bizarre hosts in the hemisphere, and the menu is declaimed aloud as a comic recitation. Showtime brings song and dance numbers plus pretty broad comedy sketches. The house specialty is the improvised segments, composed at the spur of the moment for any table that is celebrating anything. The shows are followed by disco dancing until midnight, when the chaos dissolves.

> **Prices:** Vary.

Les Girls, 2A Roslyn St., Kings Cross. ☎ **358-2333.**

This decidedly offbeat program features young and less-so female impersonators, highly talented and stunningly attired. They romp through a middling Rabelaisian variety show abrim with campy humor and awash with double entendres. All the singing is (superbly) mimed to pretaped voices, but the dancing and stripping is done in person. It has a sumptuous setting, done out in scarlet and glitz, with velvet wherever you look. All slightly hysterical and deliberately overdone. Show times are 9:15 and 11:15pm Wednesday to Saturday. Afterward you can disco-dance till 6am.

> **Prices:** Dinner and Show $A40.

⭐ **Tilbury Hotel,** 22 Forbes St., Woolloomooloo. ☎ **357-1914.**

Looking very plain on the outside, the venerable Tilbury has a separate entrance leading into a charming restaurant, open seven days for lunch and dinner. On cool nights there's a roaring fireplace, in balmy weather an open-air beer garden with shady grape vines and a retractable roof. Dinner shows are staged nightly and change frequently. The stage is minute, the vibes usually great, and the performers have included some legendary cabaret veterans as well as hopeful newcomers. Mostly you get a pleasing mix of song and comedy routines, aided by hearty, good-value pub fare described as "à la carte Australian cuisine."

Prices: You pay separately for show and food. Show price is $A20, a three-course meal comes to around $A38.

2 Kings Cross Nightlife

Sydney's night scene is Kings Cross, the down under version of Times Square, North Beach, and Montmartre, with touches of Hamburg, Amsterdam, and Bangkok thrown in. The Cross is a blatantly frank red-light district (though the lights are predominantly pink) of a breed that is almost extinct in America. It keeps the kind of hours that once prevailed on the Broadway of Damon Runyon's era—the action doesn't really get under way till 10pm and the streets are thronged around three in the morning. The milling crowds in the main thoroughfares make it a generally safe area, though the little dark alleys are somewhat less so. Watch your purse or hip pocket.

The odd thing about the Cross is that, technically, it doesn't exist. The region is merely a vague geographical definition, the area where Darlinghurst, Potts Point, and Elizabeth Bay meet and join hands in a bit of heel-kicking before going their separate ways. But the meeting is pretty hectic and produces more after-dark whoopee than you'll find anywhere else south of the equator. Within one square mile the Cross generates every conceivable type of night action, from super-svelte to ultra-sleazy.

In between you'll find many of Sydney's finest hotels, restaurants, and supper clubs, outstanding bookstores and delis, and cozy little cafes. They are all part of the same scene and keep the same late hours. And at the arterial hub of the Cross, the exquisite **El Alamein Fountain** shimmers in the floodlights like a giant thistledown, dispensing delicate beauty in all directions, free of charge.

It's useless to try to list the entertainments hereabouts; they are too many and they change names too often. Here, I'll merely pick out a few random raisins and assure you that there are many others in the pie:

The Civic Club, 44 Macleay St. (☎ **358-1211**). Charges no admission and sells drinks at bar prices. Overseas visitors sign in at the door, play rows of slot machines, and see a floorshow that frequently includes outstanding pop artists. The club stays open from 10am till 3 or 5am.

The Colosseum, 54 Darlinghurst Rd. (☎ **357-3800**). Has a DJ five nights, pretty hectic rock parties Friday and Saturday, and karaoke on Sunday nights. Admission runs from gratis to $A5, depending on what's on, and on most nights the drinks are half price 5 to 8pm. Action goes "till dawn," a nicely nebulous term.

Sight/Soho, 171 Victoria St. (☎ **358-4221**). A very popular disco-nightclub and magnet for the serious dance crowd. Different beats on different nights, mostly with labels comprehensible only to earnest ravers who distinguish between the Manchester scene and Sanctuary Gothic. Cover charge $A5 to $A7 and action all week till 3am.

Illusions, 17 Earl Place (☎ 357-3481). Small and rather intimate, has a 24-hour cocktail bar. Otherwise and on different nights it's DJ, piano bar, funk, and live soul music. Entertainment starts at 8pm, goes till 7am. Admission ranges from zero to $A7.

Picture the above establishments multiplied by five and you'll have an idea of what the area offers in terms of nocturnalia. This does not include the various strip shows, most of them with the word "pink" on their shingle. The **Pink Pussy Cat,** for instance, has leather-lunged barkers outside, relays of long-stemmed ladies dressed only in demure smiles on the inside. Somehow Aussie peelers always give an impression of wholesomeness because of their suntans.

But just down the road there's a different kind of enterprise. The **Wayside Chapel,** 29 Hughes St. (☎ 358-6577), has married more people than any other church in Australia, and probably helps more desperate souls as well. This is a 24-hour crisis center if you're in trouble or if you need a place to crash for the night.

3 Cabaret & Comedy

There are flocks of these in Sydney—birthing, dying, and virtually impossible to keep abreast of. They function in pubs, in basements, in tents, or in fairly elaborate premises. Humor is their stock in trade, but the brand of comedy they dispense depends on their audiences. These fall into two main categories, "ockers" and "trendoids," distinguished not only by what they wear but also by what they laugh about. For the ockers of both genders, comedians rely on endless series of "poofter" jokes and sketches, on beery misadventures, and on a very broad brand of hetero humor. For the trendoids they'll produce political satire with a left-wing slant, skits on TV programs and pop stars, and jokes about ockers.

★ **Comedy Store,** 278 Cleveland St., Surry Hills. ☎ 319-5731.
This place presents a wonderfully assorted bag of professional comedians, promising amateurs, and semivaudevillian entertainers. Thursday night it's an all-female show—frequently the sharpest and funniest of the week. You can come for dinner and the show or for the show only, which starts at 9pm Wednesday through Saturday.
Admission: Dinner and show $A20, show only $A10.

★ **Harold Park Hotel,** 115 Wigram Rd., Glebe. ☎ 692-0564.
This unpretentious pub hides one of Sydney's best entertainment venues. The offerings resemble a smörgasbord catering to every palate. On Monday and Friday nights you get stand-up comedy. On Tuesday it's literature, with readings by contemporary Australian authors. Wednesday is theatrical—two short plays that can be comic, dramatic, or both. On Saturday and Sunday come the bands, rock or jazz. And all week Harold's grill serves lunch and dinner at economy prices. This is Sydney's pioneer pub of literary entertainment. **Bus:** 431, 434.
Admission: $A6–$A15, depending on the night.

Comedy Club, in the Hyatt Kingsgate Hotel, Kings Cross.
☎ **268-4800**.

The entertainment lounge of one of Sydney's plushest hotels, this is a far cry from the humble interiors of most comedy settings. The Comedy Club features celebrities in the field, like the Amazing Jonathon, in shows running Tuesday to Sunday. Two shows per night, usually at 8 and 10pm.

Admission: Depends on the celebrity.

4 The Bar Scene

Boulevard Cocktail Bar, in the Boulevard Hotel, 90 William St.
☎ **357-2277**.

Perched way up on the 25th floor of a swank hotel, this cocktail bar offers panoramic vistas along with the liquor. The elevator shoots up like a silent rocket, and then there's all of Sydney unfolding below. This is also the site of a very plush restaurant. Open till midnight Monday through Saturday.

Centrepoint Tavern, Pitt Street, Centrepoint. ☎ **233-1622**.

Located in the Pitt Street pedestrian mall, this isn't so much a tavern as a complex that tries to be all things to city workers. There is a restaurant section serving counter meals, a café-pâtisserie, and no fewer than three bars. Main courses run $A9 to $A13; drinks, $A3 to $A6. One of the bars, the Pompadour Room, becomes a piano bar after dark, complete with pink lighting, romantic seating, and a wonderfully versatile pianist specializing in romance. Patrons here are mainly well-dressed, well-behaved office staffers. Closed Sunday.

⭐ **Habit Wine Bar**, 185 Glebe Point Rd., Glebe. ☎ **660-2498**.

I have no idea what the "habit" signifies, unless it's the habit of gathering here, which the patrons do with a regularity akin to addiction. This is a genuine wine bar, serving only the noble grape juice, plus tasty food at modest prices. It's one of the coziest and most comfortable imbibing spots in town, with subdued lighting, wood paneling, and a spiral staircase winding up to the restaurant above. Open seven days a week till midnight. **Bus:** 431, 434.

⭐ **Pumphouse Brewery**, 17 Little Pier St., Darling Harbour.
☎ **29-1841**.

This establishment was built around an old water-pumping station. The original pumphouse rose in 1891 to provide high water pressure to power Sydney's elevators—electricity was not considered reliable enough. The immense cast-iron water tank of the old pumphouse is still there, but alongside it today is a very pleasant roomy beer garden with upstairs balcony. As I sat with my beer I mused on the peculiar Sydney habit of wedging taverns and restaurants into sites like incinerators, funeral parlors, and pumphouses. In this case the result is a charmer, which—aside from a vast array of potables—also serves tasty and economical meals. Open seven days till 10pm and located behind the Entertainment Centre.

Sydney Hilton, 259 Pitt St. ☎ **266-0610.**

A trio of bars in the hotel form an intriguing study in contrasts. The first and most famous is the **Marble Bar,** in the basement, which was saved from destruction when laborers refused to wreck it. It's a real Victorian nostalgia nook, dating from the time when bars were retreats for gentlemen wearing mustaches, watch chains, and bowler hats, and women were barred from the premises. The bar boasts huge marble columns and a ceiling of colored glass. Decorations include buxom music-hall beauties, lovingly painted in gowns that may as well not be there. Despite its ornate splendor, the Marble Bar is quite casual, attracting a broad cross section of clients. Entertainment includes guitarists and occasional rock bands. Open till midnight during the week, till 2am on Friday and Saturday; closed Sunday.

On the second floor, the **America's Cup Bar** has the reputation of being *the* elite rendezvous in town. Cocktail prices are steep ($A5 to $A15), service is impeccable, and the decor vaguely nautical, with colored pennants and stately yachts. Open seven days till midnight or 1am, and on weekends a singer provides nonintrusive background entertainment.

Henry the 9th is on the ground floor, but has only a few Tudor touches despite its name. It's a place for after-work drinks with a convivial atmosphere and a high decibel level. Everybody seems to know each other, or pretend they do. Open seven days a week till midnight.

Albury Hotel, 6 Oxford St., Paddington. ☎ **361-6555.**

Probably the most popular gay bar in town, it gets packed and rather boisterous. Entertainment is provided by an excellent piano bar and frequent drag shows, which can be a mixed bag: very good at times, overcamped and shrill at others. Upstairs there's a Thai restaurant whose cuisine is guaranteed to raise thirsts. **Bus:** 380, 382.

5 Nightclubs & Discos

The Sydney nightclub scene is for the young, the hearing impaired, and the smoke-proof. You must be young in terms of stamina to enjoy places that roar into action around 11pm and stamp till daylight. You need tin ears to survive a decibel pitch resembling indoor battlefields. As for smoking, well, one nightspot—I won't say which—has been described as "an ashtray with exits."

Like New York and London, Sydney has a constantly shifting pattern of in, inner, and innest ventures, distinguishable by the number of hopeful patrons they keep *out.* These optimistic rejects wait in long lines outside whichever paradise is in vogue at the moment, kept from entering by doormen with the build and mentality of sumo wrestlers, whose entire vocabulary consists of a growled, "Full up, mate." This is one area where the famed Aussie egalitarianism falls flat on its face. As far as the "in" nightspots are concerned, you can't get cliquey enough. They were the only spots on the entire continent where I had to flash my credentials in order to poke my nose inside.

The ironic part of this rigmarole is its transience. Four months—or even four weeks—later the same joint may be lying semideserted while the lines of young trendies form outside some other establishment that has suddenly blossomed into fashion—and where they receive exactly the same treatment.

Basement, 29 Reiby Place, Circular Quay. ☎ **251-2797.**

An outstanding showcase for jazz and blues combos, the Basement features cavalcades of limited-run performers. The turns include a lot of first-rate overseas talent, and the program thoughtfully divides them into "early" and "late" performers. The terms, though, are fairly flexible, since the action goes from 8:30pm to around 3am.

Admission: From $A5.

★ **Bobby McGees,** South Pavillion, Darling Harbour. ☎ **281-3944.**

Splendid harbor views and highly imaginative service are pluses here. The wait*persons* are costumed actors of all genders, playing roles like Charlie Chaplin, Maid Marian, Dracula, or Lucrezia Borgia. Swings Monday to Saturday till 3am.

Admission: $A8–$A10.

Don't Cry Mama, 33 Oxford St., Darlinghurst. ☎ **267-7380.**

Known as DCM, this used to be exclusively gay, but is now a huge and happy mix of revelers of every hue and persuasion. Has several podiums for amateur exhibition dancing; occasionally brilliant, frequently woeful. An Italian restaurant is on the premises as well as a disco that plays the latest pops. Because the DCM keeps very late hours it often gets swarms of patrons migrating from clubs that have closed. Operates Thursday to Saturday only, but then from 6pm till anytime between 3 and 7 in the morning.

Admission: Free–$A7.

Juliana's, in the Hilton Hotel, Pitt Street. ☎ **266-0610.**

This is definitely a place for dressing up and being seen. It caters to the smart younger set (those who can afford it), and puts on excellent floor shows earlier in the evening, often featuring international celebrities. It becomes a disco in the late hours and goes on until around 3am.

Admission: $A10.

Kinselas, 383 Bourke St., Darlinghurst. ☎ **331-6200.**

An erstwhile funeral parlor, now a fun complex spread over three floors. Although the disco is on the top floor, most of the serious networking takes place on the stairs in between. Currently one of *the* places to mingle and meet. Alternatively to shoot pool on the ground floor or breast the cocktail bar on the second. Take time off to admire the art deco details strewn all over. The disco operates Wednesday to Saturday from 11pm to 3am.

Admission: $A10.

Mars, 169 Oxford St., Darlinghurst. ☎ **331-4001.**

Mars is gay on some nights, straight on others, but I've never figured out whether this depends on coincidence or the calendar.

Anyway, it's a big two-level operation. The first floor has a disco where the dance music changes according to the night of the week. Upstairs is devoted to live performers: local rock groups, jazz combos, and blues singers, with occasional performers from interstate and overseas. Open Monday to Saturday till 2 or 3 in the morning.

Admission: $A5.

⭐ **Metropolis,** 99 Wallner St., North Sydney. ☎ **954-3599.**

Boasts the most striking decor in Sydney, and patrons to match. This North Shore nightspot draws legions of young and medium-done execs of both sexes, particularly for the big events staged on Tuesday nights. Has an international restaurant, an outdoor terrace and a disco that starts spinning around 10pm and goes till 3, 4, and even 5am on different nights. The dress code used to be fairly strict, but now you actually get in without a necktie. Closed Sunday. **Train:** North Sydney.

Admission: Free on Mon and Wed, other nights $A10.

The New Pharaoh, in the Hotel Nikko, 161 Sussex St. ☎ **299-8777.**

This place could rank as Sydney's poshest nightclub. Built into an old maritime warehouse dating back to the 1850s, the Pharaoh boasts the latest and costliest lighting and sound equipment in town. The antique sandstone walls enclose some extremely chic interior decorating but remain just visible enough to provide an intriguing contrast. Service in the restaurant is impeccably smooth and the adjoining disco has a dance floor fit for a royal ballet. There is an even more velvet-lined VIP area, in case you don't wish to mingle with the mob. Open from 6pm to 3am Sunday to Thursday, till 4am Friday and Saturday.

Admission: $A10 entry fee or a $A20 ticket that includes four drink coupons.

OP's, 22 Central Ave., Manly. ☎ **976-2288.**

The across-the-harbor resort of Manly has a night scene all of its own, and OP's is a good sample. Glowing with chrome mirrors, lighting effects, and highly polished dance floors, the place serves international cuisine until 10:30pm, snacks until early morning. Every night features an entertainment specialty: live rock, Latin or jazz bands, plus DJs. Wednesday is "Ladies Night," presenting a male beefcake revue, with guys barred until ten. Excellent dance floors and free drinks on certain nights (they change).

Admission: Dinners $A12–$A25.

Riva, Park Lane Hotel, Castlereagh Street. ☎ **286-6666.**

Possibly the trendiest nitery in town (at the moment), Riva offers laid-back glamor, modern dance, and jazz to legions of the *jeunesse dorée* who arrive in black-garbed avalanches. Well-trained ushers equipped with headsets keep the stampede orderly. In action Wednesday to Saturday from 10pm till 5am. Periodically Riva puts on special events, like the election of the "Super Model of the Year," complete with a $A1000 cash prize.

Admission: $A12.

★ **Rogues**, 16 Oxford St., Darlinghurst. ☎ **332-1718.**
Distinctly upmarket and for the slightly older bracket. Populated by the stylishly casual and nonchalantly affluent—suits mingling with designer jeans on affectionate terms. The place houses a fine restaurant as well as a disco with relays of DJs playing the absolutely latest in dance sounds. The posh Eastern Suburbs are present in force. Open Tuesday to Sunday from 7pm to 3am.
   Admission: Free Tues–Wed, $A10 other nights.

Rokoko, 16 Argyle St., The Rocks. ☎ **251-1579.**
Sitting in the heart of tourist territory, the Rokoko offers a greater variety of entertainment than most nightspots. You get dancing to top quality jazz bands, swimsuit parades, swing nights, raffles, record giveaways, limo rides, rock groups, soloists, comedians, and half a dozen other types and turns. Open all week from 5:30pm to 3am.
   Admission: Free before 9pm.

Round Midnight, 2 Roslyn St., Kings Cross. ☎ **356-4045.**
Subtitled Latin Quarter, this suave and dressy nightspot caters to a distinctly adult clientele. The music starts a little before midnight and features live groups delivering the smoothest bossa, tango, salsa, blues, and soul. The decor is as polished as the bands, including lacquered tables and marble bars. Goes till 3 or 5am every night.
   Admission: $A5–$A10.

Studebakers, 33 Bayswater Rd., Kings Cross. ☎ **358-5656.**
A slick, American-styled operation that uses a Studebaker chassis for a shingle. Specializes in '50s and '60s dance nights with authentic period music. The atmosphere is geared for good, clean fun, and occasionally the staff dances on the tables. Open all week till 2 or 3am, and serves an excellent buffet dinner.
   Admission: $A5–$A10.

---

6   Rock, Jazz & Folk

The places listed below are primarily or entirely musical venues, though a few of them feature dancing as a sideline. They consist mainly of entertainment pubs, which play a vital role on the Australian music scene. Without the pub venues the vast majority of Oz bands wouldn't be able to exist. Alternatively, a band with crowd appeal can turn a mediocre watering hole into a gold mine.

   Numerically the music pubs overwhelm every other type of evening enterprise. There are so many of them that I could devote the rest of this book to reciting them. But since they lie scattered over the whole metropolitan area, including the far outer suburbs, few visitors ever get to see more than the handful operating in the tourist regions.

Annandale Hotel, 17 Parramatta Rd., Annandale. ☎ **550-1078.**
Located near Sydney University, this pub draws a largely collegiate crowd. Their taste is reflected in the alternative music styles offered here, though the basic fare is rock and funk. The Annandale is much

stricter in checking ID cards than most hotels. Bands or duos come on Wednesday through Sunday, starting around 8:30 and finishing at 11:30pm.

The Bridge, 135 Victoria Rd., Rozelle. ☎ 810-1260.

An outstanding entertainment hotel, winner of several industry awards, with a multilevel beer garden that is transformed into an open-air movie theater on balmy weekend nights. The interior decor ranks a few notches above the usual pub standard. The bands, mostly but not exclusively rock, often feature international greats. On celebrity nights the usual cover charge of $A3 zooms up to $A18 to $A20. Bands perform nightly, and from Thursday to Saturday the action goes till 4am. Check the newspapers to see who's playing.

Hard Rock Cafe, 121 Crown St., Darlinghurst. ☎ 331-1116.

As the name indicates, here it's rock all the way. The food served on the premises is fairly authentic American/Mexican. Drinks, including piña coladas, at a locally famous video bar. The decor leans heavily on Los Angeles and is almost a museum of music memorabilia. Which may be the reason why the place attracts as many tourists as natives. Open seven days from noon to midnight. The bands start blasting around 8pm.

Real Ale Cafe, 66 King St. ☎ 262-3277.

Not a real cafe, but a beer palace dispensing 183 varieties of brew, local and imported. One of Australia's foremost jazz venues, the Real Ale features live jazz Tuesday to Saturday. The bands, too, are local and imported and frequently include mighty names in the field. The house also has an ultra-smooth piano bar to keep you entertained during happy hour, 5 to 7pm, when all drinks come at half price. The bands strike up at 8pm, and on Friday and Saturday go till 4am. An international restaurant serves solid food at gentle prices.

★ Rose, Shamrock and Thistle, 193 Evans St., Rozelle. ☎ 555-7755.

The name, of course, refers to the English, Irish, and Scottish folk music played and sung here on Friday, Saturday, and Sunday. (Local folkies have dubbed it the "Three Weeds.") An old pub by origin, the place is unpretentiously cozy and one of the friendliest anywhere. You get a nice mix of folk, pop, reggae, and blues music, occasionally a celebrity band or vocalist. There's an inexpensive menu (main courses around $A10), and admission ranges from $A4–$A16. Open till 11pm.

Selinas, in the Coogee Bay Hotel, 253 Coogee Bay Rd., Coogee Bay. ☎ 665-0000.

One of Sydney's major music showcases, Selinas is part of a large castlelike hotel that also harbors half a dozen bars, a disco, and a vast beer garden. Selinas is likewise big—capable of holding 3,000 people—and needs every inch of space when the big-name groups strike up. Since the names won't mean anything to visitors, I'll just tell you that they usually play on Friday and Saturday nights and that audiences get fairly frenzied at times. The stage has elaborate lighting effects and the sound is good, er—mostly. Closing hours vary; Friday and Saturday it's 3am. **Bus:** 373, 374.

★ **Strawberry Hills Hotel,** 451 Elizabeth St., Surry Hills. ☎ **698-2997.**

Mainly devoted to jazz, this place also ventures into various contemporary sounds to provide well-rounded entertainment evenings. The performance space is handsomely wood-paneled, the lighting atmospheric, the band quality invariably high. Trad jazz on Saturday and Sunday, other varieties Monday to Thursday evenings. On weekend afternoons you occasionally get a western swing combo as well.

7   More Entertainment

Movies

Called cinemas in Australia (or "the pictures" by the older generation), movie theaters have dwindled in number while ticket prices have reached for the stars. In Sydney's mainstream city houses you now pay an outrageous $A11.50 (children $A7.50) and for that you must also sit through ten minutes of commercials. On Monday, however, you get in for $A5 to $A6. In the so-called "fringe" cinemas, which run revivals, obscure foreign films, and cult strips, tickets cost around $A9.50 and the movies are often better as well.

As in the United States, the popular theaters tend to cluster in complexes housing up to half a dozen screens each, with roughly equal amounts of space reserved for junk-food dispensaries. The inner-city complexes are **Greater Union Pitt Centre,** 232 Pitt St. (☎ 264-1694); **Hoyts,** 505 George St. (☎ 267-9877); **Greater Union George City,** 525 George St. (☎ 267-8666); and **Cinema City,** 545 George St. (☎ 264-6701).

The most interesting theaters are the individual houses, which include the unique **Walker Cinema,** 121 Walker St., North Sydney (☎ 959-4222). This is a luxury theater near the North Sydney train station, next door to a Japanese restaurant. For a total of $A17 you get a Japanese meal *and* a movie. **AFI Cinema,** corner of Oatley Road and Oxford Street, Paddington (☎ 361-5398), is the showcase of the Australian Film Institute. It screens a fascinating mixture of local and overseas features, controversial documentaries, children's specials, animated strips, and filmed operas. This is also the place where you can see some of the early efforts of the Australian film industry, including those the makers would like audiences to forget about. I witnessed one, titled *The Silence of Dean Maitland,* which I took to be a parody until I realized it was meant to be serious. **Valhalla,** 166 Glebe Point Rd., Glebe (☎ 660-8050), is the dean of alternative movie houses, a gathering place for cult fans of every stripe, and a social center as much as a theater. It specializes in theme weeks, such as science fiction, animation, and comedy festivals, when they show works you're never liable to see anywhere else.

The most extensive film listings and program times appear in the *Sydney Morning Herald's* Metro section on Friday.

Leagues & Other Clubs

The term "club" in Sydney can denote something quite different from what it means anywhere else. Here it signifies private premises that are permitted to operate slot machines—or one-armed bandits, or "pokeys," as the locals call them. And in order to lure customers to these contraptions, the clubs put on lavish entertainment, supply cheap liquor, and serve very good, inexpensive meals (around $9). All of which can be legally enjoyed without going near a gambling device.

The word "private" may daunt visitors, but the label is pleasantly stretchable. The majority of clubs simply look at your passport, identifying you as a bona fide tourist. Then you sign a book and—hey, presto—you're a "temporary member" for the evening. With the bigtimers, the Leagues Clubs, proceedings are a little more elaborate. You call them first, stating who you are, where you're from, and that you'd like to see their show. Your name will be left with the doorman, you will be smilingly admitted, and you become an honorary member for the rest of your Sydney stay. The Leagues Clubs are athletic associations, but also vast casinos with rows of slot machines, plus stages, bars, restaurants, and lounges.

Mandarin Club, 396 Pitt St. ☎ **211-3866.**

Huge and glittering, this Asian-Aussie melting pot operates on three levels, boasting half a dozen bars, a dance floor, and a restaurant. Shows have Chinese or local vocalists, bands, and dance acts, as well as disco dancing and slot machines. It's like three nights out rolled into one, and at pleasingly moderate prices. Goes till morning seven nights.

St. George League Club, 124 Princes Hwy. ☎ **587-1022.**

The most lavish revues in the city are staged in this club (36,000 members strong), whose glittering suburban edifice is known as the "Taj Mahal." Name artists appear; call for program and reservations (required). Shows are at 8:30pm on Friday and Saturday, jazz on Sunday afternoons.

South Sydney Junior Rugby League Club, 558 Anzac Parade, Kingsford. ☎ **349-7555.**

With 55,000 members, this is Australia's largest club. The shows are staged in a 1,000-seat auditorium and the casts include top-level entertainers—all for free! Call for current programs or consult the "What's On in Your Club" column in the Sunday papers.

Sydney Aussie Rules Social Club, 28 Darlinghurst Rd., Kings Cross. ☎ **358-3055.**

The "Aussie Rules" refer to football, not to social activities. This club rolls out a big welcome mat for overseas visitors and claims that you can win up to $A100,000 on its poker machines. Apart from the ubiquitous pokeys, it offers bingo games Monday to Friday and karaoke on Wednesday nights. Live bands every night from 10pm till around 2am.

North Sydney Leagues Club, 12 Abbott St., Cammeray.
☎ **955-6101.**

Has an impressive Celebrity Room for grand-slam concerts. The last I attended was an excellent jazz combination, featuring two of Australia's top jazz outfits. Concerts usually start around 8pm, but check by phoning ahead.

Talking Two-Up

If you're a male traveler on your own, you may be invited to join a two-up game, or "school." Don't do it—because if the organizers have failed to grease the right palms you're liable to get arrested. Two-up is Australia's national game, but it happens to be illegal *anywhere* outside licensed casinos. Only it's illegal the way whisky was during Prohibition.

Aussies call two-up *swy* (from the German *zwei,* meaning two), and consider it as much part of their military tradition as the famous digger hat. It was said that you could spot Australian trenches in both world wars by the two coins perpetually whirling in the air above them. It's a fast game and an honest one. It's fast because all you do is bet on whether two pennies tossed from a board (or "kip") will land heads or tails. And it's honest because it's safer that way. Some decades ago a game organizer tried using a two-headed penny. He was last seen locked in his car in the process of being rolled off Port Melbourne pier. There hasn't been a double-header around since.

Honest, yes. But, as stated earlier, strictly illegal.

An Entertainment Cruise

Richmond Riverboat, Pier 4 Pontoon, Walsh Bay (next to The Rocks). ☎ **247-2979.**

Not a riverboat, but a harbor cruiser, this craft combines great New Orleans-style jazz with dancing, drinking, and dining. The jazz is sometimes varied with blues and reggae, but the food served is unvariedly fine, the vibes great (helped along by an excellent bar). Cruises depart at 7:30pm on Friday, at noon and 6pm on Sunday. Call for reservations.

Prices: $A20 for the 4-hour cruise, plus food and drink.

10

Excursions from Sydney

SYDNEY IS SO LARGE, DIVERSE, AND ENGROSSING THAT IT'S EASY TO FORGET it's also the capital of a very big state—the "premier state" of Australia, in fact. **New South Wales** measures a third of a million square miles and has some 5.8 million people. Since about 3.5 million of them live in metropolitan Sydney, you can imagine how much elbow room there is for the rest.

The state boasts a greater variety of beauty spots than any other on the continent. It has four distinct geographical regions, each with its own special characteristics. First there's the 1,000-mile coastal strip, offering some of the finest surfing and swimming beaches on the globe. Then there are the inland mountain ranges and plateaus, with snowy peaks rising to over 7,000 feet, forming a winter playground with ski lifts and alpine chalets. Third, there's the golden-green lushness of the western slopes, a region of warm lazy rivers and rich wheatfields, ideal for fishing and waterskiing. And finally there is the great western plains, the "woolbelt" of the state, presenting the real outback with immense flocks of sheep, little gray-black shepherd dogs, and flat horizons that stretch into eternity.

All I can do here is to give you a quick tour of the highlights, and only a few of those, worse luck. But you'll miss a lot if you copy those Sydneysiders who only leave their city to go abroad. They think that the Sahara starts just beyond the Blue Mountains.

Getting Around

The **Countrylink** network of the NSW Railways offers a special NSW Discovery Pass. The pass is valid for one month of economy class travel throughout the state with unlimited stopovers. It costs $A249, and members of the Youth Hostel Association receive an extra 10% discount. For bookings and information, call **13/2232.**

Hazelton Air Services, a country airline covering most of New South Wales, has standby airpasses for unlimited standby travel on its network. These passes are issued for 10 or 21 consecutive days ($A279 or $A449) and only to holders of non-Australian passports. Call **02/235-1411** for bookings and information.

Air services within the state are also provided by Qantas Domestic (☎ **13-1313**), Ansett (☎ **268-1111**), and East-West Airlines (☎ **268-1166**).

Bus travel within the state is handled by Greyhound and Pioneer Coaches (☎ **286-8688** and **286-8666**), and McCaffertys (☎ **361-5125**).

1   Blue Mountains

Just 50 miles west of Sydney, these mountains rise from the coastal plain to form a background almost as spectacular as the harbor entrance. For these rolling, cliff-toothed ranges really *are* of a deep, dreamlike blue, a natural phenomenon produced by countless oil-bearing eucalypti. The trees constantly release fine droplets of oil into the surrounding atmosphere, reflecting the blue rays of the sun and wrapping the whole landscape in a vivid azure haze.

Blue Mountain National Park is fringed with resort towns, ribboned with magnificent waterfalls, and crisscrossed by hiking trails. When Sydney is steaming below, the mountains are cool and fresh. And each of the resorts has its own bag of scenic delights and attractions. For more information, contact **Blue Mountain Tourist Information Centre,** Echo Point, Katoomba, NSW 2780 (☎ **047/39-6266**).

Getting There

You can reach the Blue Mountains from Sydney by train, bus, or car. Trains run daily from Central Station to Katoomba, the mountain capital, the trip taking about 2 hours and costing $A13.10. By road you drive west on the Great Western Highway, which starts near Parramatta. This highway crosses the entire mountain range, going through virtually all the towns in the region.

Nearly all of Sydney's coach-tour companies run excursions to the Blue Mountains. The trouble is that in order to give you your money's worth they try to cram too much sightseeing into their one-day jaunts, leaving you inundated at the end. Typical is the daily excursion operated by **Great Sights** (☎ **241-2294**). The coach leaves circular Quay at 8:45am and returns at 7:30pm. You travel via Wentworth Falls and Lawson to a photo stop at Katoomba's spectacular Echo Point. Then take a ride on the Scenic Skyway (fare not included). On to the Jenolan Caves, with time to explore one of the nine caves open to visitors (admission not included). On the return drive you visit one of the fruit orchards of the region. Adults pay $A62, children $A49. You can arrange for free hotel drop-offs.

Katoomba

Heart and capital of the region is Katoomba (pop. 15,000), which offers a considerable amount of resort bustle. There you'll find the **Scenic Skyway** and **Scenic Railways.** The former is an aerial cable car, suspended over a breathtaking chasm, costing $A3 for adults, $A1.50 for children. The latter is *allegedly* the steepest rail track in the world—at least that's what it feels like when you're riding it. Adults pay $A3; children, $A1.50. The **Megalong Valley Farm** is a charming mélange of working farm and showcase. You can go for tractor rides or pet baby donkeys, piglets, and foals. Then watch the cattle show, the sheepshearing, and the heavy-horse show—in which you watch a draft horse jump a hurdle. The farm is open Wednesday through Sunday from 9:30am to 5:30pm. Admission for adults is $A6, $A3 for children.

From Echo Point at Katoomba you can see one of the most intriguing natural attractions of the region, the **Three Sisters.** These are a trio of towering stone pillars, looking uncannily like three upright female figures, particularly under floodlighting at night. According to an ancient Aboriginal legend they were once the three daughters of a mountain witch doctor. When a *bunyip* (mythical

New South Wales

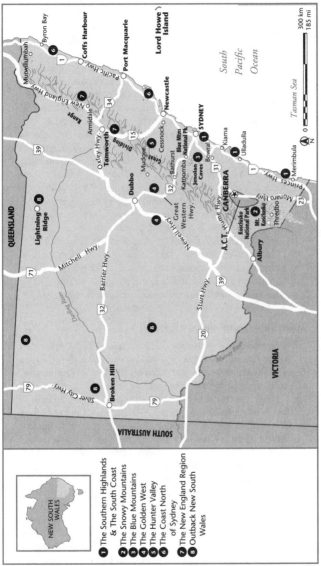

The Southern Highlands & The South Coast
The Snowy Mountains
The Blue Mountains
The Golden West
The Hunter Valley
The Coast North of Sydney
The New England Region
Outback New South Wales

6116

monster) tried to carry them off, the distraught father turned them to stone and himself into a lyrebird, since he lacked the power to turn the bunyip into anything. At midnight, the legend goes, you can still hear the lyrebird plaintively calling out to his stone children.

Adjoining the old courthouse in Katoomba is the **Renaissance Centre** (☎ 047/82-1044). This is a very attractive cluster of galleries, workshops, restaurants, museums, exhibitions, and performance space, housed on four levels of a rambling structure. There are 21 glass-fronted specialty shops selling books, pottery, antiques, handmade glass, and fashions. There are working craft studios where you can watch glassblowers, wood-carvers, hatters, and potters in action. There is a photographic museum with memorable mountainscapes on display, a fitness center, a brasserie, and periodic stage performances, making this structure an amazing all-rounder.

The neighboring town of **Leura** has a shopping mall and the magnificent mansion called **Leuralia.** This was the residence of H. V. Evatt, the Australian statesman who became secretary general of the United Nations. The house stands surrounded by glorious gardens and is furnished in art deco opulence. There is a small museum inside, dedicated to the life and work of Evatt, one of Australia's all-time political "greats." Admission is $A2 for adults, A50¢ for children, and the house is open Friday through Sunday from 10am to 5pm.

The **Everglades Gardens,** 37 Everglades Ave., Leura (☎ **047/84-1938**), bear no resemblance to their Florida namesake. This is possibly the finest cold-climate arboretum in Australia. Landscaped high above the Jamison Valley, they present a vista of tranquil beauty unmatched in the mountains. They include formal terraces, a watercourse area, a grotto pool, and a shaded Alpine reserve planted with masses of azalea. Open daily from 9am to 5pm. Admission is $A3 for adults, free for children.

More Blue Mountains Attractions

Falconbridge has the **Norman Lindsay Gallery** (☎ 047/51-1067), a large stone cottage at 128 Chapman Parade, in which the celebrated artist lived and worked for 57 years. The house and surrounding landscaped garden are filled with his paintings, sculptures, and memorabilia. It's hard to convey today just how much Lindsay's joyous nudes shocked his generation (which didn't stop anyone from buying them, nor from perusing his "scandalous" books). But let's remember that his illustrations for the classic *Lysistrata* were banned in New York as well. The gallery is open Friday through Sunday from 11am to 5pm. Admission is $A3.

Wentworth Falls is the most spectacular waterfall in a region full of rushing water. The white cascade shoots down a rugged escarpment, then plummets some 500 feet into the Jamison Valley. There is a lookout directly opposite the falls that gives a wide panoramic view of the drop. Just above Wentworth Falls, hidden away in a bush and parkland setting, stands **Yester Grange,** a Victorian country mansion that was once the home of a state premier. You can inspect the Victorian interiors and the garden Wednesday through Sunday from 10am to 5pm. Admission for adults is $A4; for children, $A2.50.

Farther to the west lies the **Jenolan Caves Resort,** a nature reserve and tourist site based around a labyrinth of world-famous limestone caves. Accommodations, wilderness walks, waterfalls, and swimming sites all abound, but the real magnet is the caves themselves. These are divided into three groups, each conveniently labeled either "strenuous" or "mildly strenuous." This refers mainly to the number of steps you have to climb in order to view their marvels—ranging from a mere 288 steps for the "Temple of Baal" to an athletic 1,332 steps for the "River." The caves offer grand adventure with an eerie beauty of their own. There are underground rivers and bleached bones, still, dark pools, and fluorescent rock walls that are sinister and eerie. You can choose from three tours, taking 2 hours each. They cost either $A5 or $A7 for adults, $A3 or $A4 for children. The third tour has a uniform price of $A10 per person and is not recommended for kids. The caves are open daily, and you can get additional information by calling **063/59-3304.**

The Hattery, 171 Lurline St., Katoomba (☎ **82-4212**), is a one-of-a-kind combination of hat workshop and tearoom. The resident "mad hatter" is Australia's leading headgear specialist, Mark O'Carrigan, and you can watch him turn out his handmade masterpieces, including suitably insane "sculptured hats." The adjoining tearooms sell Devonshire tea and light meals. Open all week 9am to 5:30pm.

Zig Zag Railway is a minor miracle of rail construction. This steam railroad was the first link to the western regions of NSW when it opened in 1869. The name indicates the way in which tracks had to be laid to enable the locomotives to haul cars over and through the mountain ranges. Today this is merely a nostalgic excursion run, with some breathtaking views en route. Trains leave from Clarence Station, on the Bells Line of the road, and take you to Lithgow in about 1¹/₂ hours. The ride costs $A7. For timetables and bookings call **047/57-3061.**

The **Explorer Bus,** one of the handiest ways of seeing the area, operates on Saturday and Sunday only. The bus starts at and returns to Katoomba railway station throughout the weekend, making a loop over the main beauty spots of the region. You can get out at any stop, sightsee, lunch or bushwalk, then rejoin another bus trip. Adults pay $A12.50; children, $A5. For schedules call **047/82-1866.**

Where to Stay

The Blue Mountains are chockablock with hotels, guesthouses, motels, cabins, lodges, and every other conceivable form of accommodation. The rate structure is typical of resort areas: nearly all the places offer special weekend deals, but in two or three-night packages only, which may be longer than you wish to stay.

EXPENSIVE

⭐ **Lilianfels,** Lilianfels Avenue, Katoomba, NSW 2780.
☎ **(toll free) 008/02-4452.** Fax 047/80-1300. 86 rms and suites. TV TEL.

Rates (including breakfast): $A235 double midweek; $A524 double for two nights weekends. Major credit cards.

A beautiful mountain mansion overlooking the panoramic Jamison Valley from Echo Point, the hotel houses an award-winning restaurant, a chic lobby lounge, and a library with 400 volumes. Elegant blue and amber bedrooms, open fireplaces, as well as a heated swimming pool, saunas, and steamroom make this a velvety refuge from city stress.

MODERATE

The Little Company, 2 Eastview Ave., Leura NSW 2781. ☎ **047/82-4023.** 40 rms and suites. TV Tel.

Rates (including breakfast and dinner): $A115 single or double midweek; $260 single or double for 2 weekend nights. Major credit cards.

Formerly a nuns' retreat and built in 1906 amid acres of landscaped grounds, this guesthouse serves wonderful soufflé breakfasts and gourmet dinners. Ringed by tennis court, putting green, and croquet lawns, it also offers a saltwater pool, open wood fires, and a pleasantly personalized welcome.

BUDGET

The Cecil, 108 Katoomba St., Katoomba, NSW 2780. ☎ **047/82-1411.** Fax 047/82-5364.

Rates (including breakfast): $A47.50 per person midweek; $A120 per person for 2-night weekends.

A large guesthouse with private parking, hot tubs, children's playground, TV lounges, laundry, a games room, and library. Locally famous for its sumptuous country breakfasts. Shared bathrooms only.

Norwood, 209 Great Western Hwy., Blackheath, NSW 2785. ☎ **047/87-8568.** Fax 047/87-8944.

Rates (including breakfast): $A55 single or double Sun–Thurs; $A75 single or double Fri–Sat.

A charming mountain-style guesthouse that also houses a well-known steak restaurant. Some rooms have private baths. A retreat with homey atmosphere, set in splendid scenery. The establishment dates from 1888.

Where to Dine

VERY EXPENSIVE

⭐ **Cleopatra,** Cleopatra Street, Blackheath. ☎ **047/87-8456.**
Cuisine: FRENCH. **Reservations:** Required.
Prices: Fixed-price dinner for two persons $A130. No credit cards.
Open: Lunch Sun only; dinner Thurs–Sun from 7:30pm–10pm.

Probably the most celebrated restaurant in the region, French to the fingertips and appropriately expensive. Serves classic Galloprovincial fare in a rustic setting that has almost as many flowers inside as out. The only uncharacteristic touch is the BYO label.

MODERATE

Stirlings, 38 Waratah St., Katoomba. ☎ **047/82-1298.**
Cuisine: INTERNATIONAL. **Reservations:** Accepted.
Prices: Appetizers around $A6; main courses around $A17.
Open: Dinner only, Tues–Sat 6:30pm.

Cozily romantic with candles flickering on the tables and a changing menu chalked on the blackboard, this BYO serves a wide range of dishes—pork in blackcurrant sauce, barramundi in tomato purée, breast of chicken in plum and orange sauce.

18 Govetts Leap, 18 Govetts Leap Rd., Blackheath.
☎ 047/87-7507.

Cuisine: AUSTRALIAN/FRENCH. **Reservations:** Accepted.
Prices: Appetizers around $A12; main courses $A18. Major credit cards.
Open: Dinner daily; Lunch Wed–Sun.

A shopfront establishment with a plain interior, amiable service and cuisine that swings intriguingly between Aussie and French. You get venison kidneys, freshwater yabbies, pheasant, or filet of beef in mushroom sauce, concluded by golden syrup pudding.

2   Holiday Coast

The stretch of New South Wales coastline that runs from Port Macquarie, north of Newcastle, to Tweed Heads on the Queensland border has been voted the most pleasant part of Australia to live in. It has a live-cheap climate, towns large enough to provide entertainment but not so big as to create urban problems, endless beaches, and a subtropical background to add color. It's a region where the taxis come fitted with surfboard racks, where protesters actually *won* their fight to save the rain forests, and where the fish bite so eagerly that the locals say you have to hide behind a rock in order to bait your hook.

It's so easygoing that the influx of practitioners of "alternative lifestyles" didn't raise an eyebrow among the natives. They simply incorporated the newcomers as part of the scenery—beards, headbands, hip-hugging babies, hash pipes, reed flutes, and all.

Getting There

You can reach the Holiday Coast by direct rail connection from Sydney, and also by direct coach service daily from Sydney to Port Macquarie ($A39). If you're driving, head for Newcastle first, then take the Pacific Highway (National Route 1) all the way.

Port Macquarie

Some seven driving hours north of Sydney, this port at the mouth of the Hastings River was established as a convict settlement in 1821. A few historic buildings are left from the bad old days, but Port Macquarie is mainly a resort town, blessed with beautiful surfing beaches plus a lot of tourist "fun attractions" that amount to a lesser blessing.

The most interesting—and touching—sight is the **Koala Hospital and Study Centre.** The clinic, the only one of its kind in Australia, caters to the koalas who live wild in the area and get sick, hit by cars, or attacked by dogs. Staffed by local volunteers, the hospital nurses them back to health before releasing them again. (Unfortunately the little cuddlies are slow learners. Several have been back a number of times because they persist in crossing heavily used highways.) The Study Centre features an educational display on koaladom, and you can visit the hospital and view the furry patients daily between 8am and 5pm.

Timbertown

Some 15 miles inland from Port Macquarie, on the Oxley Highway near Wauchope, stands Timbertown (☎ **85-2322**). This is an enthralling re-creation of a 19th-century logging village, complete to the trailing skirts and pinned hats worn by the female inhabitants. The houses are made of sawed slab and shingle roofs, creaking bullock teams haul giant logs to the working sawmill, and you can ride a puffing open-car steam train over a spectacular trestle bridge.

The village store sells licorice by the yard, and the blacksmith hammers out horseshoes and iron tires for wagon wheels, exactly as his forebears did a century ago. The woodturner makes carved chair legs from rosewood, the steam mill operates a dragsaw, and open wagons, drawn by mighty Clydesdales, rumble over bush tracks. Timbertown is open for visitors seven days a week from 10am to 5pm. Admission is $A13.

Coffs Harbour

An unusual combination of resort and deep-water port, Coffs Harbour started out as a harbor for the timber trade, then gradually drew in more and more tourists until it achieved its present dual existence. The big ocean freighters still dock almost in the town center, while the other end of the foreshore belongs to the swimmers. On Orlando Street is a famous **Porpoise Pool,** where the porpoises are so tame they stick their heads out to be patted and respond with friendly puffs from their blowholes. Open daily from 10:30am to 5pm, with porpoise and trained-seal performances.

At Micalo Island, east of Yamba, lies an attraction you'll find hard to believe—a **prawn stud farm.** This is no joke, but a serious and lucrative business. The "farm" consists of huge saltwater ponds where millions of succulent prawns are bred from specially selected stud prawns. The offspring are exported to Sydney and Tokyo restaurants, but the studs stay on to breed further exports. You can pick out those prawny Casanovas by their sheer size (like small lobsters) and aquatic arrogance. Open 10am to 5pm.

And just north of Coffs Harbour is another unlikely show— **Merino Mac's Agradrome,** on Pacific Highway (☎ **066/49-4405**). This is a sheep show to beat all others, where the sheep act both as passive objects—being shorn, displayed, and herded by sheepdogs— and as star performers. Sheep are supposedly not stage material, but at least two of these performing rams have obvious theatrical personalities. You also learn a lot about Australia's wool industry while admiring those splendid merinos romping around the stage. An indoor, all-weather attraction, open seven days in shearing season.

Nimbin & Byron Bay

In the area around Nimbin and Byron Bay you become aware of the influence of the so-called counterculture. Only here it doesn't run counter to anything—it's just part of the scene. The "straight" farmers, fishermen, and tourists mingle easily with saffron-robed Hare Krishnas, long-bearded and maned fiddlers, and couples with babies, all wearing homespun sacking, or what looks like it.

Seaside pubs stand next to shops painted with transcendental designs, community centers blaze in atmospheric murals, and half the cafes advertise vegetarian or Hunza fare. At the aptly named **Friendly Bar** in Byron Bay there are usually bearded musicians strumming, fiddling, and fluting bush ballads, rebel songs, and blues. The town is bursting with artisans and craftspeople in a dozen different branches, and some of their top-quality work in pottery, leatherware, sculpture, glassware, weaving, and painting is displayed at the **Cape Byron Gallery.**

Market days (Saturday and Sunday) in Byron Bay are an old-fashioned delight. You can get some real bargains (and equal amounts of junk) at the crafts stalls, especially in the jewelry line, although some of the homemade clothing defies description. But you'll find it hard to resist the local fruit on display, representing the riches of the subtropics: avocados, mangoes, lychees, sugar bananas, pawpaws, macadamia nuts, pecans, nectarines, and the most luscious peaches you've ever tasted.

At Casino, a few miles inland, is a **Platypus Pool** below the bridge on Summerland Way, where you can watch that incredible little beast in its natural surroundings. The platypus has a duckbill but is covered in fur, lays eggs but then suckles its young, and spends all its time in the water but is an air-breathing mammal. When the early explorers brought back descriptions of this critter, the Royal Zoological Society flatly refused to believe its existence.

Tweed Heads

The northern tip of the Holiday Coast is Tweed Heads, which straddles the Queensland border (the borderline runs right down the main road, Boundary Street). One side is Tweed Heads, New South Wales; the other is Coolangatta, Queensland.

Officially Tweed Heads and Coolangatta are twin cities, but periodically they march to a different drummer. The period is summertime when New South Wales, in tune with most of Australia, puts its clocks ahead by one hour. Queensland does not. Thus, Coolangatta lags an hour behind Tweed Heads during the hot season, which means that whenever you cross Boundary Street, you have to set your watch back. A minor annoyance for you, but it creates havoc in transportation schedules, especially since the major airport of the region lies on the Queensland side of the border.

Quite apart from the time difference, the borderline has other than academic distinction. In fact, the distinction is something from which Tweed Heads makes an annual bundle.

WHAT TO SEE & DO

The Tweed Heads bonanza stems from the legal technicality that Queensland does not permit poker machines, whereas New South Wales does. On the NSW side there's a cluster of luxurious clubs whose revenues depend on the one-armed bandits. They happily subsidize meals, transportation, drink, and lavish entertainment to entice tourists over from Queensland to feed those insatiable slots. Whole caravans of "pokey buses" come all the way from Brisbane and points in between, loaded with visitors who make straight for the clubs. Ostensibly these institutions are "private"—that is, for the use of members only. But in practice they admit "bona fide" visitors. Either you or any Queenslander simply has to show some proof of identity (driver's license or passport) to the doorman and the gates fly open. You're welcome to partake of some of the best—and cheapest—victuals on the coast, and watch first-class floor shows at no extra cost. And nobody forces anybody to gamble.

Clubs

Seagulls Rugby League Club, Gollan Drive, ☎ **075/36-3433.**

Here you'll find the Stardust Room, the most modern extensive auditorium on the national club scene, with elbow room for 2,000 people to enjoy the spectacular stage presentations. There is also a range of luxury bars and a row of dining spots, as well as gymnasiums and play and training fields for those actually practicing rugby.

Terranora Lakes Country Club, Mara St., ☎ **075/90-9223.**

This club features a show band plus selected solo performers. In the bistro dining room, roast beef, pork, or chicken go for very little.

Tweed Heads Bowls Club, Florence St. ☎ **075/36-3800.**

Besides bowling, this club also offers a revue show, famous stage and television comedians, a French restaurant, and six bars, plus 300 slot machines. There's a $A2 cover charge, and bistro meals hover around the $A9 mark. It's the scene of world-class bowls tournaments.

Twin Towns Services Club, Pacific Hwy. ☎ **075/36-2277;** for show reservations, **008/36-1977.**

This club presents a galaxy of Australian and overseas stars every afternoon and evening. The lineup changes, but the plush cocktail bar, smörgåsbord bistro, sports room, and air-conditioned lounges are permanent fixtures. Dinner will cost you from $A9.50 up.

More Attractions

In fairness it must be stated that Tweed Heads offers considerably more than a dazzling club scene. This little fishing village, which has grown into a sprawling resort, still retains its local fishing fleet and processing plant, but has added a huge shopping mall and residential complex. Most of the funds for these developments came from the $A73 million spent annually by Queenslanders crossing the border for you-know-what.

The **Minjungbal Aboriginal Museum,** Kirkwood Road, South Tweed Heads (☎ **075/54-2109**), features displays on Arnhem Land

and Central Australian Aborigines. Open Tuesday to Friday from 10am to 3pm. Admission \$A2.

Natureland Zoo, on Binya Avenue, has one of the largest private animal collections in Australia, including lions. Open daily from 9am to 4pm. Admission \$A4.

3   New England

Forget all about the New England you know. This region, inland from the Holiday Coast, looks nothing like it. It's lushly green countryside, dotted with large, prosperous sheep and cattle holdings, waving with silver birches, elms, oaks, and willows, and moistened by tumbling waterfalls. It does, however, share a certain academic flavor, stemming from an almost British-style university town.

The entrance, so to speak, is the Oxley Highway running from Port Macquarie over the Great Divide through the grandiose **Apsley Gorge National Park.** This is highland country with awe-inspiring scenery, where the roaring waters of Apsley Falls drown out conversation.

At **Uralla** you come into "Thunderbolt Country," so called after the legendary Captain Thunderbolt, one of the most famous of Australia's bushrangers. Thunderbolt, whose real name was Frederick Ward, plundered travelers on the roads between Newcastle and the Queensland border for six years from 1864 onward. He was not an ordinary thief and his courtesy toward the mail-coach passengers he held up became legendary. When one of his victims complained of nervousness and wanted to smoke, Thunderbolt not only gave him a cigar but lit it for him.

In May 1870, Thunderbolt was surprised during a robbery by two mounted troopers. During a furious gun battle, the polite bushranger received a bullet through the heart. He lies buried in Uralla Cemetery, and the locals regularly place flowers on his grave. In 1970 they even held a Thunderbolt Centenary Celebration at which he was honored by a plaque in the Uralla Shire Council Chambers.

Armidale

Some 352 miles north of Sydney on the New England Highway, Armidale is reached from Sydney by express train every Monday, Wednesday, and Friday. The trip takes 8 hours and costs \$A100 round-trip.

WHAT TO SEE & DO

Armidale is seat of the **University of New England,** a miniature down under version of Oxford. Of the town's 22,000 inhabitants, more than 2,000 are students and staff of the university. True, inside the campus park deer mingle with kangaroos in a most un-Oxonian fashion, but the collegians make up for it by having officials called yeoman bedells and talking in terms of "Town and Gown," just like in the Old Country. And the town is sprinkled with cathedrals with dreaming spires and excellent and numerous pubs, and enjoys the crispest, most multicolored autumn in the state. For visitors interested in educational facilities, there is also Australia's first country teachers' college.

The college houses a remarkable art collection, including a Rembrandt etching, given to the institution by a shipping tycoon who wound up being worth about $A50 because he spent all his fortune on paintings that he gave away to galleries.

Armidale Folk Museum, at the corner of Rusden and Faulkner Streets (☎ **067/72-8666**), features interesting displays of Victoriana, including room settings, kitchens, lighting fixtures, and 19th-century transport vehicles. Open daily from 1 to 4pm; free.

New England Regional Art Museum, Kentucky Street (☎ **067/72-5255**), housed in an impressive building set in beautiful grounds, exhibits a large collection of Australian art spanning more than a century. Open seven days from 10am to 5pm. Admission is $A3 adults, free for children.

Other museums in Armidale specialize in antiquities, zoology, and rural life and industry.

On the New England Highway toward the airport lies the **Berry Patch,** the largest hydroponic berry farm in Australia. Try the fruit pies and strudels every day from 8:30am to 6pm.

WHERE TO STAY

Moderate

Cattleman's Motor Inn, 31 Marsh St., Armidale, NSW 2350. ☎ **067/72-7788.**

Rates: $A90–$A110 single; $A95–$120 double. Major credit cards.

This motel has a spa, pool, sauna, video movies, and no holiday surcharges.

Inverell

About an hour's drive northwest of Armidale, Inverell features **Pioneer Village,** one of the best of its kind in Australia. The historic buildings were transported here, intact, from their original sites, which were scattered all over the place. Now they form a compact and authentic outdoor museum, spanning the period from roughly 1840 to 1930. There's a tiny church, an equally tiny school (complete with battered and carved-up desks). The village store still has some of its archaic merchandise on the shelves. Paddy's Pub, with a bark roof, was once a stopover for the Cobb & Co. stagecoaches regularly held up by Captain Thunderbolt. There's *The Times* printing office with its old flatbed presses, and the Aberfoyle Telephone Exchange, about the size of a dog kennel, and a couple of dozen other buildings and homesteads. Call **067/22-1725** for information.

At the Serpentine River on the New England National Park Road, about 50 miles from Armidale, is the **L. P. Dutton Trout Hatchery.** This is a series of huge tanks containing the region's famous trout varieties in various stages, from fingerlings a couple of inches long to sleek, fat, and hefty beauties. The hatchery is open every day from 9am to 4pm, and conducted tours of the breeding ponds take place every half hour. Admission is free.

Tenterfield

Tenterfield, north of Armidale on the New England Highway, was founded by Sir Stuart Donaldson, who later became premier of New South Wales and the last man in Australia to fight a duel. This happened in 1851 and had an unbloody conclusion—one of the pistol balls passed through Donaldson's hat, so the seconds wisely called it a draw.

One of the town's attractions is **Hillview Doll Museum,** Palham Street (☎ **067/36-1491**), displaying more than 1,000 dolls from all parts of the world, including the locally made "Appleheads." Open daily from 9am to 5pm. Admission $A2.

About 25 miles north of Tenterfield stretches **Bald Rock National Park,** a vast bushland reserve, full of flora and wildlife, which harbors one of the state's most spectacular—and least known—natural wonders. **Bald Rock,** the focal point of the landscape, is the largest exposed granite monolith in Australia and (after Ayers Rock) the second-biggest rock in the world. It's an awesome sight—sheer gray granite rising 170 feet above the surrounding bushland. You can climb up a marked walking track—it's hard going at first, but easier in the later stages. From the peak the view is breathtaking—you can see all the way across the Queensland border and to the ocean.

4 The Outback

The term "outback" is more of a mental image than a geographical definition. It means the bush, the remote countryside, the land "beyond the black stump," and a different area in every state. In New South Wales it refers to the extreme western portion up to the border of South Australia. It's not quite the "great Australian loneliness," but close enough to give you the flavor.

It's a dramatic landscape of brown and green, furrowed with dry riverbeds, studded with gnarled ghost gums—endless plains extending to the far horizon, with an immeasurable pale blue sky hanging above, blurred with heat mirages that trick your eyes into believing that a giant body of water lies only a few miles off. There are sprinklings of isolated homesteads, white-walled with rust-brown corrugated iron roofs, a windmill pumping artesian water on the side. Where the Darling and Murray Rivers run, their banks burst into dark-green tangles, and here and there the rocks are engraved with ancient Aboriginal markings, telling of hunts and ceremonies staged long before the white man came. You see occasional groups of kangaroos and strutting emus, and up in the crystal clear sky the wedge-tailed eagles float on hot air currents. The suburbs of Sydney seem as distant as Mars.

Broken Hill

Hazelton Airlines has flights from Sydney to Broken Hill every Monday, Wednesday, Friday, and Sunday. By rail it's a comfortable but long 18-hour trip from Sydney, on air-conditioned sleeping cars departing three times a week.

Broken Hill (population 25,000) transformed Australia from a pastoral nation to the industrial hub of the South Pacific. The town sits among an immense chain of hills that hold some of the most valuable lead, zinc, and silver deposits in the world. The 130 million tons of ore that were mined here acted as the propellant that shot the continent from the agricultural to the factory age. The first thing you notice in Broken Hill is the huge machinery atop the pits, producing the annual 5.5 million tons that keep Australia's smelters roaring.

WHAT TO SEE & DO

Broken Hill, which lies 717 miles west of Sydney, was made by the mining industry, and the mining industry made modern Australia. You can visit some of the mines in operation and get a glimpse of what the industry is all about. **Delprat's Mine** (☎ **080/88-1604**) takes you on underground tours 90 feet below the surface and shows you the initial stages of ore extraction. Tours start at 10:30am Monday through Friday and at 2pm on Saturday and cost $A18. Cameras are permitted. **North Mine** (☎ **080/97-325**) has a surface tour starting at 2pm Monday through Friday; no cameras allowed.

Beyond the mines, Broken Hill is quaint in some parts, ultramodern in others, fascinating everywhere, and completely *different* from anything you might have expected. It has wonderful old country pubs, a huge civic-center complex staging top theatrical performances and symphony concerts, Victorian buildings that look like birthday cakes baked from bricks, stone cottages with wide verandas, and an astonishing number of art galleries and museums.

These galleries owe their existence to the "Brushmen of the Bush," a world-famous group of artists like Jack Absalom, Pro Hart, Eric Minchin, and Hugh Schulz, who epitomize Australian contemporary painting. Their work, and that of their less renowned contemporaries, can be seen in more than a dozen galleries. To mention a few, the **Ant Hill Gallery,** 24 Bromide St. (☎ **080/88-1551**), features the cream of the local artists as well as local crafts such as pottery and china (open daily till 5pm); the **Pro Hart Gallery,** 108 Wyman St. (☎ **080/87-2441**), houses the work of the artist and is one of the largest private collections in Australia (open daily till 5pm); the **Absalom Gallery,** 638 Chapple St. (☎ **080/5881**), has works by Jack Absalom, plus a large collection of opals (open daily till 5pm); and the **Hugh Schulz Gallery,** 51 Morgan St. (☎ **080/87-6624**), displays paintings by a range of local artists as well as craft works (open weekdays, except Wednesday).

The **Gladstone Mining Museum,** at the corner of South and Morish Streets, South Broken Hill (☎ **080/87-6277**), is a replica of a working mine built into an old hotel, showing past and current mining procedures by means of life-size models. Open daily from 2 to 5pm. The **Daydream Mine,** on the other hand, is not a replica but the real thing, circa 1880. Visitors can walk down the underlays to the workings. For open hours, call **080/2241.**

Broken Hill has a great many other attractions, unrelated to mining. There is a **Muslim mosque** (☎ **080/6060**) dating back to the earliest days of the town. It was built as a place of worship by the Afghan camel drivers on the site of the former camel camp. Camels handled most of the land transport in the region before the advent of railroads and automobiles. Later the camels ran wild, and proliferated, in the saltbush deserts, the Afghans scattered to other towns, and the mosque lay abandoned until it was restored by the local historical society. Open for visits every Sunday afternoon from 2 to 3pm.

A few miles out of town, beside the Barrier Highway, lies the base of the **Royal Flying Doctor Service.** Made famous (and fictionalized) by films and TV, this remarkable organization maintains radio contact with more than 400 outposts, providing medical assistance by way of long-range diagnosis and advice on treatment, dispatching doctors and removing patients by air. For thousands of bush dwellers this is the sole medical help available. The annals of the Flying Doctor Service are full of landings and takeoffs under the most appalling conditions imaginable, the little mercy planes staggering in and out of grazing paddocks and half-cleared scrubland, undeterred by floods, tropical thunderstorms, or bushfires. Inspections of the base are conducted at 10am and 4pm Monday through Friday and at 10am on Saturday. All reservations must be made at the **Tourist Information Centre** (☎ **080/87-6077**). Admission $A2.

Almost equally famous is the **School of the Air,** headquartered at Broken Hill. This unique school conducts lessons via two-way radio for the children of isolated homesteads scattered over hundreds of square miles of bush. At the receiving end the radio sets are often powered by foot pedals, but the educational standards are equal to, if not better than, those of normal classrooms. You can visit the facilities during school terms at 8:40am Monday through Friday. Arrangements must be made in advance at the **Tourist Information Centre,** corner of Blende and Bromide Streets, Broken Hill (☎ **080/87-6077**).

WHERE TO STAY

Broken Hill has about 20 tourist hotels, motels, and guesthouses, plus a couple of caravan parks.

Budget

Overlander Motor Inn, 142 Iodide St., Broken Hill, NSW 2680.
☎ **080/88-2566. Transportation:** Courtesy car to and from the airport and bus depot.
Rates: $A62 single; $A70 double. Major credit cards.

Small and centrally located, this modern inn provides a sauna and spa, laundry, and free in-house movies.

Silverton

Some 18 miles northwest of Broken Hill lies Silverton, a semi-ghost town that has become a kind of outback Hollywood. Originally Silverton was a rip-roaring mining community of about 3,000 people, digging for valuable ore in the 1870s. But the ore petered out and the people drifted away, leaving the place nearly deserted. Then, about a century later, movie producers discovered some magic in the quality of the light at Silverton, as well as the cinematic charisma of its antique buildings. So the town began its second career as a backdrop for any script requiring a romantically dramatic bush setting. A score of films, such as *A Town Like Alice, Mad Max, Hostage, Razorback,* and *Wake in Fright* were shot here, as well as TV shorts and countless commercials. The native population stays at around 100, but film crews, actors, tourists, and visitors from Broken Hill swell it to several times that number.

Sooner or later they all drift into the wondrous old **Silverton Hotel,** whose staff has grown somewhat blasé about serving beer to screen deities. They're more concerned about Misty the movie horse, who trots up to the bar to get a hot scone with jam, followed by tea (Misty despises beer).

The **Silverton Gaol,** the restored old hoosegow of the town, is one of the grizzled structures camera crews love for picturesque backgrounds. Instead of imprisoned drunks it now houses a collection of relics from the town's past.

Camels no longer transport much in the region, except a great many tourists. For a ride around the area on a swaying hump, contact **Camel Treks** (☎ 080/91-1682).

Menindee

For a complete change of environment you only have to go to Menindee, about an hour's drive southeast of Broken Hill. This is a gigantic lake region with a water area eight times that of Sydney Harbour. There you can fish from the shore, ride in speedboats, or swim and generally wallow in this tranquil green oasis that makes it hard to recall the stark dryness you've just left. But there is a reminder. In the township of Menindee is the camping ground of the tragic explorers Burke and Wills. Here they rested and fished and swam before setting out on their last journey into the deserts in the north, where both perished.

5 Snowy Mountains

Covered from about June to September in superbly skiable snow, the Snowy Mountains start their climb some 300 miles southwest of Sydney, and their tallest peak, **Mount Kosciusko** (7,314 feet), is the highest point in Australia. Mount Kozzie, as the natives call it, forms part of a vast winter playground that embraces all 2,100 square miles of **Kosciusko National Park** and looks like a portion of Switzerland transported to the southern hemisphere.

Getting There

Nearly all Snowy Mountains sightseeing tours operate out of Canberra, southwest of Sydney. You can fly from Sydney to Canberra (Ansett or Qantas) for about $A143, taking roughly an hour, then catch a bus for the two-hour road trip to Cooma. Alternatively, there is daily rail service from Sydney to Canberra. The train leaves Sydney's Central Station at 9:30am, gets to Canberra at 2pm, and links up with a bus to Cooma. The train trip costs about $A41 one way.

Thredbo

This skiing capital is a new, all-modern-conveniences-included resort village. The brainchild of former Czechoslovakian ski champion Tony Sponar, **Thredbo Alpine Village** was built in the image of famous European winter-sports resorts. In similar style, it offers outdoor and indoor fun in roughly equal quantities, but at less than European prices. You can share a room in an economy lodge or rent a holiday flat. All-inclusive six-day snow-holiday packages start as low as $A500 to $A600. In season (that is, *out* of season for Sydney) the whole village merges into one big party, scattered between the thumping disco of the Keller and half a dozen more intimate—but just as swinging—restaurants, bars, and bistros. Maybe it's the marvelously bracing mountain air, but most of the swingers manage to stumble onto a 2,000-foot chair lift next morning to zoom down 25 miles of ski trails, jet-turning and paralleling as if they hadn't rocked through the night.

Off season, the attractions include glorious views—a 1 1/2 mile chair lift operates the year round to the top of **Mount Crackenback** (6,350 feet)—and such relaxing diversions as fishing, swimming, hiking, barbecuing, campfire nights, and dinner dances. Prices relax too, slipping well below the winter rates. You reach Thredbo by bus, train, car, or plane to Cooma, which is 56 miles away. Coaches then take you to the ski fields.

Snowy Mountains Hydroelectric Scheme

Formerly a drowsy little mountain hamlet, **Cooma,** about an hour by air from Sydney, burst into cosmopolitan life when it became the launching pad and headquarters of the Snowy Mountains Hydroelectric Scheme. Today the village proudly flies the flags of 27 nations, one for each country whose citizens took part in this titanic project. To see it you must cross the border of New South Wales into neighboring Australian Capital Territory (ACT). This is a kind of federal enclave (not a state) like the District of Columbia, drawn around Australia's capital, Canberra.

The Snowy Scheme, as Aussies call it, was named by the American Society of Civil Engineers as one of the "Seven Wonders of the Engineering World." It is the mightiest technological task ever accomplished in Australia and has become an almost mystical focal point of national pride. For sheer magnitude the Snowy can only be compared with America's Tennessee Valley Authority water and power development projects.

The significance of the SMA (Snowy Mountain Authority) stems from the fact that Australia is the driest of all continents, mainly because it has few massive mountain ranges to precipitate rain and give rise to rivers. The basic idea of the scheme was to divert the Snowy River from its original path into three new rivers that would flow west into water-needy country, and in so doing provide not only irrigation and thus fertility, but also a colossal amount of water-generated electricity for power and lights for homes, industry, and transport in the plains below. If you've seen the movie *The Man from Snowy River* you'll have an inkling—no more—of what kind of tiger country the project was tackling.

Begun in 1949, the project took 25 years to complete and cost $A800 million, the labor of 6,000 men, and the lives of 54 killed by rockfalls and misfired tunnel blasts. This was the price paid for the astonishing speed of the tunneling operations, which frequently reached a rate of 541 feet per week. (The previous world record, set by the Swiss, was 362 feet of tunneling a week.)

The SMA boasts a mass of dazzling statistics—90 miles of tunnels hewn through the mountains, 80 miles of aqueducts, 1,000 miles of road, and seven power stations with a generating capacity of 4 million kilowatts of electricity! The entire scheme embraces an area of over 2,000 square miles and has created a chain of huge artificial lakes, the largest of which, **Lake Eucumbene,** contains nine times the volume of water in Sydney Harbour!

But better than all these figures is the loving care with which the whole undertaking has been blended into the scenery. Far from marring the beauty of the mountain ranges, the Snowy Scheme has enhanced the natural environment. Many of the power plants are underground and invisible until you reach the entrance. The immense silvery-white dams blend with the snow-capped peaks like natural waterfalls. The lakes—cold, blue, and crystal clear—have been stocked with rainbow trout and provide some of the best game fishing in the country. And somehow even the masses of sightseers attracted by the project are absorbed with a minimum of blatantly commercial tourism.

Khancoban, situated west of Cooma, halfway between Sydney and Melbourne, is the Cooma story in reverse. During the construction of the hydroelectric project this was a beaver-busy work camp and boomtown housing around 4,000 people, nearly all construction workers. Then, when the scheme was completed, Khancoban became a restful little mountain retreat catering solely to holidaymakers. The village nestles in the foothills of the Great Dividing Range that marks the border of New South Wales and Victoria. All around rise the forested alpine peaks crisscrossed by foaming rivers and placid lakes and teeming with wildlife (no hunting in this nature reserve, but the trout fishing is superb).

Where to Stay

Most of the accommodations in this region double as summer sports and winter ski chalets; the winter rates offer ski-package deals covering several nights and may include rented snow gear. There are also several working stations (ranches) that offer guests a chance to participate in tending mobs of sheep or cattle in weeklong droves on the "long paddock"—traditional stock routes.

San Michele Resort, Snowy Mountains, Adaminaby, NSW 2630. ☎ 064/54-2229.

Rates: $69–$89 adults; $A32–$A50 children (including all meals).

In the foothills of the Snowy Mountains, one hour by car from Thredbo, San Michele has a restaurant with country cooking, swimming pool, tennis courts, trout fishing, and horses for any type of rider.

Reynella Homestead, Adaminaby, Snowy Mountains, NSW 2630. ☎ 064/54-2386. Fax 064/54-2530

Rates: (Full board and riding) $A99 adults; $A54 children. Special packages for ski season.

This is a working sheep and cattle property set in the hills about 35 miles west of Cooma. Offering country meals in lodge-style accommodation and an emphasis on horseriding that includes alpine horseback jaunts along the trails of the high country, Reynella Homestead makes tenderfoot guests feel like the legendary *Man from Snowy River*.

---

6 Hunter Valley

Lying northwest of Sydney in a wonderfully lush landscape is Australia's oldest wine region. Although the bulk of the continent's wines today come from South Australia, the Hunter had an operating winery as early as 1828—long before California. Today the region boasts more than 40 wineries, including some of the most famous brand names in the country—Wyndham Estate, Saxonvale, Lakes Folly, Rothbury Estate, Hermitage, Lindemans, Tuloch, McWilliams, all music to a wine-lover's ears.

A visit to Hunter Valley naturally turns into a wine-tasting tour. Since about half a million people come with the same idea, you can do yourself a *big* favor by timing your visit for midweek, when the restaurants have spare tables and the tasting sessions of the wineries can focus on individual visitors. During weekends they're packed. Another point—if at all possible, don't drive yourself. The Hunter highway police keep a sharp eye on motorists, and prolonged tasting tours do have certain side effects. Better to join one of the coach trips where the driver has to stay stone cold sober, which will make it all the easier to enjoy the Hunter's unofficial motto, "Say G'Day to a Chardonnay."

Newcastle

Gateway and springboard to Hunter Valley is **Newcastle** (metropolitan pop. 430,000), the second-largest city in New South Wales and a heavily industrialized steel and coal producer. But Newcastle also has great surfing beaches right near the city center, a fine art gallery, and just to the north, Port Stephens, one of the most magnificent and unspoiled waterways found anywhere in Australia.

Newcastle is certainly industrialized—among other things it is home to part of BHP (Broken Hill Proprietary Co.), Australia's biggest steel producer. All the plants are contained in one specific area, separated from other districts by the broad Hunter River. The commercial center of the city is a wide, tree-lined pedestrian plaza, the *Hunter Mall,* a lively and colorful market square with an amazing variety of department stores, boutiques, restaurants, and specialty shops. Just south of the city stretches **Lake Macquarie,** the largest saltwater lake on the continent. This is a mecca for thousands of lake sailors, yachtsmen, and fishers or for folks who just enjoy lazing about in the sun. The spectacle of hundreds of bright sails on the sparkling (and unpolluted) water gives the area the appearance of a vacation resort.

North of the city lies the "Blue Water Wonderland" of **Port Stephens.** This is the name of a large peninsula blessed with an exceptionally agreeable climate that acts as a weekend playground for Newcastle's population. Port Stephens offers everything you'd expect from a resort region, including two sizable peaks for climbing. Below them lie patrolled surfing beaches, secluded fishing coves, commercial centers with restaurants and shops, and any number of motels and holiday units.

One of the best features of the region is the fishing fleet, which brings large catches of fish, prawns, and local lobsters to the restaurants, guaranteeing a supply of fresh seafood. Port Stephens's claim to national fame is **oyster farming.** The young oysters are grown in the Salamander and Soldiers Point waters, then gathered and moved to quieter waters to mature and grow fat. A plate of local oysters in a shoreline restaurant is a treat well worth the short trip from Newcastle. And at **Mofiat's Oyster Barn,** Swan Bay (☎ **049/97-5433**), you not only learn how oysters are raised but also get to eat them, seven days a week, for lunch.

Cessnock

The center of the Lower Hunter region is Maitland, a rural trading township dating from the 1830s. But the most important town is **Cessnock,** a place unique among urban centers the world over. Cessnock is the only city on the globe that lives simultaneously by coal mining and wine growing, two activities usually regarded as mutually exclusive. This was the region of the mining empire run by the legendary John Brown, with the largest shaft mine in the southern hemisphere, which set world records for coal production.

Just outside the town lies **Poholbin,** where the first commercially successful vineyards of the young colony were established by pioneer vignerons from 1830 onward. Today the area embraces more than 30 wineries, thriving literally next door to the "black diamonds" that feed coal furnaces. The contrast makes visitors shake their heads in disbelief, although the locals take it for granted.

Dungog

For yet another contrast there is Dungog, the gateway to the magnificent **Barrington Tops National Park.** This is an unspoiled bushland reserve, a land of rugged timbered ridges, deep-green rain forests, and rushing streams. The animals are quite tame—you can actually feed the wild rosella parrots, possums, scrub turkeys, and kangaroos.

The Wineries

The Hunter Valley stretches northwest of Newcastle and is divided into the Lower and Upper Hunter. It doesn't really matter which one you visit as both abound in wineries, in restaurants serving excellent food (and wine, of course), and in Tourist Information Centres supplying invaluable guidance.

The wineries vary greatly in size and reputation, but most of them have tasting rooms, several give conducted tours of their premises, and all want you to stock up on as many bottles of their product as possible. The examples below will give you a general idea.

Note: The wines are cheaper when bought in lots of a dozen, but rough prices for single bottles are $A12 for cabernet shiraz, $A13 for sauvignon, $A14 for chardonnay, $A9 to $A18 for port, and $A7 to $A14 for rieslings.

Hunter Valley Wine Society, 4 Wollombi Road, Cessnock (☎ 049/90-6699), is a coordinated enterprise that lets you taste (and buy) the products of 36 Hunter wineries, and also serves a charcoal-grilled lunch seven days a week. It's a good on-the-spot comparison opportunity—providing your palate holds out.

McWilliams, Mount Pleasant, Pokolbin (☎ 049/98-7505), offers guided tours Monday through Friday four times daily, and also cellar-door sales of "limited release" wines, which really are limited.

Wyndham Estate, Branxton (☎ 049/38-1135), is reputedly the oldest winery on the continent. Beautifully situated on the banks of the Hunter River at Dalwood, via Branxton, five miles off the New England Highway, it has four restaurants on the grounds, cellar-door sales, and tastings seven days a week till 5pm.

Hungerford Hill Wine Village, Broke Road, Pokolbin (☎ 049/98-7666), in the self-proclaimed "Heart of the Hunter Valley," has a motor inn, farmers market, swimming pool, restaurant, and gift store, as well as wine-tasting and sales rooms. Open daily till 5pm.

Marsh Estate, Deasys Road, Pokolbin (☎ 049/98-7587), is a family property known for growing only classic varieties: traminer, hermitage, pinot noir, chardonnay, and cabernet sauvignon. Small, friendly, and more personalized than most wineries, with an exceptionally comfortable tasting room, it's open all week: till 4pm Monday through Friday, till 5pm on Saturday and Sunday.

In the Upper Hunter region, on the banks of the Hunter River, lies **Arrowfield,** Highway 213, Jerrys Plain (☎ 065/76-4041). Huge, modern, but scenic, this winery has barbecue facilities and is open for tasting and single-bottle sales seven days a week (Sunday from noon).

Rosemount Estate, Denman (☎ **065/47-2467**), the largest winery in the area, has an international reputation for high-quality chardonnay, sauvignon blanc, and Sémillons. Tastings and sales seven days a week.

Horderns, Yarraman Road, Wybong (☎ **065/47-8127**), is small, with limited output, but both historic and charming. Some of the buildings were constructed with stone taken from the ruins of nearby Bengala prison. The winery is famous for its wood-matured Sémillon whites. Open daily till 5pm (Sunday till 4pm).

WINE TOURS

For an inexpensive and nicely varied tour, pick the Hunter Valley Winetaster, operated by **AAT King's** (☎ **02/252-2788**). The tour coaches leave Circular Quay in Sydney at 8:45am on Thursday, Saturday, and Sunday, returning at 7:30pm. You visit the Hungerford Hill estate for a tasting and a steak lunch, and get a browse through the Farmers Market and a scenic return journey. Adults pay $A77; children, $A52.

If you prefer touring with a touch of style, you can travel with the exclusive day tours run by **Christopher Buring** (☎ **02/875-4720**), a celebrated wine maker and consultant. He'll pick you up at your Sydney hotel at 8am and deliver you back around 6pm. En route you'll learn more about the Australian wines in general and Hunter Valley in particular than you'll need to impress any number of grape experts back home. The trip includes a gourmet lunch in the valley. Call for reservations and prices.

Where To Dine

Casurina, Hermitage Road, Pokolbin. ☎ **049/98-7562.**

Cuisine: ASIAN.

Prices: Appetizers around $A10; main courses around $A20. Major credit cards.

Open: Lunch Sat–Sun; dinner daily from 7pm.

Despite the Latin label of the establishment, the fare leans more toward Asian gourmetry, except for the wine list, which is local, extensive, and partly magnificent. You can dine in air-conditioned comfort indoors or outside in the courtyard. Offerings range from fresh fish to beef teriyaki and hot Thai seafood mixtures.

The Old George And Dragon, 48 Melbourne St., East Maltland. ☎ **049/33-7272.**

Cuisine: FRENCH.

Prices: Appetizers around $A13; main courses around $A22. Major credit cards.

Open: Dinner only. Wed–Sat 7pm–midnight.

This award-winning dinery has the reputedly finest wine list in the valley—which is saying something. It also boasts what may be the most tasteful decor in the region. The cuisine is mainly French and includes several outstanding venison specialties as well as a renowned crab broth.

7 Illawarra

The region stretching inland from the Pacific shore about 50 miles south of Sydney takes its name from Lake Illawarra, but its oceanfront is known as the Leisure Coast. It's not a strictly accurate label because the entry points, **Wollongong** and **Port Kembla,** are highly industrialized and far from leisurely. Port Kembla, in fact, boasts the largest steel mill in Australia. Wollongong, however, is undergoing an interesting transformation, adding strings of tourist attractions to its industrial backbone. The central part of the main street was rebuilt as a splendid pedestrian plaza with soaring steel arches, hanging gardens, and glittering water displays. The Wollongong North Beach Hotel is a three-star, international-style establishment.

Getting There

Wollongong is only an hour by road from Sydney, but if at all possible, do the trip by train. The track follows one of the most scenic routes on the continent, skirting the edge of Royal National Park, then winding along the Escarpment, where the mountains seem to push into the sea with only the narrow track in between. The New South Wales Railway operates the **South Coast Spectacular,** the first and third Tuesday of every month. Trains leave Central Station at 8am and return at 4:15pm. At Wollongong you transfer to coaches and ride to Mount Kembla, then on to the Blowhole at Kiama. The tour costs $A35 for adults, $A31 for children.

What to See And Do

At Helensburgh, just before you reach Wollongong, lies the **Symbio Koala Garden,** on Lawrence Hargrave Drive. Nestling in a large bushland setting, this nature park houses dozens of koalas as well as other grazing, nibbling, and flying Oz critters. There is a special nocturnal house for observing the night denizens. The garden is open daily from 9:30am till dusk.

Located five miles west of Wollongong is **Mount Kembla Historic Village.** Not colonial this time, but early industrial, this is a preserved mining community from the turn of the century. It has a group of arts and crafts workshops, including a working smithy, and a monument to a pit disaster that occurred in 1902.

Along the South Coast the scene becomes a true leisureland, with small villages facing the blue ocean where main pastimes consist of swimming, waterskiing, hang-gliding, bushwalking, and horseback riding. At Kiama the top attraction is a natural phenomenon known as the **Blowhole.** This is a tunnel running through solid rock inland from the oceanfront. As heavy seas crash into the tunnel entrance, they force huge sprays of water up the tunnel opening at the other end, sending geysers into the air as high as 80 feet. The Blowhole was discovered by Europeans in 1797, but nobody has yet explained how and why the water hollowed out this narrow pipe through the stone.

Wilton has quite another kind of attraction in **Macarthur Winery,** Mount Keira Rd. (☎ **046/30-9269**). A large estate winery, this place has country music and bush dancing on Saturday nights, and serves sumptuous lunches on Sunday. Wine tastings are held daily from 10am to 6pm.

Southwest of Wollongong, on the Hume Highway, lies **Berrima,** the oldest village of its type in Australia. Founded in 1829 by the colony's surveyor-general, the place retains 40 historic buildings constructed from local sandstone during the convict days. And you can still down a middy at the **Surveyor-General's Inn,** Hume Hwy., the oldest continuously licensed pub on the continent. It was a brutal place in those early days—the ancient Berrima Gaol was built by chained convicts driven by the lash. Laggards were habitually chained up in cells measuring 3 by 6 feet, heated to the temperature of bake ovens by the sun. A solemn Royal Commission was instituted to look into these cruelties, but the honorable commissioners of the time preferred to disregard all such claims made by the convicts.

Today Berrima is a placid little country hamlet, proud of its antique Court House, which now houses a video display of early Berrima, and Australia's first trial by jury, which was held there (as distinct from the usual administrative courts-martial, which were held everywhere). You can wander into the quaint general store, with signs for century-old newspapers costing one penny, faded calendars dated 1880, and yellowing posters advertising Beechams Pills (for your liver) and Parsons Infant Powder (for another place).

Joadja, just off Hume Highway on Wombeyan Caves Road, is a ghost town with a resident—and quite benevolent—ghost. The whole town actually belongs to an American woman, Pat Lee, who bought it for a song when she migrated here from her native Georgia more than 30 years ago. The ghost's name is Robert McGregor and he allegedly wears hobnailed boots you can hear at night. Joadja is open for visitors till 4pm on weekends only, but it's best to call ahead and make sure (☎ **048/71-2888**). A row of miners' cottages, the old schoolhouse, and some ancient kilns are still standing. And after dark there's Mr. McGregor. . . .

8   Lightning Ridge

A real Australian outback town, sunbaked and flat, but with a tourist lure few others possess—you just *might* leave it richer than you came—Lightning Ridge, some 480 miles northwest of Sydney, is the only place in the world where the most beautiful and valuable type of opal is found, the so-called black opal, which actually blazes in a rainbow of colors, and which some connoisseurs consider the finest gem on earth. The first black opal was discovered here in 1907, but production peaked in 1914 and has been declining ever since—hence the rising value of the stones. The local population of around 2,000 sifts through the old mullock, the residue excavated by pioneer miners, by means of a puddler, a type of metal sieve. Puddlers are for rent and visitors are invited to fossick on the heaps or dig down in any unoccupied holes. Do they find anything? Many don't, but some gather enough rough opal pebbles (called nobbies) to pay for their vacation. A very few strike it rich, such as the schoolboy who picked up a nobby worth $A3,000.

Even if you leave with no souvenir other than the dirt under your nails, you'll be richer for the experience. For this is the frontier Australia so many of us come seeking. At least half the residents here came to find opals and stayed on because they liked the vibes. The place is easygoing friendliness personified. It's taut, hot (broiling for five months of the year) countryside where you can sip an ice-cold Fosters in a grand old pub called **Diggers Rest** beside men called Crank Joe, Shameless, and Spider Brown. For your creature comforts there are several motels, a spa pool, and a caravan park with on-site vans for overnighting. You can browse through two museums with gemstones on display, and the quietly amiable townsfolk are only too willing to talk prospecting lore with anyone who'll listen. It's a long, long way to the rat race.

The nearest town of any size to Lightning Ridge is **Walgett,** with all of 2,700 people. It has an airfield, the railroad terminal for the trains from Sydney, and several cabs that will take you the 46 miles to the Ridge. **Hazelton Air Lines** (☎ **02/235-1411**) runs three flights a week from Sydney to Walgett. For organized tours to Lightning Ridge, contact the **Travel Centre of N.S.W.,** 19 Castlereagh St., Sydney (☎ **02/231-4444**).

Lightning Ridge lies at the center of what is known as the **North West Country,** a very large and extremely varied region. It changes from scenic mountain ranges in the east to vast flat plains in the west, from rich agricultural land to semi-desert. The North West includes the little town of **Bourke,** and "back o' Bourke" in Oz phraseology is where the Outback starts.

A unique feature of the country is the artesian basin that provides a constant flow of *heated* subterranean water, in contrast to normal artesian bores that run icy cold. This basin feeds the spa baths in the country towns (including Lightning Ridge), and you can see the thick jet of hot water gushing out of **Dunumbral Bore,** one of the attractions of the North West.

At **Moree** stands one of Australia's four OTC Satellite Earth Stations, operated by the Overseas Telecommunications Commission, which provide telephone, telegraph, telex, and TV service between Australia and the rest of the world. Moree also boasts the most luxurious of the artesian spa baths, with two Fiberglas hot pools and every modern spa facility.

The largest town of the region is **Tamworth,** on the Peel River at the junction of the New England and Oxley highways. Tamworth, with a population of 35,000, was actually the first city in the southern hemisphere to have its streets lit by electricity (1888). Today its fame is derived from being the Country Music Capital, with an annual country music festival held every January. Tamworth also has the **Gallery of Stars Wax Museum,** a must for country music fans from everywhere.

9 The Golden West

"Golden West" was the title bestowed, rather optimistically, on the central region of New South Wales during the big gold rush of the 1870s. Here, at **Hill End,** the immense Holtermann Nugget was found—the largest chunk of reef gold ever unearthed anywhere. News of the find brought 60,000 people from all over the world to the area. When the gold petered out—as it always does—the prospectors settled down to farming, but the name stuck. You can still do a bit of fossicking in the valleys around Bathurst, but I wouldn't bet on another Holtermann.

Today the Golden West, about 180 miles west of Sydney, is strewn with the relics and structures of the wild goldhunting days, but these are overshadowed by newer attractions. Several trains a day run from Sydney to Bathurst. The trip takes around four hours and costs $A23. Drivers follow Great Western Highway past Penrith, Katoomba, and Lithgow to Bathurst and Orange.

Bathurst

With a population of 28,000, Bathurst lies close to the gold-rush village of Hill End. The town is Australia's motor-racing capital and bursts at the seams with motor maniacs every Easter, when the internationally famous Bathurst 1000 race takes place. Victors' Walk, outside the town's Civic Centre, displays rows of brass plaques commemorating the winners of this race.

The actual racing circuit is at Mount Panorama. When no races are being held visiting motorists can drive around, imagining, no doubt, they're behind the wheel of a roaring Ferrari. In Pit Straight, Mount Panorama, stands the **Bathurst Motor Racing Museum** (☎ 32-1872), an edifice filled with motoring memorabilia and anything connected with the sport. Open daily 9am–4:30pm (to 2pm on Friday). Admission is $A3.

North of Bathurst lies **Mudgee,** which produces two very pleasant commodities: honey and wine. The Mudgee Honey Company conducts inspection tours and hands out samples. And there are around a dozen wineries in the area, most of them open for tastings. One of them is **Craigmoor Wines,** Henry Lawson Drive (☎ 063/72-2208). Open Monday to Friday 9am–5pm, Saturday and Sunday 11am–4pm.

Dubbo

Northwest of Bathurst on Great Western Highway is **Dubbo** (pop. 33,000), the largest city in the area. Here is **Western Plains Zoo,** Obley Road (☎ 068/82-5888). This was the first Australian zoo without bars—a daring experiment that has visitors view the inhabitants from elevated roadways, safe but unobstructed. There are thousands of animals, including tigers, bears and cheetahs, living in the closest thing to their natural environment. Open daily 9am–5pm. Admission $A13 adults, $A6 children.

A Somber Memorial

Southwest of Bathurst, on the banks of the Lachlan River, lies the little country town of **Cowra.** Here, of all places, you'll find the largest traditional Japanese garden outside Japan. Covering 25 acres, it forms the **Japanese Cultural Centre** and serves as a living reminder of one of the grimmest tragedies of World War II. Cowra was then the site of a huge Japanese prisoner of war camp, and the captives included Imperial Guards who were determined not to remain prisoners. In 1944 the camp inmates threw themselves against the surrounding barbed wire fences in a series of sudden, frenzied *Banzai* charges. Hundreds were machine-gunned from the watch towers, but several dozen made it over the top. They were hunted down in the bushland by army patrols and civilian vigilante squads. Some were killed on the spot, some committed suicide, a few were returned to the camp. To this day nobody knows the exact casualty figures. It was the largest and most tragic prison break of the war.

10   Penrith & Windsor

Let's conclude our survey of excursions by looking at two towns on the fringes of the Sydney metropolitan area.

Penrith

One hour west of Sydney on the suburban train line lies the old pioneer town of Penrith. This is where the foothills of the Blue Mountains meet the winding Nepean River, providing an enchanting patch of wooded hills and riverland. The little town dates back to the 1830s and the whole district is sprinkled with stately mansions, colonial homes, and quaint churches. The hills are ideal for bush-walking and camping, the sparkling clear (and pretty cold) river for rowing, sailing, and canoeing.

Penrith has the **Q Theatre,** the **Nepean Belle Showboat** (on the river), and **Panthers,** on Mulgoa Rd. (☎ **047/21-7700**), a motor inn housing the Casino Royale gambling facility and surrounded by a vast entertainment park. **Cables Fun Park** embraces two lakes equipped for cable waterskiing, a thrill sport that operates without boats. All you need bring along is a swimsuit and a taste for water-whizzing. If you're driving, Panthers is located just off the F4 freeway.

For a family style pub restaurant there is **Grey Gums,** at the corner of Malgowa and Blaike streets (☎ **047/33-1801**). The place has a welcoming beer garden (with children's play area) and serves surprisingly cosmopolitan repasts, such as curried prawns or satay lamb. Appetizers go for around $A5, main courses for around $A12. Open for lunch all week, for dinner Tuesday to Sunday. Reservations are recommended on weekends. BC, MC, and V accepted.

Windsor

Windsor lies on the northwest boundary of the Sydney metropolitan area, more than one hour by train from Central Station. Settled in 1791, Windsor was linked to Sydney 30 years later by a road built with the sweat and blood of 1,200 convicts who toiled in clanking leg irons and dropped like flies by the wayside. A lot of buildings in the town lay claim to being the oldest on the continent—and some of the claims may be true.

Windsor is the gateway to **Hawkesbury Country,** a string of towns and resorts along the broad Hawkesbury River, surrounded by no less than five national parks. The Hawkesbury is Sydney's freshwater play and sportsground. For details of river activity contact **Hawkesbury Regional Tourist Centre,** at the corner of Windsor and Graves Roads in Vineyard (☎ **045/87-7388**).

The core of Windsor is the shaded and landscaped mall at the end of George Street. Surrounding the mall run the narrow, strangely old world streets of the original settlement, studded with antique dwellings, inns, and churches (as well as antique shops). The **Macquarie Arms Hotel,** at 99 George St., one of the claimants for the "oldest" title, was built by convicts in 1815 and today serves counter lunches and Sunday roast dinners. The Court House in Thompson Square, designed by the convict-architect Francis Greenway, has the 1817 trial record of Mary Reibey (see The Rocks walking tour in Chapter 7), when that formidable lady was found guilty of assaulting an individual who had owed her money for too long.

For dinner try the **Do Drop Inn,** at 135 George St. (☎ **045/77-4208**). You get an Italian three-course meal, including a complimentary glass of wine, for about $A25. Open seven days.

Appendix

A The Metric System

Length

1 millimeter (mm)	=	0.04 inches (*or* $^1/_{25}$ in.)
1 centimeter (cm)	=	0.039 inches (*or* under $^1/_2$ in.)
1 meter (m)	=	39 inches (*or* about 1.1 yards)
1 kilometer (km)	=	0.62 miles (*or* about $^2/_3$ of a mile)

To convert kilometers to miles, multiply the number of kilometers by 0.62. Also use to convert kilometers per hour (kmph) to miles per hour (mph).

To convert miles to kilometers, multiply the number of miles by 1.61. Also use to convert speeds from mph to kmph.

Capacity

1 liter (l)	=	33.92 fluid ounces	=	2.1 pints
	=	1.06 quarts	=	0.26 U.S. gallons
1 Imperial gallon	=	1.2 U.S. gallons		

To convert liters to U.S. gallons, multiply the number of liters by 0.26.

To convert U.S. gallons to liters, multiply the number of gallons by 3.79.

To convert Imperial gallons to U.S. gallons, multiply the number of Imperial gallons by 1.2.

To convert U.S. gallons to Imperial gallons, multiply the number of U.S. gallons by 0.83.

Weight

1 gram (g)	=	0.035 ounces (*or* about a paperclip's weight)		
1 kilogram (kg)	=	35.2 ounces		
	=	2.2 pounds		
1 metric ton	=	2,205 pounds	=	1.1 short ton

To convert kilograms to pounds, multiply the number of kilograms by 2.2.

To convert pounds to kilograms, multiply the number of pounds by 0.45.

Temperature

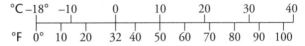

To convert degrees Celsius to degrees Fahrenheit, multiply °C by 9, divide by 5, and add 32 (example: 20°C × 9/5 + 32 = 68°F).

To convert degrees Fahrenheit to degrees Celsius, subtract 32 from °F, multiply by 5, then divide by 9 (example: 85°F − 32 × 5/9 = 29.4°C).

B   Clothing Sizes

Clothing measurements in Australia are probably quite different from those you're accustomed to. For shoes and hats the best move is to get yourself measured in the shop. For other items you can use the tables below.

Women's Dress, Blouse, and Skirt Sizes

Australian	8	10	12	14	16	18	20
American	6	8	10	12	14	16	18

Men's Suit and Sweater Sizes

Australian	92	97	102	107	112	117	122
American	36	38	40	42	44	46	48

Men's Shirt Sizes

Australian	36	37	38	39	40	41	42
American	14	14 ¹/₂	15	15 ¹/₂	16	16 ¹/₂	17

C Road Distance Chart

	Adelaide	Albany	Ayers Rock	Brisbane	Broken Hill	Cairns	Canberra	Darwin	Melbourne	Perth	Port Hedland	SYDNEY
Adelaide	—	2675	1597	1992	513	2858	1230	3261	747	2720	3847	1475
Albany	2675	—	3636	4269	2790	5135	3905	3735	3422	409	2105	3791
Ayers Rock	1597	3636	—	3472	1712	2753	2827	2152	2344	3681	3737	2873
Brisbane	1992	4269	3472	—	1479	1710	1315	3672	1718	4314	5289	1031
Broken Hill	513	2790	1712	1479	—	2345	1100	3376	861	2835	4531	1161
Cairns	2858	5135	2753	1710	2345	—	2938	2953	3039	5180	4570	2636
Canberra	1230	3905	2827	1315	1100	2938	—	4233	651	3950	5646	302
Darwin	3261	3735	2152	3672	3376	2953	4233	—	4008	4206	2510	4095
Melbourne	747	3422	2344	1718	861	3039	651	4008	—	3467	5286	889
Perth	2720	409	3681	4314	2835	5180	3950	4206	3467	—	1696	3996
Port Hedland	3847	2105	3737	5289	4531	4570	5646	2510	5286	1696	—	5692
SYDNEY	1475	3791	2873	1031	1161	2636	302	4095	889	3996	5692	—

Distances are in kilometers. To convert to miles, multiply by 0.62.

Index

Accommodations

EXCURSIONS

Restaurants

EXCURSIONS

Key to abbreviations *E*=Expensive; *I*=Inexpensive; *M*=Moderately priced; *VE*=Very expensive

Now Save Money On All Your Travels By Joining FROMMER'S™ TRAVEL BOOK CLUB The World's Best Travel Guides At Membership Prices!

Frommer's Travel Book Club is your ticket to successful travel! Open up a world of travel informationand simplify your travel planning when you join ranks with thousands of value-conscious travelers who are members of the *Frommer's Travel Book Club.* Join today and you'll be entitled to all the privileges that come from belonging to the club that offers you travel guides for less to more than 100 destinations worldwide. **Annual membership is only $25.00 (U.S.) or $35.00 (Canada/Foreign).**

The Advantages of Membership:

1. Your choice of **three free** books (any **two** *Frommer's Comprehensive Guides, Frommer's $-A-Day Guides, Frommer's Walking Tours* or *Frommer's Family Guides*—plus **one** *Frommer's City Guide, Frommer's City $-A-Day Guide* or *Frommer's Touring Guide*).
2. Your own subscription to the **TRIPS & TRAVEL** quarterly newsletter.
3. You're entitled to a **30% discount** on your order of any additional books offered by the club.
4. You're offered (at a small additional fee) our **Domestic Trip-Routing Kits.**

Our **Trips & Travel** quarterly newsletter offers practical information on the best buys in travel, the "hottest" vacation spots, the latest travel trends, world-class events and much, much more.

Our **Domestic Trip-Routing Kits** are available for any North American destination. We'll send you a detailed map highlighting the best route to take to your destination—you can request direct or scenic routes.

Here's all you have to do to join:

Send in your membership fee of $25.00 ($35.00 Canada/Foreign) with your name and address on the form below along with your selections as part of your membership package to the address listed below. Remember to check off your three free books.

If you would like to order additional books, please select the books you would like and send a check for the total amount (please add sales tax in the states noted below), plus $2.00 per book for shipping and handling ($3.00 Canada/Foreign) to the address listed below.

FROMMER'S TRAVEL BOOK CLUB
P.O. Box 473
Mt. Morris, IL 61054-0473.
(815) 734-1104

[ ] **YES!** I want to take advantage of this opportunity to join Frommer's Travel Book Club.

[ ] My check is enclosed. Dollar amount enclosed   *
(all payments in U.S. funds only)

Name _____

Address _____

City _____ State _____ Zip _____

All orders must be prepaid.

To ensure that all orders are processed efficiently, please apply sales tax in the following areas: CA, CT, FL, IL, IN, NJ, NY, PA, TN, WA and CANADA.

*With membership, shipping & handling will be paid by Frommer's Travel Book Club for the three free books you select as part of your membership. Please add $2.00 per book for shipping & handling for any additional books purchased ($3.00 Canada/Foreign).

Allow 4-6 weeks for delivery. Prices of books, membership fee, and publication dates are subject to change without notice. Orders are subject to acceptance and availability.

Please send me the books checked below:

FROMMER'S COMPREHENSIVE GUIDES

(Guides listing facilities from budget to deluxe,
with emphasis on the medium-priced)

	Retail Price	Code		Retail Price	Code
☐ Acapulco/Ixtapa/Taxco, 2nd Edition	$13.95	C157	☐ Jamaica/Barbados, 2nd Edition	$15.00	C149
☐ Alaska '94-'95	$17.00	C131	☐ Japan '94-'95	$19.00	C144
☐ Arizona '95 (Avail. 3/95)	$14.95	C166	☐ Maui, 1st Edition	$13.95	C153
☐ Australia '94-'95	$18.00	C147	☐ Nepal, 2nd Edition	$18.00	C126
☐ Austria, 6th Edition	$16.95	C162	☐ New England '95	$16.95	C165
☐ Bahamas '94-'95	$17.00	C121	☐ New Mexico, 3rd Edition (Avail. 3/95)	$14.95	C167
☐ Belgium/Holland/ Luxembourg '93-'94	$18.00	C106	☐ New York State, 4th Edition	$19.00	C133
☐ Bermuda '94-'95	$15.00	C122	☐ Northwest, 5th Edition	$17.00	C140
☐ Brazil, 3rd Edition	$20.00	C111	☐ Portugal '94-'95	$17.00	C141
☐ California '95	$16.95	C164	☐ Puerto Rico '95-'96	$14.00	C151
☐ Canada '94-'95	$19.00	C145	☐ Puerto Vallarta/ Manzanillo/ Guadalajara '94-'95	$14.00	C028
☐ Caribbean '95	$18.00	C148			
☐ Carolinas/Georgia, 2nd Edition	$17.00	C128	☐ Scandinavia, 16th Edition (Avail. 3/95)	$19.95	C169
☐ Colorado, 2nd Edition	$16.00	C143	☐ Scotland '94-'95	$17.00	C146
☐ Costa Rica '95	$13.95	C161	☐ South Pacific '94-'95	$20.00	C138
☐ Cruises '95-'96	$19.00	C150	☐ Spain, 16th Edition	$16.95	C163
☐ Delaware/Maryland '94-'95	$15.00	C136	☐ Switzerland/ Liechtenstein '94-'95	$19.00	C139
☐ England '95	$17.95	C159	☐ Thailand, 2nd Edition	$17.95	C154
☐ Florida '95	$18.00	C152	☐ U.S.A., 4th Edition	$18.95	C156
☐ France '94-'95	$20.00	C132	☐ Virgin Islands '94-'95	$13.00	C127
☐ Germany '95	$18.95	C158	☐ Virginia '94-'95	$14.00	C142
☐ Ireland, 1st Edition (Avail. 3/95)	$16.95	C168	☐ Yucatan, 2nd Edition	$13.95	C155
☐ Italy '95	$18.95	C160			

FROMMER'S $-A-DAY GUIDES

(Guides to low-cost tourist accommodations and facilities)

	Retail Price	Code		Retail Price	Code
☐ Australia on $45 '95-'96	$18.00	D122	☐ Israel on $45, 15th Edition	$16.95	D130
☐ Costa Rica/Guatemala/ Belize on $35, 3rd Edition	$15.95	D126	☐ Mexico on $45 '95	$16.95	D125
☐ Eastern Europe on $30, 5th Edition	$16.95	D129	☐ New York on $70 '94-'95	$16.00	D121
☐ England on $60 '95	$17.95	D128	☐ New Zealand on $45 '93-'94	$18.00	D103
☐ Europe on $50 '95	$17.95	D127	☐ South America on $40, 16th Edition	$18.95	D123
☐ Greece on $45 '93-'94	$19.00	D100	☐ Washington, D.C. on $50 '94-'95	$17.00	D120
☐ Hawaii on $75 '95	$16.95	D124			
☐ Ireland on $45 '94-'95	$17.00	D118			

FROMMER'S CITY $-A-DAY GUIDES

	Retail Price	Code		Retail Price	Code
☐ Berlin on $40 '94-'95	$12.00	D111	☐ Madrid on $50 '94-'95	$13.00	D119
☐ London on $45 '94-'95	$12.00	D114	☐ Paris on $45 '94-'95	$12.00	D117

FROMMER'S FAMILY GUIDES

	Retail Price	Code		Retail Price	Code
☐ California with Kids	$18.00	F100	☐ San Francisco with Kids	$17.00	F104
☐ Los Angeles with Kids	$17.00	F103	☐ Washington, D.C.		
☐ New York City			with Kids	$17.00	F102
with Kids	$18.00	F101			

FROMMER'S CITY GUIDES

(Pocket-size guides to sightseeing and tourist
accommodations and facilities in all price ranges)

	Retail Price	Code		Retail Price	Code
☐ Amsterdam '93-'94	$13.00	S110	☐ Nashville/Memphis,		
☐ Athens, 10th Edition			1st Edition	$13.00	S141
(Avail. 3/95)	$12.95	S174	☐ New Orleans '95	$12.95	S148
☐ Atlanta '95	$12.95	S161	☐ New York '95	$12.95	S152
☐ Atlantic City/Cape May,			☐ Orlando '95	$13.00	S145
5th Edition	$13.00	S130	☐ Paris '95	$12.95	S150
☐ Bangkok, 2nd Edition	$12.95	S147	☐ Philadelphia,		
☐ Barcelona '93-'94	$13.00	S115	8th Edition	$12.95	S167
☐ Berlin, 3rd Edition	$12.95	S162	☐ Prague '94-'95	$13.00	S143
☐ Boston '95	$12.95	S160	☐ Rome, 10th Edition	$12.95	S168
☐ Budapest, 1st Edition	$13.00	S139	☐ San Diego '95	$12.95	S158
☐ Chicago '95	$12.95	S169	☐ San Francisco '95	$12.95	S155
☐ Denver/Boulder/Colorado			☐ Santa Fe/Taos/		
Springs, 3rd Edition	$12.95	S154	Albuquerque '95	$12.95	S172
☐ Dublin, 2nd Edition	$12.95	S157	☐ Seattle/Portland '94-'95	$13.00	S137
☐ Hong Kong '94-'95	$13.00	S140	☐ St. Louis/Kansas City,		
☐ Honolulu/Oahu '95	$12.95	S151	2nd Edition	$13.00	S127
☐ Las Vegas '95	$12.95	S163	☐ Sydney, 4th Edition	$12.95	S171
☐ London '95	$12.95	S156	☐ Tampa/St. Petersburg,		
☐ Los Angeles '95	$12.95	S164	3rd Edition	$13.00	S146
☐ Madrid/Costa del Sol,			☐ Tokyo '94-'95	$13.00	S144
2nd Edition	$12.95	S165	☐ Toronto '95		
☐ Mexico City, 1st Edition	$12.95	S170	(Avail. 3/95)	$12.95	S173
☐ Miami '95-'96	$12.95	S149	☐ Vancouver/Victoria		
☐ Minneapolis/St. Paul,			'94-'95	$13.00	S142
4th Edition	$12.95	S159	☐ Washington, D.C. '95	$12.95	S153
☐ Montreal/					
Quebec City '95	$11.95	S166			

SPECIAL EDITIONS

	Retail Price	Code		Retail Price	Code
☐ Bed & Breakfast Southwest	$16.00	P100	☐ National Park Guide, 29th Edition	$17.00	P106
☐ Bed & Breakfast Great American Cities	$16.00	P104	☐ Where to Stay U.S.A., 11th Edition	$15.00	P102
☐ Caribbean Hideaways	$16.00	P103			

FROMMER'S WALKING TOURS

(With routes and detailed maps, these companion guides point out the places and pleasures that make a city unique)

	Retail Price	Code		Retail Price	Code
☐ Berlin	$12.00	W100	☐ New York	$12.00	W102
☐ Chicago	$12.00	W107	☐ Paris	$12.00	W103
☐ England's Favorite Cities	$12.00	W108	☐ San Francisco	$12.00	W104
☐ London	$12.00	W101	☐ Washington, D.C.	$12.00	W105
☐ Montreal/Quebec City	$12.00	W106			

FROMMER'S TOURING GUIDES

(Color-illustrated guides that include walking tours, cultural and historic sites, and practical information)

	Retail Price	Code		Retail Price	Code
☐ Amsterdam	$11.00	T001	☐ New York	$11.00	T008
☐ Barcelona	$14.00	T015	☐ Rome	$11.00	T010
☐ Brazil	$11.00	T003	☐ Scotland	$10.00	T011
☐ Hong Kong/Singapore/ Macau	$11.00	T006	☐ Sicily	$15.00	T017
			☐ Tokyo	$15.00	T016
☐ Kenya	$14.00	T018	☐ Turkey	$11.00	T013
☐ London	$13.00	T007	☐ Venice	$ 9.00	T014

Please note: If the availability of a book is several months away, we may have back issues of guides to that particular destination. Call customer service at (815) 734-1104.